BEHOLD
THE
WEST INDIES

BOOKS BY AMY OAKLEY
Illustrated by Thornton Oakley

———————

Henry Christophe
King of Haiti 👑

BEHOLD
THE
WEST
INDIES

by
AMY OAKLEY

Illustrations
by
THORNTON OAKLEY

LONGMANS, GREEN AND CO.
New York   London   Toronto
1951

LONGMANS, GREEN AND CO., INC.
55 FIFTH AVENUE, NEW YORK 3

LONGMANS, GREEN AND CO. LTD.
6 & 7 CLIFFORD STREET, LONDON W 1

LONGMANS, GREEN AND CO.
215 VICTORIA STREET, TORONTO 1

BEHOLD THE WEST INDIES

PUBLISHED SIMULTANEOUSLY IN THE DOMINION OF CANADA BY
LONGMANS, GREEN AND CO., TORONTO

Printed in the United States of America
VAN REES PRESS • NEW YORK

MISCERIQUE PROBAT
POPULOS ET FŒDERA
JUNGI

TO
WILSON MINSHALL
whose enthusiasm for Trinidad
we share

COLOMBVS
LYCVR NOVI ORBIS REPTOR

Table of CONTENTS

ix

Sir Henry Morgan

⟨⟨ List of Illustrations

Introduction

RELEASE from petty or business care, the rigors of a northern winter, the artificialities of city life, even, perhaps, from self—by the wider interests engendered—is a paramount reason for a voyage or flight by air to the West Indies. The beholder can hardly fail to be entranced with the variety of contour and natural beauty of the islands, the luxuriance of tropical foliage, the quality of sunlight, the glamour of that American Mediterranean—the Caribbean.

The plan of a book on the West Indies was developed to include for good measure, the Spanish Main. This volume, is, then, the result of four journeys undertaken by my Illustrator and myself during two winters and also several springs. The initial adventure was made by cruise and stopover: transportation was by Furness Line, the Canadian National, Royal Netherlands, French Line, Grace Line, and United Fruit Company.

Travel, on two other trips, was exclusively by planes of Pan-American Airways, with the exception of a brief voyage by Bull Line steamer. Certain discrepancies of season, in the text, may be accounted for by the fact that places were not actually seen in the sequence given, although it appeared more logical so to present them in book form. Islands were frequently revisited.

The Bahamas, nearest to the United States, seem, in the natural order of things, to be an appropriate starting-point, followed by the Greater Antilles: Cuba, Jamaica, Hispaniola (Haiti and Dominican Republic), Puerto Rico; and by the Lesser Antilles: Virgin, Leeward, and Windward Islands, the French islands of Guadeloupe and Martinique; as well as by Barbados, and the equally British Trinidad and Tobago; also the Dutch West Indies; and, lastly, glimpses of the Latin-American republics of Venezuela, Colombia, and Panama. The variety of racial background, an unfailing source of interest, should be noted. British, American, French, Dutch possessions include, among their citizens, as do all the islands, a large proportion of Negro, as well as white nationals. In the case of the independent republics, one, Haiti, is peopled by those of African or Africo-French descent; while, in the others, Spanish-Indian blood predominates. Danes are still to be found at St. Thomas, and Hindus form, approximately, a third of the population of

Trinidad. Exclusive of patois, therefore, the
languages encountered include English, French,
Dutch, and Spanish.

On our most recent visit to the Antilles, by
means of Furness Line and airplane, the most
noticeable changes were to be found on the Island
of St. Thomas and at Trinidad. The American
bases have added to the Cosmopolitan quality that
Trinidad already possessed. Americans, stationed
on the island during the war, now returned as
tourists, may often be seen sharing the scenic
wonders with their families. At St. Thomas the
building of immense hotels on the island has not
marred the intrinsic quaintness of Charlotte
Amalie. The influx of wealthy Americans, some
attracted by the new divorce laws, has perhaps
created the need for the charming Antilles School
for young children, the transformation of disintegrating Danish warehouses along the Caribbean
into delectable gift shops, separated by alleys such
as the one living up to its name, Hibiscus Alley,
leading to the Art Center of the Virgin Islands.
My Illustrator has noted the contrast between pre-
war and modern planes.

AMY OAKLEY

Unless the soul goes out
 to meet what we see
we do not see it ; nothing
do we see, not a beetle, not
a blade of grass.

W. H. Hudson.

BEHOLD
THE
WEST INDIES

Nassau ‡
Bay Street abounds in shops

BEHOLD THE WEST INDIES

Chapter I

Nassau of the Bahamas

Our take-off from Miami to Nassau was in a Caribbean Cruiser. The wind being against us we averaged a mere hundred miles an hour. Incredibly low we flew, hovering over banks of coral, barely veiled by sunlit water rippling into visibility.

Later came currents of turquoise, expanses of cobalt, while, toward the end of the second hour, as we neared our destination, the cerulean shade dubbed Bahama blue blurred remembrance of fainter Bermuda seas.

Nassau, capital and seat of government of the Bahamas' three-thousand-odd isles and islets, was the Charles Towne of pirate days. It is situated on the island of New Providence, which derives its name from the providential preservation from death of one Captain William Sayle, an English navigator, shipwrecked upon its shores.

Charles I claimed the Bahamas for England, granting rights of settlement to Sir Robert Heath in 1629—the tercentenary of this date was duly celebrated. In 1670 Charles II sanctioned a grant to the Duke of Albemarle, but in 1717 the whole was surrendered to the crown. English settlers from Bermuda established themselves first on the island of Eleuthera and later on New Providence. As is obvious, the name of Nassau dates from the reign of William III of the house of Orange and Nassau. Turbulent as were the years of the colony's beginnings, when one governor was deported to Jamaica, another to Cuba, one deposed, another—on his own initiative—actually returning to England (having found the island depopulated, following a French and Spanish raid), later years have been hardly less sensational. Periods of buccaneers and of slave-traders were to be replaced by eras of blockade-runners of the American Civil War, and of sales on the high seas to the rum-runners during Prohibition in the United States. Daring and extravagance have been flaunted along the water-front. Perhaps the outstanding example of Nassau pageantry was in 1718 when George I sent Captain Woodes Rogers to govern the colony. Rogers (the rescuer of Alexander Selkirk) had not, at one time in his career, been averse to marauding the Spanish Main. With all the zeal of a convert and backed by British soldiers, he set himself to his task. A motley assembly of pirates, whom he had been sent to capture or reform, stood at attention as he stepped ashore. Two hundred were to take the oath of allegiance. Eight of the more notorious he chose to hang at Fort Nassau. This was the time when, as Howard Pyle puts it, piracy was in "the flower of its days."

The history of New Providence could no more spare Blackbeard than Shakespeare's masterpiece its Hamlet. At the foot of Mathew Avenue, on the Eastern Parade, once stood the immense fig tree (cut down in 1807 and made into souvenirs) beneath which the freebooter used to hold his council and hang his prisoners. There is a legend that the tree was festooned with ribbons and that the birds in its branches were shot with coins extracted from the pockets of victims. Captain Teach was known as Blackbeard from the bushy growth on his face, worn braided into tentacles—transforming him to the semblance of an octopus. To add to his diabolical appearance, in time of action, it is recorded, in addition to three brace of pistols, "he stuck lighted matches under his hat, which, appearing on each side of his face, and his eyes naturally looking fierce and wild, made him altogether such a figure that imagination cannot form an idea of a Fury from hell to look more frightful." Not Captain Kidd himself

could rival in notoriety this most piratical of
pirates. Teach was past master in the art of ma-
rooning—as his confederates learned to their
sorrow. No less was he an adept at concealing
doubloons and other treasure.

Born in Bristol, serving an apprenticeship
aboard privateers in the East Indies, plying his
trade on the Spanish Main, blockading Charles-
ton, taking advantage of a royal proclamation in
North Carolina, but relapsing to his chosen career,
Blackbeard met his end with his boots on. Lieutenant Maynard of the man-of-war *Pearl* was sent
to Ocracoke Inlet to take him. It was not without
the loss of many men that the lieutenant—after a
hand-to-hand conflict in the course of which Blackbeard was riddled with shot and cutlass wounds—
was able to sail back to Virginia with the pirate's
head a "bloody trophy nailed to the bow of his
battered sloop."

Memories of like sort haunted us at sight of
Blackbeard's Tower, approached by way of the
drive to the East Point. At a villa known as
Towerleigh we were informed that the path uphill
was overgrown but, persevering, we drove to a
group of houses on the adjacent knoll and found a
path through the thicket to where the watch-
tower stands. On its walls we read:

"This Tower according to Legend is the Lookout Built and occupied by Edward Teach ("Blackbeard") the notorious Pirate who infested this

Blackbeard

Island and the surrounding Seas in the early part
of the 18th century. In the Creek near-by he Careened his Ships.''

How near the apparition of Blackbeard draws!
... as in life his face covered with a ''large quan-
tity of hair, like a frightful meteor.''

The protection of Nassau was obtained by the
erection of fortifications. The New Colonial Hotel
has supplanted Fort Nassau. (Beneath this imposing edifice the curious are still shown Blackbeard's well, where the pirate was wont to obtain
water for his ships.) Dominating the town is Fort
Fincastle, reached by vehicle or by the Queen's
Staircase—a flight hewn from the coral rock. Fort
Charlotte—bearing the name of George III's
Queen—like Fincastle has become a signal station.
Its traditional rôle was to guard the western en-

trance to the port, while Fort Montagu, a small
redoubt, two miles east of the town, commanded
the narrows between Athol and Hog Island. This
smaller fort, now dismantled, was erected in 1742.
Near-by is the site of the landing of the expedition under Colonel Deveaux who, with only 220
men armed with 150 muskets, so terrorized and
deceived the Spanish Governor that he capitulated. It is told how Deveaux caused his men to
be rowed backward and forward between the ships
and the shore to give the impression of numbers.
"On their way to the shore they stood up; but as
they rowed back to the brigantines they hid below the gunwales." Dummies were strategically
placed, and soldiers impersonating Indians.

Of late years cruise ships may enter the harbor
of Nassau formed by the narrow channel between
New Providence and the south shore of Hog Island. Larger vessels ride at anchor, while lesser
dock in the neighborhood of the Prince George's
Wharf—named for the Duke of Kent, in 1928,
when he visited the Bahamas on his honeymoon.
Here throngs assembled, on Good Friday morning in the spring of 1934, when Mr. Vincent Astor's yacht *Nourmahal,* flying the Presidential
standard of the United States, received a salute
of twenty-one guns from H. M. S. *Danaë.* Photographs are still shown of Mr. Roosevelt waving
to the populace as His Excellency the Governor
and Lady Clifford left the yacht after returning

Mr. Astor's call. The incident came as the climax of the President's fishing trip among the "out-islands."

The "out-islands" found an unexpected champion during the régime of the royal governor of the Bahamas. The Duke of Windsor and his Duchess visited outposts where no governor had hitherto ventured. The most smartly dressed American women habituées of Nassau have for years vied with one another in rather slavishly copying the styles, including coiffure, of the chic Duchess. *A King's Story: The Memoirs of the Duke of Windsor* has proved a lively topic of conversation to all sorts and conditions of men and women, its photographs of the Duke rivaling in popularity those of the Princess Elizabeth and her children. Only the stony-hearted could fail to be moved by this poignant and dramatic human story.

Roughly speaking only a quarter of the inhabitants of the Bahamas dwell at Nassau, but it is equally true that the vast majority of travelers to the archipelago never venture beyond the confines of Nassau's island of New Providence. The population of the latter was doubled in 1784 when subjects loyal to the King, accompanied by their slaves, immigrated from Georgia and the Carolinas.

Owing to the Gulf Stream, Nassau has a subtropical ocean climate, varying from an average of seventy degrees in winter to perhaps eighty or ninety degrees in summer. Over a period of thirty years fifty-three degrees is the lowest and ninety-eight degrees the highest on record.

Sponges vied with the tourist trade as a source of income during the palmy years of prohibition in the United States. During the present epidemic of sponge disease which has closed the sponge banks, and the upset condition of affairs in the British Empire, Nassau has languished. In the time of the town's prosperity, on a single day, cruise ships have been known to disgorge five thousand passengers. (Today Nassau prospers!)

Adversity has, we thought, its compensations! as we sauntered along a Bay Street almost devoid of foreigners. The north side of Nassau's chief thoroughfare is taken up largely with wharves and markets and with such institutions as the Royal Bank of Canada and Vendue House, once the scene of slave auctions, now headquarters of the telephone and telegraph. The south side abounds in shops tempting the American devotee of things British with a lavish display of English tweeds, Burberrys, Fownes gloves, Kent brushes, liquors, Yardley's soaps and perfumes, vying with native displays of tropical fruits and home-industry baskets. Nassau coconut-palm hats having taken New York by storm, the novelty is less than it would have been a few years ago, but sisal hemp confections and shell ornaments still tempt the searcher for the exotic or bizarre. At the basket

Anything from a handbag to a hamper

market beside the landing-dock soft-voiced natives call the attention of "Missus" to "anyting" from a handbag to a hamper. Luscious are the colors chosen to harmonize with sunburnt skins, skilful the dusky fingers of weavers. Caressing drawls pluck at the heart-strings, aiding and abetting the intrinsic merit of the wares to loose the purse strings.

At the foot of Frederick Street the sponge fleet from Andros still lines the quays at certain hours, but deserted are the packing houses, unemployed the hundreds of sponge trimmers. A mammy sitting on the quay informed me, between puffs on a clay pipe, that trimming was all the work she ever knew. Nowadays the boats bring firewood, corn fodder, and conch shells—gray as to exterior when alive, but the lips delectably pink. Shells were often shipped to Italy for the use of cameo makers. "Right here in Nassau," a native epicure told me, "is the place to sample the part we care for. Conch soup at the Prince George Hotel is an experience."...No less an experience is watching the boatmen knock the spiral shells with machetes and draw forth limp conchs.

The most popular vehicle in Nassau is known as a "carriage." It is a lightly built and ramshackle conveyance of uncertain age, but given a youthful and debonair appearance by gay red curtains—whose chief use may be to detract attention from the nag's inadequacies. As my Illustrator and I lingered on the docks, to my dismay, one of these indigenous vehicles almost ran us down.

"He won't hurt you. He won't bite anything,"

the white-whiskered Negro driver reassured me, flicking his whip in the direction of his cadaverous little horse.

"Yes, he will. He will bite grass!" remarked a native bystander, thereby giving us a fair example of local pleasantry.

Opposite the landing-place stands Rawson Square (named for a former governor), and opposite Rawson Square, with his back to the statue of a youthful Victoria and to public buildings forming three sides of a rectangle—government offices, post-office, Legislative Council and Assembly —sits for the greater part of the day a superb figure of a man on an animal the like of which is not to be found elsewhere in all New Providence. This is none other than Major Hawkins (a retired sergeant of Cavalry) who waits like a spider in the web of the law—the courts lie immediately behind the post-office—ready to pounce upon any beast unfit for work and to fine its owner. In other words the sergeant-major is inspector for the Bahamas Humane Society. Of a poor inbred stock are the creatures who pull the carriages. Jamaica ponies are imported for the races and are frequently to be seen on the roads, ridden by colored jockeys and, more often than not, owned by Negroes.

Government House tops an eminence known as Mount Fitzwilliam. The vista of it obtained from George Street—skirting the colossal New Colonial

Hotel—is impressive. A flight of steps leads to the ample gardens. Dominating the approach stands a statue of Columbus modeled in London—so Mary Moseley, the astute historian of the Bahamas informed us—with the aid of Washington Irving, and presented to the Colony by Governor James Carmichael Smyth. Although the American winter residents build beside the sea, the British first families of Nassau have always preferred to ensconce themselves in sheltered gardens inland. Miss Moseley herself possesses a quaint domicile, on East Street, filled with evidences of the scholarly living of her grandfather, her father, and herself, each in turn editor of that leading newspaper, the *Nassau Guardian*. Prints found in London adorn the walls. One showed the Hotel Royal Victoria (the favorite of Nassauvians) before it received additions at the hand of Flagler. This hotel (of which the brother of Grover Cleveland was once proprietor) and many dignified residences skirt the ridge known as East Hill Street. From the veranda of the Victoria's upper stories one overlooks the very heart of Nassau: Shirley Street with its Green on which the octagonal prison stood—the building (since 1879) converted into a unique Library; Parliament Street leading to the public buildings ... all surrounded, like the hotel itself, with luxuriant vegetation. Mockingbirds carol in the green oasis of ancient tamarinds —a sun-flecked world almost as much removed from mundane intrusion as the world of one's lost youth or as the realm of fish, anemones, and branching coral beneath the surface of Nassau's mirrory seas.

Imagination has been given full scope in the planning of the Royal Victoria's garden. Haughty palms, planted in a jungle of tropical growth, lead to the climax of a ceiba, to see which is in itself reward for a journey to Nassau. The spread of its branches, like those of famous "Peace Trees" in, for example, Cuba and Venezuela, reaches out as though to shelter all mankind. This tree, worthy to be a symbol of fraternity, has made itself host to birds and creeping things. Lilies and orchids, ferns and dangling lianas form appropriate members of its community. By daylight its beauty is reminiscent of others remembered (to me of a certain saman in far Tobago), but at night! At night fairyland takes shape within the precincts of Victoria's garden. Veiled lights glimmer from the heart of trees, concealed, revealed, as breezes stir the fronds. Rapture fills the hearts of young romantics as they dine or waltz beneath the palms.

The New Colonial Hotel, that modern caravansary beside the sea, like the Fort Montagu Beach Hotel is obviously an outgrowth of American prohibition. The Jungle Club, an upstart offspring in the vicinity of Fort Montagu—on the grounds of the hotel of the name—can not compare in ele-

gance with that aging aristocrat, the Royal
Victoria.

The Fort Montagu Beach Hotel started life in
1926 as the Hotel Waterloo, a name scarcely designed to lure the American tourist to whom
Waterloo implies not victory but defeat. Despite
the repeal of the Eighteenth Amendment and the
deflection of travelers in a war-torn world the rechristened hotel has, to date, avoided meeting its
Waterloo.

Nowhere could be found a more striking contrast in housing than between the palatial hotels
of Nassau and the hovels of Grant's Town, the
native quarter "over the hill." The vast majority
of Bahamians are, of course, African Negroes
with, in some cases, a strain of Moorish blood, a
fact stressed by Major Bell in his *Bahamas: Isles
of June.* "The police of Nassau," he avers, "are
descendants of those warriors of the Congo Delta
and hinterland who led by Arab princes carried
chain mail of the Royal Guard." It seems not too
high a claim, judging by the appearance of the
dark-skinned veterans who now, in lieu of mail,
sport red-striped blue trousers, impeccable white
coats and pith helmets.

Between the parasol-decked tables, gay at noon
with convivial lunchers, in the Montagu's garden
and the parasol-decked bathing beach of the hotel,
runs the highway, a continuation of Bay Street—
at this point over two miles from the heart of the

A buttressed ceiba of Nassau .

town and a greater distance from Blackbeard's
Tower and the extreme East Point. Hotel buses
ply at intervals, passenger-laden, to and from
Rawson Square; private motors draw up to load
and unload wealthy owners and their multifarious
baggage; others spin to links and distant beaches.
Beneath shade trees tables display basketry,
tempting even the wary.

Yielding to persuasions we seated ourselves in
a carriage and turned in the direction of "de
village."

" 'De village,' dah's what we call it, yassus,
yassum," our cheerful driver (who had introduced himself as "David, de Shepherd Boy"), a
mason's apprentice out of the tourist season, informed us. " 'De colored section' others call it,
but not the people who live dere, no suh."

Beginning on the edge of the residential quarter
of Nassau, "de village" stretches over a vaster
extent than we cared to traverse. Trees were heavy
with sapodillas—brown as the faces of the inhabitants. It was a source of wonder that tidily-garbed
individuals could emerge from palm-thatched
shanties where, we were told, a dozen occupants
will share a room rented for two or three shill-
ings a week. The scent of roses and orange
blossoms enveloped us. The sun shone hotly on
the just and the unjust, those that lolled at the
local bar and those headed with their offspring
for the Church of God.

Buttressed as their omnipresent ceiba trees are the African Bahamians in their faith. Outgrowth of darker primitive beliefs though their religion may be, it keeps them, on the whole, law-abiding, and forms their chief diversion, as well as giving them an unwavering trust in "de Lawd," an unquestioning child-like devotion unparalleled by their pale-faced Christian brethren. The morals of these people are, however, the despair of monogamists.

"Have you bin to de Holy Rollers?" was the question asked by all our colored friends. "You suttenly would enjoy you'selves."

The night was dark, a high wind blowing, when Labrin called with his carriage personally to conduct us to the Church of God. We complimented him on his well-kept horse.

"Dah's Lion." We could see a Cheshire-cat grin in the faint light of the lantern. "Lion 'cause he's de strongest."

As we neared "de village" Labrin broke into song, the same meandering ditty known to all the "boys"; " 'My Mammy don't want no peas, no rice, no coconut oil!' "

"I tries my level best to amuse you," Lion's driver muttered, as boys, caroling from other carriages lit by fire-fly lanterns, called out as we passed: "You got a good singer, suh, Labrin a good singer."

The streets, for the most part deserted by day,

now swarmed with life. The air was close even before we entered the crowded precincts of the Church of God.

"Dere's never any cold wind in de village," Labrin commented, abandoning Lion at the church door and transforming his lank form into a human wedge—by means of which we gained access through the milling throng.

After registering we were ushered into the visitors' gallery—at the back of the edifice—from which we looked down upon a turbulent sea of color. Banners and signs of welcome greeted us, the American flag was conspicuously displayed, and the blare of a brass band stationed below the speaker's platform. How many American choirs could surmount such an accompaniment? But it was no obstacle to hymn-singing Bahamians. To the clapping of hands they marched, to and fro, led by women captains, white-clad and blue kerchiefed.

"Success Comes in Cans," one sign read. "Failure in Can'ts."

Spider-like from the ceiling hung the names of the "out-islands," under which the delegations were assembled, for this was Annual Colonial Convention, leading up to the climax of mass baptism.

The General Overseer, a formidable black man, led the host in prayer: "The Devil is roamin' along the river ... roamin', roamin' .... Pack your

grip for Hell or Heaven, there's no other place
to go!''

Sister Ruth of Texas was the preacher ... vital
as a mountain lion. Her face—surrounded with
ardent, pressing black ones—was strangely pallid.
For a moment we sensed how ghostly, fearful, the
white man looks to the African bushmen who flee
in terror at his approach. Yet Sister Ruth was of
their race. A satin blouse topped her abbreviated
black skirt. Her person seemed charged electri-
cally. Her words rang throughout the auditorium,
challenging her hearers to deny the truths she
yelled, her theme the ''Advantages of Salvation.''

''Paul knows!'' she shouted, without need of
amplifier, leaping into the air, with forceful gesticulation, her voice gaining in volume as the
emotion of the crowd found outlet in frequently
shouted: ''Praise God!'' ''Praise de Lawd!''

''Job knows!'' hurled back the evangelist.
''Ruth knows!''

As the stentorian voice ceased, the preacher,
dripping from the ordeal, became, instantaneously,
a limp and, one would say, fragile woman.

Color, music, motion, there was nothing static
about the assembly. Its assets were at all times
fluid—perhaps for this reason the coins flowed
so merrily into the proffered plates. Who could
resist a loosely-built usher approaching in cake-
walk rhythm, while the men's choir assembled on
both sides of the platform and the women captains

on the stage all clapped in unison, nodding their heads and even indulging in a few cake-walk maneuvers?—not a black man, "no suh," not a black man.

Homeward bound.

"Suah, boss," Labrin had responded—though obviously disappointed that we were not stopping at Weary Willie's Hotel Roof Garden to see "de Ole Sly Mongoose" in person.

In the impenetrable pall of night the dim light of the smoking carriage-lantern half revealed barely visible jostling forms ... lives, we sensed, as remote from ours as had been the Hindus of India, yet sinister only in proportion to our own lack of comprehension. Melodious voices were heard in the bushes, then stillness reigned where had been sound. Were these highwaymen who startlingly waylaid us? No, they were merely youths with guitars, to whom Labrin was emphatic: "We goin' home," he announced.

"O.K., boss, O.K.," they accepted with the simplicity of children.

Dolce far niente is a mood dear to Bahamians, especially those of color. New-comers at hotels and on cruise ships frequently expend all their energy upon swimming, golf, and tennis, with dancing thrown in for good measure. Sight-seeing plays a minor rôle in the daily round. There is, however, one tour which, in total or in part, should not be overlooked by the visitor who enjoys being a conscious part of his environment. The expedition consists of encircling, in so far as roads will permit, the elliptical island. The start will be from Nassau, continuing as far as Bay Street extends and beyond to Clifton Point and Bluff, on the west, and homeward via the pine barrens.

My Illustrator and I set forth in a chugging car on the kind of day of which Nassauvians boast. The salmon-pink walls of the fantastic New Colonial Hotel, decked in garlands of bougainvillea, rose like a palace of Arabian Nights above the blue of the sea. Passing scenes already known to us—the Persian residence of Professor Charles Dolley (the Beebe of Nassau), the walls of "Ship Ahoy," the tasteful abode of another American, Mr. Austin Levy of Rhode Island (collector of and performer upon fine violins, successful experimenter with crops and cattle on his vast estates on the island of Eleuthera)—we came to the Golf Club on Cable Beach. Here we paused to watch an exhibition of water skiing—youths and maidens, five abreast, riding a towed surf-board as grandly as though it were a dolphin charger and they gods and goddesses of Ancient Greece.

Through woodlands we next chugged on past the remnants of old slave quarters to the extreme western point of the island and from there to the fishing pier of Clifton Bluff. Then followed the pine barrens, scattered cabbage-palms—forlorn and undernourished in comparison with those remembered deep-rooted in the fertile soil of Cuba.

Geologists haggle as to the exact formation of the Bahamas. The islands are conceded to be formed of coral reefs and Æolian deposits. In the rocky soil of the pine barrens of New Providence the surface rock is honey-combed, offering obstacles to walking. So-called "banana holes," of uniform pattern, occur in the limestone, reaching, in certain cases, to a depth of more than forty feet.

Being amateurs of lonely, melancholy pools, my Illustrator and I had tried unsuccessfully to obtain information, more exact than its mere position on the map of *The Bahamas Handbook*, as to the whereabouts of Mermaid's Pool. The road appeared to lead no nearer than a mile to the object of our quest, and there was no indication of a path. As we approached the region, we accosted a bearded black man carrying on his head a load of pinebrush. His manner led us to believe that he knew but would not tell. Do the natives, we wondered, fear to go there? It was after continued scouting that we came upon the trail, the words "Mermaid's Pool" scrawled upon an arrow much askew. Single file we snaked through the short-cropped brush, minding pot-holes and giving thanks for thick-soled footgear.

There was an unearthly stillness—not a bird nor an insect chirruped. Not since the dew pools of Britain, not since Dozmary in Cornwall—where

we had all but seen Excalibur—had we been so
moved at sight of still, forgotten water. Indeed
we had been about to give up the search, discouraged, when the dark circle of the pool's mirror
unfolded, set amid treacherous pot-holes, framed
by a protective phalanx of pines. Cornwall? Brittany? Were we not near to Merlin and Vivian
now? Were we not close to the throbbing heart of
nature, to the mysterious legendary gods—
spurned by man for those of lesser worth? The
sun was sinking . . . still we lingered at Mermaid's
Pool, rechristening it, in our minds, the Pool of
the Water Sprite.

In the Bahamas the legendary and the historic
meet. Ponce de León, fresh from the conquest of
Puerto Rico, sailed the seas in quest of the "Fountain of Youth." A fount with healing powers, according to tradition, exists in the isle of South
Bimini. Another insignificant island, now marked
by an Imperial Light, was long known as Watling's for a religious buccaneer who sang hymns
of a Sunday. San Salvador was the name given by
Columbus to his landfall in the New World and,
with the identification of Watling's and San Salvador, the original name has been restored. "For
lust of knowledge and for love of the cross, he
sailed," says Rosita Forbes in her inimitable book
A Unicorn in the Bahamas—rich in impressions
of the out-islands. Clad in armor and wearing a
scarlet cloak, the admiral stepped ashore and

knelt to hear the Mass—the first to be celebrated in the western hemisphere. Here the gentle Lucayans greeted the white man whose coming was to seal their doom. In the year 1509, so soon after the landing of Columbus, Ovando, governor of Española, received a permit from Ferdinand to procure, from other islands, laborers for the mines. It is said that forty thousand Indians were transported, unresisting, to what they had been told by the Spaniards were the "heavenly shores" ... An expression that was to take on a sinister meaning.

Three channels flow in the archipelago of the Bahamas: the Florida Channel, followed by the Gulf Stream; the Providence Channel, with two branches and a depression known as the Tongue of the Ocean, reaching a depth of 2,700 fathoms; and the Old Bahama Channel between the islands and the Cuban shore. On the west, almost to Cuba, a vast submerged bank limits the depth to a few fathoms.

Information about the out-islands is easily obtained from the Development Board at Rawson Square. By far the largest of the group, over a hundred miles in length, is Andros (the former Isla del Espirita Santo), but it is, in addition, one of the least frequented. Bush blacks as primitive as their brothers in the Congo inhabit the interior, where are vast forests of mahogany and other valuable hardwoods. There is even a tradition that a lost tribe of the Lucayans has found shelter here. The children of the forest-dwellers are said to flee from the white man. Andros, named for a governor of Colonial Massachusetts, is famed for two things: its "rookeries" of flamingoes, and the fact that there Neville Chamberlain managed for some years a sisal-hemp plantation owned by his father. The failure of the sisal estates on Andros is notorious. It was from Andros that the senior Curry, father of the author of that enchanting book *Bahamian Lore,* hailed as a member of the Assembly.

Even on the out-islands contrasts obtain, although to a lesser degree than on New Providence. There is a smart club at Cat Cay. North Bimini, near the Florida coast, with its Compleat Angler inn and millionaires' camps, is headquarters of wealthy fishermen who charter boats to troll for such big game as sailfish, swordfish, and marlin. "The swordfish is really a natural submarine, U-boat and torpedo combined," says Rosita Forbes; but she does not consider swordfish to be as beautiful "as their fabulous cousins with sails upon their backs."

Settlers may be tempted by the lure of the New England Colony on Eleuthera, accessible in good weather by plane to Hatchet Bay or in three and a half hours by motor vessel from Nassau; fishermen, as I have said, feel the call of Bimini; aristocratic names of Old England still exist among the inhabitants of Exuma, and the Exuma Cays are popular for sailing cruises; but, for the most part, the twenty-nine islands, not to mention the 661 cays and 2,387 rocks (the *Encyclopædia Britannica* has had them counted), are undisturbed by the white man. Salt Cay, indeed, has found an American owner and has been rechristened Treasure Island; Sandy Cay, with its straggling palms, is beloved of picnickers; and the name of Rum Cay should be enough to tempt the convivially minded.

Justice in the out-islands is administered by commissioners frequently as dusky as other descendants of sires who were slaves a hundred years ago but whose offspring, educated at English Universities, now sit in the House of Assembly at Nassau and grace the legal and medical professions. Bahamian Negroes, on the whole, are gentle and law-abiding. The beat of the tom-tom is rarely heard, the fire dance is forbidden. Poverty of soil, inaccessibility to markets, the ravages of the recurring hurricane are all factors to prevent the prosperity of out-islanders. Although the sophisticated may sneer at the emotionalism of the Holy Rollers (not all natives of African descent are members of the "Church of God"), yet the Christianity of the devout, in all its primitive simplicity, may be nearer the way of the Master than is that of the so-called Christians to be found in the capitals of the globe. What the Red Cross means to a stricken world the Cross of Jesus means to the poverty-stricken islanders.

The length of the narrow New Providence is twenty-one miles, and of Hog Island, which shelters Nassau to seaward, only three. The best view to be had of the latter is from the roof of the Fort Montagu Beach Hotel. How the wind, almost continuous in the Bahamas, rattles the shutters and lashes the coconut palms in the garden below! Across the white-flecked expanse of blue lies the shimmering island with its famous beaches, its immense mansion belonging to the Swedish millionaire, Axel Wenner-Gren, where Greta Garbo, having flown in a privately chartered plane from Miami, had found an unpublicized retreat.

Paradise, Nassau: Nassau, Paradise—with some the terms are synonymous ... meaning, of course, Paradise Beach. My Illustrator and I had long been familiar with the blue of the Mediterranean at Marseilles and the French and Italian Rivieras, at Algiers and en route to Suez, yet, when confronted with the blue of the Caribbean we had confessed that never before had we known water seemingly of pure cobalt. On the north shore of Hog Island we came, overwhelmingly, upon Nassau blue, that is to all other blues as crimson to rose pink. Leaving, for the nonce, the gaily parasolled tables where we would lunch, the populated breakers where we would swim, we strove to forget all but the lonely curve of gleaming coral

sand inviting our feet. Beyond the sight and sound
of man, with only quivering jelly-fish and conchs
as our companions, we stretched upon the dunes
and gazed oceanward.

"H. P.!" exclaimed my Illustrator—the magic
letters standing for none other than Howard Pyle.

"Marooned"! I echoed—the caption of one of
our favorites in the *Book of Pirates*.

Beyond a turquoise foreground combers rolled
and broke, tossed sapphires transformed beneath
the gaze to diamonds and pearls—as though to
whet the greed of Blackbeard and his lusty crew.
Had not these adventurers, like us, lolled upon
these burning sands, smelt the salt breath of ocean,
let their eyes rest upon spray flying hither and
yon as though in pursuit of tireless gulls? Did not
the same raucous cries beat upon their ears? Did
their world rise and fall with the beat of their
hearts, with the pulse of the sea? Did their globe
tremble and threaten to burst like a fabulous
bubble?

"A penny for your thoughts!" my Illustrator
called.

"Toss me a doubloon," said I, "if I lift the
lid of my coffer."

Talk turned to Winslow Homer ... to Steven-
son, and, inevitably, to Joseph Conrad.

What a shock to come again to pained-looking
athletes ... daubing coco oil on backs of sun-tanned
Amazons, par-boiled to the waist, ogling through

black glasses. It was a relief to find ourselves at last in the shady allée of Australian pines leading dockward. Obviously the beauty of this earthly Paradise is not echoed by the hosts who find shelter there; refugees, to judge by their half-roasted appearance, from a distinctly hotter location.

Sea gardens seen from glass-bottomed boats! ...How I had for years marveled at travelers' tales! Not until we actually stepped into a sturdy craft at the dock at Rawson Square could I believe in my own good fortune. The experience combines with the outing to Hog Island, as the Marine Gardens (natural but protected) lie at the Narrows, between that island and Athol.

"Always ask for Willum's boat," said our soft-voiced darky at the helm.

Past the *Tioga of Marblehead* we threaded our way; past *Stormy Weather,* owned by William La Brot of the Annapolis Yacht Club, four-time winner of the Miami-Nassau ocean race; past the substantial ketch of the Lord Bishop of Nassau— his has been called "a diocese of the sea"; and past Axel Wenner-Gren's famous *Southern Cross,* gleaming in sunlight, almost as svelte, we thought, as our beloved *Stella Polaris.* A Swedish sailor swam at the bow, as though to display his prowess beneath the intent gaze of the flaxen-haired figure-head. On every hand sails caught the wind. The salmon-pink Hotel Montagu rose starkly above

its beach. A plane, having taken off from the
harbor, zoomed overhead on its daily flight to
Miami. Interest had, so far, centered on the element of air, but with the stopping of our engine
and the lifting of floor boards to disclose trans-
parent glass, we forgot that our element was not
water.

Seaweed swayed in the current; minnow-like
fish, brilliant as Brazilian butterflies, darted
among the long grasses. Although the surface of
the bay around us was rippled, perfect calm prevailed beneath our boat. The clarity and purity
of the water was unsullied. With the drifting of
the craft the seascape changed. Rooted in beds
of white sand, fabulous growths resembling plumes
waved continuously; gigantic sea fans of velvety
purple, veined white, and canary yellow, and stag-
horn coral completed the foliage. Studded with
anemones of various colors was the garden; brain
coral, gorgonian sponges, poisonously barbed
urchins—known locally as sea-porcupines. Unlike
Paradise Beach, the Marine Gardens are peopled
with angels ... angel fish, flat as flounders, heavenly hosts in white and yellow or Spanish angels
in black and sunlit gold. Among the feathery sea-
plumes out-of-scale groupers wandered and large
gray snappers, trigger-fish, grunt (the fish that
grunts like a sucking-pig when taken from the
water), luminous parrot-fish—those blue parrakeets of the sea. One with the fish we seemed, an

uncanny experience. Peeping Toms, we felt, with no need of fern seed, for never a fish turned its glassy eyes upon us.

A new world had opened its portals. Bermuda, Woods Hole, and the Bronx hereafter would no longer seem mere aquariums but would have power to transport us in spirit beneath tropical waters. Now doubly significant are memories we guard of Naples and Monaco! Even the Brooklyn Museum has taken on added fame from Herbert Tschudy's reminiscent set of Sandy Cay reef, and Beebe's *Beneath Tropic Seas* has become our deep-sea Bible.

Havana ‡   †   †
The Cathedral has an air of extreme antiquity

Morro Castle: Havana

CHAPTER II

CUBA, EDEN OF THE AMERICAS

HAVANA had taken me unawares. No one had told me of its beauty; or, perhaps, I had not listened in those pre-war days, when Europe's voice called with overwhelming insistence to the would-be wanderer. Arriving in June, fresh from oppressive Panama, aboard a United Fruit Company's steamer, I received the revelation. Here was an ancient, seemingly old-world city—reminiscent of the temperate zone yet tropical withal, bearing earmarks of time and yet subtly modern—comparable to the globe's most far-famed capitals.

Returning to Havana the following January, I dwelt lingeringly upon our more leisurely first approach. El Morro, with its guardian light, had risen toweringly against the blue of summer skies. An almost Moorish picture it had presented— indeed, its sixteenth-century Spanish builders had

used as model a fort erected by the Moors at
Lisbon. El Morro, La Punta, fellow-guardians of
the narrow channel, La Fuerza, oldest fortress of
the Western Hemisphere, had dominated the pre-
vailingly ocher buildings of Havana's old town.
We had glimpsed the New-Yorkish looking Hotel
Nacional upon its cliff, the monumental Malecon,
skirting the sea-wall, the leafy Prado—stretching
to Cuba's Capitol.

Swifter was our second coming to Havana than
once-dreaded onslaught of pirate or buccaneer.
The whirring engines of the "clipper ship" that
bore us had hardly announced the arrival of our
Pan-American plane before, Morro and Prado
passed, it swooped into the land-locked harbor.
No time was there for ceremonious salutation to
familiar landmarks. A mere condescending nod
from our aloof point of vantage had to suffice;
an oblique recognition of an intenser blue, of flying-fish—like ourselves joyously on the wing.
With deafening roar the monster neared the
water, quiveringly alighted, to cleave passage to
its goal.

Havana! Once more we felt the onrush of the
city's Latinity, its European background, its
American foreground, wave after wave of emotional contact, as tangible as those that, at first
impact, had seemed about to engulf our sea-land-
ing plane.

To a native the center of Havana, the zero kilometer from which all Cuban roads depart, is the twenty-four-carat diamond embedded in the floor of the Capitol. To the traveler, however, the center of his universe is his hotel. The summer resident may decide upon the Presidente; the transient sportsman, the business magnate, the creature-comfort-loving pleasure seeker will probably find what they desire at the so-American National Hotel or the more accessible Sevilla-Biltmore; but, for those who go along with me, who wish to imbide deep draughts of the bouquet of the traditionally Spanish, there is no other hotel than the Inglaterra. From it I stretch my measuring rods in Cuba, not from the adjacent Capitol, for is not the Inglaterra a diamond without price, a jewel of a hotel?

Our balcony gave upon the square, the Parque Central: those less athirst for local color might prefer rooms on the Moorish court. There was a similarity about the apartment to our familiar base in Paris. The first, tiled, high-ceilinged, was built for the tropics; glassless French windows, open to breeze unless shutters (if need be reinforced by hurricane bars) were drawn. From the balcony of the second can be seen the Sacré Coeur; but, from the Havana balcony, the dome of the Capitol rises beyond the ornate National Theater on one hand and, on the other, the Prado leads to a glint of sea, where surf flies as high as the lighthouse of El Morro.

Were the cuisine of the Inglaterra not so rich
in local delicacies it would hardly be remembered,
so varied are the accompaniments to meals.
Adolph, the Hungarian maître d'hôtel, had no
sooner helped us to the choice of moro crab, sauce
tartare, for a first luncheon, than the distractions
(second only to Shepheard's in the opinion of my
Illustrator) commenced. Three itinerant guitar-
ists, stationed in the arcade within coin-tossing
distance, began the wistful strains of "Siboney,"
to be followed by "La Paloma," "Estrelita,"
and songs which, like the singers, were presum-
ably of Negro origin. Venders of maracas shook
their leaded gourds. A civilian, lunching with a
toplofty officer of police, seizing castanets, assumed the conductor's rôle. Angora guinea-pigs
(apparently produced from a conjurer's hat)
were, to the delight of Cuban youngsters, peddled,
surreptitiously, indoors.

Spectators crowded the pavement, jostling outside the windows: sailors, tourists, the turbaned
mammy whose doleful wail attracted attention to
the newspaper she sold, merchants of bead-chains
swathed like Hawaiians, walking scarecrows of
sallow countrymen festooned with high-peaked
straw hats, youths with trays of orchids, lottery-
sellers, as everywhere in Cuba, enamoured of lucky
numbers, thrusting whole series forward to tempt
the spectator. Only an iron grille separated us
from the hotel lobby where varied types—Cuban,

Lottery!

American, European, even Chinese—passed fit-
fully. At the Inglaterra life does not stagnate.

The most historic site in the once-walled portion of the city, now spoken of as Old Havana,
is the Plaza de Armas. Here stands the Fuerza
fortress from which de Soto sailed...as he
thought to the conquest of Florida. From La
Fuerza tower his loyal wife, the Doña Isabella,

watched, four years on end, until, convinced at
last of her husband's doom, she had no will to
live. Near-by El Templete, a memorial chapel,
marks the spot where the victorious Spaniards,
under Diego Velázquez, first landed, in the year
1519, celebrating Mass beneath a sheltering ceiba
tree. To-day a bust of Columbus stands where
his supposed remains (now thought to have been
those of his son) were deposited before transfer
to the cathedral. Royal palms ornament the
square, and a statue, with undeservedly eulogistic
inscription, to Ferdinand VII of Spain. Opposite
El Templete is the famed Ayuntamiento, formerly
Government House, but now the seat of Havana's
local administration. The patio possesses a serene
Colonial quality—though at noon its statue of
Columbus looks down upon politicians bickering,
probably, as violently as their forebears did in the
Admiral's day in Spain.

The buildings on the Plaza de Armas have preserved the spirit of their illustrious past—unlike
the Santa Clara Convent and the Franciscan
Church, used respectively as Department of Public Works and as post-office. The former Bishop's
Palace, then Senate Chamber, and now Supreme
Court is an embodiment in stone of law and order.
Within the columned entrance court a heroic head
of Martí (work of the Cuban sculptor Sicre)
presides.

Tranquillity is to be found, if anyhere, in turbulent Havana, on the plaza of the Cathedral erected to the Virgen Maria de la Concepción. The European aspect is overwhelming. Due to the crumbling limestone of which it is constructed, the edifice, erected in 1704 by the Jesuits, has a wholly unwarranted air of extreme antiquity. The sight of its towers and façade, from the arcade of the Café de Paris or from the shops displaying native wares, is heart-stopping to one famished for a glimpse of the Old World.

The renown of Havana's Cathedral need not depend upon its transitory connection with the oft-discussed bones of Columbus. Despite the protestations at Havana and Seville, the scales seem to be tipping in favor of Trujillo City. When Spain lost possession of her colony of Santo Domingo, a vault containing the supposed remains was opened and the contents were sent to rest in Havana. But Spain has made a habit of losing colonies. In 1899 the relics were transferred to Seville. At Dominican Republic we were to hear of the discovery of the true casket.

If Cuba's churches, if indeed Cuba's much-vaunted shops on Obispo and O'Reilly streets of the Old Town leave something to be desired, not so her restaurants. Perhaps only Paris can show any rivals to them, although the cuisine is more that of Marseilles. Not Hispano-American, like the style of architecture, is the traditional Cuban food but, shall we say, Franco-Hispanic.

"Go," had said our burly yachtsman friend, "at once to the oldest and best restaurant in Havana. It's called La Zaragozana."

Following this advice my Illustrator and I stood outside the modest exterior of the place and this is what we read:

"The fish we serve to-day slept in the Ocean last night."

Explaining the origin of the restaurant's name, the son of the house, a student at the University, showed us to a table.

"A century ago," said he, "the houses in Havana had no numbers. The founders of this place were from Saragossa, so their patrons would say: 'We are going to the restaurant run by the Saragossans.' Will you try our local fish, *Pampane sote Maître d'hôtel?* or perhaps *Cangrejos à la Catalana*—moro crab?"

"Why," I exclaimed to my Illustrator, "with such native offerings and such prices as these and those of the Paris, the Florida, the Inglaterra, do tourists to Havana flock to 'Hunt Breakfasts' and 'Smörgåsbord' in caravansaries run by Americans?"

"They're like my friend who scorns the Inglaterra," he said. "Says he likes to keep local color at arm's length."

"After all," I admitted, "Lions and Rotarians, coming as they do four thousand strong, could hardly be accommodated here!"

Perhaps no question is more annoying to a well-bred Cuban than inquiries where best to see a rumba—note the spelling. There is no more need for an "h" in rumba, the saying goes, than a cockney has for an "h" in 'ouse! The true rumba, it seems, is based on African voodoo dances, and, like the tango of Argentina, is considered by Cubans most unsuitable material for ballroom adaptation. At Sans Souci in Havana it is danced by mulattoes and staged after the fashion so popular in New York night-clubs. The admirable dolls in rumba costume, for sale at Snider's Antique Shop, aroused my interest.

"Where can we see rumba dancers in such costumes?" I inquired, to be told, uncompromisingly: "Nowhere at all. These dolls were made by a decent woman."

With some trepidation, having left our valubles at the hotel, and escorted by a Cuban, we ventured forth in the hours of darkness to see the black African version. Hot Dog Alley reached, we threaded our way through phalanxes of shabby citizens, of all degrees of color, who probably did not deserve their reputation of being, in large number, thugs and pickpockets. Palefaces, like ourselves, were few and timorous. Our escort was well known. He clapped on the back the scrawny woman who led us, during a momentary lull, to our drumside table. At the sound of the tom-tom waves of horror engulfed us, so black, so sinister

the rhythm. It conjured darkest Africa...un-
visited by white men. Before the mind's eye
flashed imagined voodoo rites, obscene fetishes,
human sacrifice. The pulsating sound, breaking
all hitherto known bounds, beat upon us, as though
to destroy our white serenity. The dance began. A
black couple—the most renowned of their kind
in Cuba—went through their paces. The word is
well chosen for, in this case, the act was known
as "shoeing the mare"...danced with the abandon of an uninhibited race. Sordid? Yes, and—to
eyes conversant with the art of Shan Kar—neither
graceful nor alluring, despite the agility displayed
by the buxom painted damsel in wielding her
rumba train, and the hip contortions of the danse
à ventre. Small wonder that Cubans do not wish
themselves identified with a dance prohibited upon
the streets, save at Carnival.

Night-life in Havana, as in Paris, has been
stressed to a degree out of proportion to its relation to life as a whole. The notoriety engendered
has appealed, in both cases, to the most frivolous,
if not vicious, element of American tourists who,
especially during prohibition in the U.S.A., frequently disgraced themselves on Cuban soil. There
is intrinsic merit in the blue tropical nights of the
capital and, granted youth and congenial companions, they may be enjoyed to the full at the
Gran Casino Nacional. There is a dignity about
its dimly lighted halls where dancers dine and

players for high stakes gather at gaming tables. On moonlit nights, within sight of the illuminated fountain, amorous couples stroll.

Our most enjoyed evenings were spent at the old Fronton. In contrast to the pelota games we had watched under Pyrenean skies, in the Basque provinces, the kindred game of jai-alai was played in a rectangular indoor court. The ball is hurled against a wall to be caught on the rebound by the wicker *pala* (the *shistera* of the Basques). Three walls are used in jai-alai, contrasting with the single wall—originally of a church—in the Basque pelota. One chilly January night the dampness penetrated to the bone. Mucous membranes were irritated by the density of tobacco smoke, added to by a delegation of policemen—to whom free admission is given. The fifty-cent bleachers are of stone, while higher priced seats tempt the extravagant. Wire netting protects the public. At the front of the cage burly men in starched white suits and scarlet bérets vociferously registered the bets of the largely masculine crowd. Music blared. There was a hush as the players entered, comparable only to that moment at a bullfight upon entrance of the bull. The silence was to be broken by cheers. The first set, three players in white against three in blue, was, my vis-à-vis informed me, composed of Cubans.

"Wait till you see the champions," he chortled, between puffs of a stogie. "They're always

Basques... big names to-night—Guillermo and Ituarte!''

The big six entered, lithe as panthers. Cheers and shouts of "Ituarte!" "Guillermo!" resounded. Umpires, seated within the enclosure, were, after the nature of their kind, eagle-eyed. For sheer poetry of motion a tanned Basque champion of the Fronton outstrips, to my mind, even the least effeminate of male dancers.

"A tie! Do you bet on *blanco* or *azul?*" my neighbor queried. He was dumbfounded to hear we were not betting.

"Come to watch the game?" said he, "I've known others to do the same, but most Americans bet."

"Hope to see you again," he said at parting. "My name is López," handing us his card, "and my business, rum."

Jostling our way to a taxi after the game we noticed a pitiful derelict reeling in the path of the car.

"They take rum," muttered the driver, turning up his coat collar, "because of the cold."

There is a serpent in the Cuban Eden—the same that rears its malevolent head in other lands than Cuba—the serpent poverty. Disease and crime lurk within Havana's limits in the squatter-constructed shacks, forming "villages" on government land. Conditions are worse than it has been my misfortune to observe elsewhere, save among famine-sufferers outside the walls of Nanking. In soul-troubling contrast to these festering centers of unrest is the splendor of the National Capitol of the new Republic.

The pearly whiteness of this building suggests, at first glance, the Capitol in Washington. Its lofty dome is unsurpassed in height by any but Saint Peter's and Saint Paul's. An immense flight of steps leads to the Reception Hall where hundreds banquet to celebrate the opening of Congress. Sixty-five kinds of marble have been used in the building's construction—the most in any one edifice in the world. The rose-colored floor of the vast Reception Hall (the Hall of Lost Steps, where the President of the Republic takes his oath of office) recalled to us, by its mirrored reflections, the Diet at Helsinki. Gold leaf has been lavished on the Florentine ceiling; thirty-two candelabra washed with gold lead the eye to the central point in all Cuba, the Kimberley diamond, embedded in the floor beneath the dome, given by those who constructed the building—architects, engineers, and laborers—at a cost of $8,500.

"There was no duty to pay," our informant explained, "and, in those days, a dollar was worth a dollar! On the Central Highway one says: 'How many kilometers are we from the diamond?'"

The stone is not as incongruous in its unique setting as might be supposed. It is placed dramatically, as befits the hub of Cuba's universe, not only beneath the dome but in the center of an eight-pointed black onyx star, encircled by gold from the pens used in signing documents for the construction of the Capitol and the Central Highway. The diamond has thirty-two main cuts, and the marble consummation of the stone's remarkable placement has, likewise, thirty-two points, signifying those of the compass. Although Machado's pockets may have bulged in consequence of this dual enterprise, yet, it must be conceded, Cuba benefited by these two outstanding achievements.

Like the diamond—above which an immense personified "Cuba" in bronze and gold stands guard—the Capitol derives added distinction from the lavish beauty of its setting. Here two parks combine to form the Parque Fraternidad. Here fountains play and sun-exposed cannas flame; here royal palms form the foliage for that heaven-aspiring efflorescence, the golden dome. Here, too, stands the Pan-American Peace Tree (a thriving ceiba), visible token of solidarity, planted with much ceremony in 1928 in soil brought from the twenty-one countries taking part in the Sixth Pan-American Conference, this time held in Havana; Mr. Hughes, Mr. Kellogg, and Mr. Coolidge representing the United States of America.

A statue of José Martí (the George Washington of Cuba) stands in Central Park, from which the Prado or Paseo de Martí leads. "It is not a very imposing monument,'' says the indispensable *Blue Guide to Cuba,* ''but his true monument, Cubans will tell you, lies in their hearts.'' As a leader of the Revolution of 1895, Martí—the poet and idealist—was not willing to remain an exile in New York, but returned to Cuba and was killed in the first military engagement. Martí is said to have embodied all the human virtues.

January twenty-eighth dawned cold and fitful. On this day the president of the republic was to review the school children of Havana, who, in honor of Martí's birth, would place wreaths at the base of the statue in the Parque Central. The balcony of our room at the Hotel Inglaterra was opposite the presidential grandstand. Palms had been massed around the pedestal of the monument. Beginning before the scheduled hour of nine, and continuing until after noon, the delegations marched. From the Prado they came, from the direction of the Capitol, from the heart of the Old Town, passing before the arcaded headquarters of the Regional Society of the Central Asturiano. Marshaled by nuns were those of rightist tendencies, while others—of the extreme left judging from the mammoth hammer and sickle on red field incorporated in their floral offerings—were led by Communists. Black-faced, colored, white, harmoniously uniformed, the children passed, to the sound of Army or Navy bands or marching school performers, skilfully drum-majored.

Flashing sunlight emphasized the blues and reds and greens, gleamed on full white skirts and gold and silken banners. Youthful patriots staggered beneath the weight of Cuban flags, cadets carried likewise the "Chinese" flag of Batista. The president of the republic, in sombrero, smiled approval as saluting youth deposited floral expressions of patriotism. Vivid, tropical were the blossom-formed confections of cannas, bougainvillea, lilies—framed in palm or silvered laurel, ribbon-bedecked. The statue of Martí was surrounded. It seemed no space remained, yet, even after the noon gun had sounded from the fortress of La Cabaña, belated delegations elbowed their way through milling throngs.

"Guests will receive visitors only in the Public Sitting Rooms or Parlors. It is strictly prohibited to do so in their Rooms or Private Parlors...." So read Article 7 of a notice posted in our bedroom at the Inglaterra. Enforcement of the ruling would seem to be in the same class as certain Articles of the League of Nations or of the Thirty-nine Articles of Religion.

"Have you a balcony on the Square?" had been the first question of the new-found friend to whom we had borne a letter from a member of the Commission on Cuban Affairs organized by the Foreign Policy Association.

"Splendid," he had said, in reply to our affirmative and hospitable answer. "Several of us who will be on the speaker's platform for the Opposition meeting to be held on Martí's Birthday did not know how our wives could hear the speeches.''

Thus it was that, as night fell, there was unsuppressed excitement within our apartment, as well as on the plaza. Throngs poured into the illuminated Square. From all points of the compass they came—afoot, by car, by caravans of motor buses. Bunting fluttered from balconies. Outside the National Theater, outlined with electricity, machines for peeling oranges were set up. Above the heads of the multitude venders carried Aaron's rods, blooming with lollypops. Amid cheers and jeers a political ''sound-wagon'' passed, blaring mechanical propaganda. Eagerly seized leaflets of the Opposition bore portraits of the speakers—three ex-presidents of the Republic.

Raps, not always audible above the din, came upon our door. Ladies in chic fur jackets overwhelmed us with their appreciation of our hospitality. A matron, formerly a leader in the movement that had won the suffrage for Cuban women, was escorted to the door by her fourteen-year-old son, protesting: ''My son is as Spanish as my father!''

Lone señoras and emancipated señoritas used our telephone to reassure families of safe arrival. Calls came for the editor of *Accion*...several husbands had remained with their wives. In all we numbered seventeen: every one able to speak

English with vivacity, the ladies vivid-cheeked, pearls at ears, and jauntily hatted; the gentlemen woolen-socked, with overcoats, as a Yale man put it, "once worn to the Yale-Harvard game." Their ice-cold hands clasped sheaves of rockets.

"We are the Revolutionists," said one, on entering. (It had a heart-stopping sound, until one remembered Washington and that, in Cuba, the powers that be were reckoned Fascist or Communist.)

"Anything may happen to-night!" said another.

A fiery-haired member of the ABC (the Revolutionary Party) bolted repeatedly from the balcony at the boom of rockets set off by the throng which numbered, *Accion* was next day to state, one hundred thousand.

"I've been through so many shootings," the lady apologized. "I saw a dozen killed in 1934, when our demonstration of ABC's was fired upon."

Hour after hour the orators harangued insatiable listeners. Loud-speakers amplified their sonorous voices which were carried by radio to the ends of the island ... an eleventh-hour permission having been granted by presidential intercession. Midnight passed and still the applause of the people was roared and bellowed.

"Votes will prove the success of our meeting," a fire-brand professor, who had endured years of

exile for his convictions, told us, lingering over
farewells: "For us this will mean prison or the
president's palace."

Modern Havana is riotous with color. The imposing ocher buildings of the University dominate
Vedado: the multi-hued houses are framed by vegetation. Beyond the gardens of the Tropical
Brewery lies the park, El Bosque, where the gorge
of the Almendares River separates Vedado from
the still less urban municipality of Mariano.
Palms, rubber trees, laurels, afford shade to boulevards unsurpassed in any capital of the world.
Scarlet, crimson, vermilion, even magenta delight
the painter's eye. This is true at all seasons, owing
to the wealth of flamboyants, poinsettias, bougainvilleas. Window glass is rare. Perpetual summer (frost is unknown despite the biting winds
of "unusual" winter weather) encourages the
growth of climbing roses which festoon stucco
walls and enhance the gaiety of sunlit iron grilles.
"The magnitude of Havana and the fullness of
life which was going on there entirely surprised
me," wrote James Anthony Froude, in 1887, com-
paring the city to Burgos or Valladolid. How
much more astonished would Froude be if he
could drive to-day along the Malecon and Fifth
Avenue—a distance of about ten miles—to the
municipal beach, the Playa de Mariano. It was
under the American régime, when Leonard Wood
was governor of Cuba, that the now famous prom-

enade of the Malecon was built. The San Lazaro
tower (a sixteenth-century lookout against pirates) would be the only object Froude would
recognize. Standing in its accustomed place it is
now overshadowed by an equestrian statue to
the incredible Maceo—politely known as the
"bronze" hero of the Revolution. Beyond Maceo
Park, on the drive skirting the sea, the towers
of the Hotel Nacional look down upon the
monument, erected by Cubans, in memory of the
officers and men who perished when the *Maine*
exploded (from causes as yet unproved) in the
harbor of Havana. Palaces of Americans vie with
those of Cuban millionaires along a Fifth Avenue
more exclusively residential than its prototype in
New York. Mariano beach is a delight. The sand,
we are told, has been brought from Florida—these
Cubans spare no pains. The entrance fee is low.
Here the public may enjoy bathing the year round,
lounging beneath tropical almonds, dancing in a
palm-thatched pavilion, pausing to partake of
coconut ice, served in the shell, or that frothy
speciality, Cuban-style pineapple juice—food for
gods. More exclusive Cubans frequent the sea-
pool of the Habana Yacht Club, whose spacious
clubhouse, decorated with trophies and with pennants, forms a brilliant setting for Cuba's élite
during the time of the regattas.

Guanabacoa, a resort to the east of El Morro,
prides itself upon the fact that here, in 1508, Se-

bastian de Ocampo, discoverer of Havana harbor, careened his ships, obtaining pitch from the near-by hills. His reception by the Siboney Indians was a friendly one. Columbus had sighted the island on October 28, 1492, landing upon the north shore and, ten years later, upon the south shore. He was unaware at the time of his death, in 1506, that he had not discovered a continent. Cuba—for so the Indians called it—was first circumnavigated by de Ocampo.

"The most beautiful land that human eyes have ever beheld," Columbus wrote of Cuba, thereby alining himself with connoisseurs in centuries to come. It was not until 1511, at a time when the son of the Admiral was governor of Española, that an expedition under Diego Velázquez was sent for the settlement of Cuba...Baracoa, Bayamo, Trinidád, Santiago, and lastly, in 1515, on the south shore at the mouth of the Gunies, San Cristóval de Havana—to be moved four years later to its more healthful present site.

Batabanó—port of departure for the Isle of Pines, noted for its sponge fisheries—occupies the approximate position of the original Havana. The expedition to Batabanó, made by motor of an afternoon, should not be overlooked. It is well to arrive before the closing of the sponge factories. Male and female sponges (the latter in this case without sarcasm "the better half," awaiting bleaching like other chemical blondes of their sex) are divided into separate bins. A monstrosity measuring about six feet has been hung pridefully from the ceiling of one factory. Remnants of sponge litter the beach. Salt water canals, scarcely wider than gutters, edge the main street of Bata-banó. Spanned by little bridges leading to dwellings, these canals give the village an especial quality. Children on roller skates herald even the mild distraction of a car's arrival. Mosquitoes, it is said, have been the undoing of the seaport of Batabanó.

Not because of the village itself, a poor place, do I extol this trip to lovers of rurality. Near Batabanó are plantations of sugar cane—ready to cut in January; pineapple fields where carts are laden; and oxen ploughing the red soil we were told was composed of iron, manganese, and lava dust. But it is not for any of these reasons that I recommend the jaunt but solely for the revelation of the beauty of royal palms. I had known these trees as courtly denizens of tropical gardens. Never had I met them as princelings out of bounds; reconnoitering, as it were, in windblown battalions or celebrating, at sunset, a rhythmic carnival. To understand a native, visit him in his own home. Cuba is the habitat of these svelte palms—the royal offspring in a democratic land where regality ceases to be a virtue save in the vegetable kingdom.

Havana is not Cuba. With the opening of the

In Cuba tobacco is King

Central Highway travelers are no longer obliged
to limit their knowledge of the island to ports of
call. Our own method was so successful as to be
worthy of imitation. Nine days were spent on the
road with José Duque Estrada, known to the
Hotel Inglaterra, at the wheel of a Packard car.
Trains in Cuba are slow, buses crowded; local
color is often missed in a foreign land without the
coöperation of a native chauffeur. One day, upon
return to Havana, was spent on the drive to the
"West Turn"—the region of Pinar del Rio, famous for its tobacco. Here plants are sheltered
from birds and insects and, especially, from
change of temperature, by coarse netting—a draw·

back from the painter's point of view, but he has his innings on arrival at Vinales.

My outstanding impression of the entire week of the expedition to Santiago was wonder at the number of horsemen encountered along the way. Planters, cowboys, farmers with bulging saddle-bags and, perhaps, a brace of chickens—firmly seated on Mexican saddles, or less prosperously perched, in my mind's eye they pass again. Most vividly of all I see once more a funeral cortège near Madruga. Two horsemen set the pace. The hearse, an automobile, was followed by mourners on stocky Cuban ponies. There was something infinitely touching about the leathery tanned faces of these farmers—expressive of the odds against which they struggle to wrest a living from the soil in which they, too, will one day lie.

"There is not a woman among them!" I exclaimed to Estrada. To which he replied: "Women never go to funerals in Cuba."

"Could a woman not go to that of her own husband or child?"

"It is not the custom."

Even to-day most Cuban women do not travel unattended and rarely go out alone at night. I was assured, however, that other fiancés are not as exacting as one, of whom we heard, who did not permit his beloved to leave her house at all! The medieval Spanish attitude of mind toward women dies hard, even though they are now voters

in Cuba. When, with the coming of new roads and
more democratic legislation, men feel it safe to
undertake a journey without firearms, perhaps
women will emerge more fully from their enforced
domesticity.

Another episode in the region of Madruga was
our first visit to a Cuban sugar-mill, the Central
San Antonio. Erected in 1921 this modern enterprise is, in these parlous times, running only two
months of the year. The mill was one of those
owned by Mr. Hershey, who is also the proprietor
of a refinery—the one used in the production of
Hershey chocolate is in the United States. (Seventy-five per cent of the active sugar-mills in Cuba
are said to be in American hands.) Grinding continues day and night while the mill is in operation. At short intervals carloads of cane are
dumped into chutes and passed, by means of mechanical conveyers, to be sliced and crushed in
rollers and finally squeezed. The juice, after
straining, neutralization of acid, and settling, is
sent to the evaporator.

Workmen were stripped to the waist in the portion of the mill to which, despite the heat, we penetrated to watch the final processes. From the cen-
trifugal machines pours forth a foaming liquid;
this fluid goes to the boilers, finally to emerge divided into sugar and a molasses used in distil-
leries. The entire procedure from cane to sugar is
accomplished, we were told, in twenty-four hours

—the usual rate of cane received being almost a hundred tons an hour. The unrefined sugar, of which our guide garnered a sample, was the off-white variety preferred by Cubans. The delectable dark brown sugar, known locally as "black," can not be stored, as it turns to liquid.

A hundred million dollars is considered the approximate value of Cuba's annual crop, although double that amount was paid during 1914 to 1915. Following unscrupulous speculation in sugar the 1919 to 1920 crop sold for over a billion dollars, with subsequent disastrous decline in price of sugar.

The rustling of the wind, seemingly perpetual in cane-fields, comes back to me, and the remembrance of a vast sea of beckoning plumes. Especially do my thoughts fly to the shipping station of the Maria Antonio Mill, near Santa Clara. Dozens of groaning bullock carts were to be seen. So heavy was the ripe cane, so rough the fields, that, although eight beasts were harnessed to a team, there was much straining at yokes.

Matanzas prides itself upon its Yumuri Valley. Viewed as a panorama from the Hermitage of Montserrate the plain is, perhaps, less striking than it might be to a horseman hedged within the valley walls. This was the scene, in 1511, of the massacre of the Arawaks. The harbor of Matanzas, with its crescent shores, blue waters, and dominating hill, is compared by the imaginative to Naples, while one not unduly modest suburb is

Groaning carts of cane +

known as Versailles. All seemed well in the realm
of Cuba while we lunched beside the fountain of
the Hotel Gran Paris; and yet our friend Inez
insisted upon showing us the latest copies of
Carteles. In these Liborio (like our own Uncle
Sam) represents the people. But our friend explained times were so bad that Liborio had become in the cartoons Liborito, a miserable little
fellow, who in one case tugged at the sleeve of a
fat politician only to be told: "No time for you
till after the elections."

Cardenas is another north coast town. Familiar names made us feel at home. First were the posters with the face of our friend Jean Andres Llitéras, "Delegado a la Constituyente"; then was the recognizable form of Columbus on the Cathedral Square; and, opposite the Hotel Europa, a bandstand decorated with the names of Chopin, Wagner, and Verdi. The climax was, however, on the peninsula of Hicacos—near the far-famed Varadero Beach resort hotel—where the massive gates of Xanadu swung wide in welcome. Spears of henequen bristled guard as we sped, mile on mile, toward the towered mansion of the American Kubla Khan whose "pleasure gardens" (not to mention golf links) are sprinkled by water piped beneath the bay, a distance of ten miles. Beaches were in a state of flux, owing to winds and waves fetching and carrying the sands hither and yon at Neptune's will, but what was that to one who had, after the way of potentates, said: "Let there be soil"... and soil covered the rocky links and terraced garden coves? Through a wind-blown forest of interlacing sea-grapes we tramped with our hosts, to come at last upon a conch-strewn shore as remote from habitation as those of Trinidad or Tobago. Leaf-cutting ants, in procession, scurried to mammoth nests; lizards viewed us with suspicion. Here sailed Portuguese men-of-war, sky-blue fairy galleons rounding cliffs undermined by an insidious sea. On a nearer beach fishermen, dwellers in caves, where buried treasure has been hid, spread drenched nets. The sun neared the horizon as we reached the sheltered terraces of citrus fruits...the coral grottoes blossoming with unexotic daisies, pansies, dahlias, sweet-williams, and sweeter roses.

The Cuban architect of the mansion was also sculptor of the head of a Carib Indian on the mantel of the baronial salon. Mahogany, resisting termites, has been used undeviatingly, and wrought-iron lavishly in grilles. The dining-hall re-created the atmosphere of medieval Spain... hung with tapestry, candle-lighted, with our patrician hostess a legendary queen. Noiseless servitors emerged from and were swallowed up by shadows—robed Moors, perhaps, if not, indeed, the turbaned vassals of Kubla Khan.

After the tumult of seemingly interminable nights spent in Havana we reveled not alone in the stillness but in the diminutive chirrup of crickets, the faint night-stirring of birds. Sensational had been the sunset, Turneresque, but the splendor of the night at Xanadu was of surpassing beauty. As we stepped from "marble halls" into the mysterious garden, among rustling palms, the heavens appeared within man's reach, obtainable to men of good will; below Orion's splendor shone an unfamiliar star—unheralded by angelic choir—that filled our hearts with wonder . . . the illustrious Canopus.

The Hotel Perla de Cuba, fronting on the park
Serafin Sánchez, advertises thus:

"Come to Sancti-Spíritus a full of attractives city
foundred in the year 1514," and, lauding the "service
insuperable" of the hotel itself: "The bes tin the City
... sorprenidid Restaurant, prices are reanduable, we
furinsh garage."

Was the translator perhaps in his cups, like a
planter in a ten-gallon hat who accosted us at
lunch? Probably not ... certainly banal words
would not so well serve to express the nonchalant
mood of this Alice-in-Wonderland town. Estrada,
to whom the place was unfamiliar, had, on his own
initiative, employed an imp-like lad, who, knowing the labyrinth of narrow streets, could steer
us while discoursing in Spanish. The first step was
to rid the running-board of urchin sellers of chattering parrakeets or cowhorn crocodiles. The next
was to drive to the church, with medieval tower
from whose belfry the ancient city resembles a
prototype in Spain. The formal square is Cas-
tilian, as are the corner harness shop—where the
construction of studded trappings held our interest—the conspicuous theater, and, most especially,
the antique bridge ... my Illustrator's delight. Beside the bridge looms the "House of Two Hundred Doors," doors to turn whose keys would be
to unlock no-longer-cherished reminders of forgotten centuries, doors opened rarely nowadays,

The ancient bridge of
Sancti-Spíritus

for the richest families in Sancti-Spíritus, owners alike of sugar-fields, of tobacco plantations, and of cattle, dwell in Havana.

Sancti-Spíritus is set among *vegas* of tobacco. Whichever way one turns the scene is of broad leaves growing in luxuriant profusion, hanging to dry on outdoor racks, or stored in vast barns— the very thought of which brings memory of pungent odor. It is a world apart. If sugar be queen in Cuba, no less is tobacco king.

It is said that when Columbus first came to Cuba he found the Cubenos (the native Siboney Indians) dwelling in *bohíos* (huts) of the same type but cleaner than those used in the interior to-day. For beds the aborigines employed *hamacs*. Although the West Indian origin of tobacco is remembered, few seem to realize that hammocks were first used in Cuba.

The island was at one time divided into three provinces: Havana, Camagüey, and Santiago; latterly into six: Pinar del Rio, Havana, Matanzas, Santa Clara, Camagüey, and Oriente. Of these the central province of Camagüey prides itself upon being the "whitest," while the coffee-growing province of Oriente, the nearest to Haiti, is, unquestionably, the "blackest."

Camagüey—so named by the Indians—has been called "Cuba's Kentucky," famed both for its horses and for the beauty of its women, descendants of Spanish settlers. Despite vicissitudes the prosperous town of the name has guarded reminders of its historic past. The town was sacked in 1668 by the pirate Morgan, who imprisoned the population in their fortlike churches until they bought their ransom with five hundred head of cattle, to be delivered, with salt for the curing, aboard ship. The Cathedral and the Soledad have been rebuilt, but the Merced, founded by missionaries of Our Lady of Mercy about 1628, remains intact.

Garlands festooned the walls of the Merced on the day of our visit, relics, so said our cicerone, of the fiesta of the Niño Jesus de Praga. Our guide, a daughter of Camagüey and, therefore, one who would have graced a mantilla, opened doors to disclose the golden images carried in procession on feast days, especially on that of the patron of Camagüey, San Juan.

"Long, long ago," the señora told us, "there lived a rich Cuban who had one son and who adopted a waif. The boys grew up and both loved the same señorita. The adopted son slew the father's only child. In order that the murderer should not benefit by his wealth, the man left all his money to La Merced."

The señora led us to the monument, an elaborate model, in dull silver, of the Holy Sepulcher, made, according to the donor's wish, from the actual forty thousand Spanish dollars of his fortune.

During its Colonial prosperity, and until the restoration of the original name in 1902, the city was known as Santa Maria de Puerto Principe. The Spanish barracks for two thousand men, built in 1849 in what was then the outskirts of the town, had, in 1903, become the renowned Hotel Camagüey. Its fame rested no less upon its cuisine than upon the attraction of its patio, where once were quartered the horses of the cavalry but where nowadays is to be seen an infinite variety of tropical foliage. From roof gardens the outlook is upon rare palms, bread-fruit trees, and spreading poincianas. Here, where bougainvilleas overhang ancient iron grilles and sunlight checkers Ali Baba jars—once the town's only reservoirs, standing beneath roofs to catch rain-water—peace prevails yet, in this very patio four martyrs of the Revolution of 1851, including the leader Joaquín de Agüero, were executed.

Camagüey being over five hundred feet above sea level is blown upon by the trade winds. The labyrinth of its streets was said to exist to baffle pirates, not, as at Arles in Provence, to withstand the mistral and to outwit the devil. That tropical hurricanes can not easily be withstood is proved by the loss of two of the original four palms planted in the park in honor of the martyred heroes of Camagüey. Behind the near-by bandstand an awe-inspiring ceiba lifts its branches heavenward. It has been fittingly dedicated by the

Alumni of the Public Schools as a monument to the founding of the Republic on May 20, 1902.

The mighty ceiba, undisputed potentate dominating the landscape, replaced to the West Indian slave the baobab worshiped with fantastic rites by his African ancestors. Solitary stark trees loom incongruously even in sugar-fields, for no Negro will fell a ceiba.

Santiago de Cuba, sheltered by its hills from the winds which sweep Havana, faces the Caribbean. The distance from the capital to this second city of Cuba is twenty-two hours by train or eighteen by omnibus. Trucks ply the route habitually. Private cars are few, and those holding American licenses are so rare as to be almost non-existent.

As we rolled toward Santiago, Estrada entered with amusement into our sport of identifying trees. The royal palm and the ceiba were lords of all the country-side. In kaleidoscopic succession followed exotic date-, coco-, and cabbage-palms, and palmettos. We were later to make the acquaintance of such burly fellows as the hickory-palm, barrel-like and unshaven. The incongruity of familiar woodpeckers ("carpenters" to the Cubans) hammering beneath coconut blossoms was surpassed only by smooth trunks of elderly royals belted with paint emblazoned, ignominiously, with the words *Pasta Gravi.*

On we whirled. Banana plantations, groves of

Palms in kaleidoscopic succession,

lords of the country-side

blossoming orange or mango, alternated with un-
settled regions where forests had been uprooted
by hurricane. Hogar Infantil Campestris—schools
built by order of Batista and, by the same token,
flying the Batista ''Army'' flag, side by side with
the star and stripes of Cuba; cockpits in the form
of roofed circular grandstands; *bohíos,* lonely or
in pseudo-African villages flashed by. Ever the
theme song was the same: above the purr of our
car, the repeated beat of horses' hoofs. Not until
we entered the hills and approached Santiago did
we out-distance horsemen.

Santiago is indeed vastly more tropical than
Havana. The proximity to Haiti is sensed in the
increased number of black faces. What can be put
off until mañana is not done to-day. We had
thought it poor psychology for the Casa Granda
Hotel (an establishment under the same railroad
management as the lamented Camagüey) to adver-
tise itself as ''earth-quake proof,'' but our ideas
changed on arrival. It is heartening to be reassured on this point by the survivor of the same
shock which, in 1933, gutted the establishment of
a competitor across the square who had not had
the decency to put his house in order. Our windows looked down upon the restored statue of
Saint Michael, guarding the Cathedral which
dates from the year of Santiago's founding by
Velázquez, 1522. Of all the attractions in this former capital none can compare with the view of the

city seen from the roof of the Casa Granda. This hotel is commercial, but, upon the refuge of this exalted lookout, we forget the blatant commercialism, the traveling salesmen and mosquitoes, the crickets the size of whistling frogs, the beggars, the black men in the lobby. The clangor of bells enhances the whole, connotes the continuity of Catholicism in the land of Cuba since Columbian times.

Within easy radius of the hotel are the birthplaces of the military hero Antonio Maceo and of José Maria Heredia, famed as a poet in the French language, and the theater where the youthful Adelina Patti made her début. Farther afield is the Calle Padre Pico, a picturesque flight of steps at the bay's end; the cemetery of Santa Ifégenia, where Martí is laid to rest. In the adjacent lot Martí's friend, Palma, first president of the republic, is mourned by a bronze figure symbolizing Cuba. Day after day flowers nod, the wind rustles the palms, sunset tinges the hills, harmony is in the very air; but the justice of which Martí dreamed does not yet prevail.

The Peace Tree (a ceiba, it is hardly necessary to add), on the road to San Juan Hill, spreads its mighty branches over commemorative tablets and silenced cannon. Its custodian, offering me a scarlet hibiscus, endeavored to dispel persistent gnats so that I might tarry long enough to look at the inscriptions:

CAMPAIGN SANTIAGO DE CUBA, 1898
MAJOR GEN. W. R. SHAFTER, COMMANDER
5TH CORP U.S.A.
THE LIBERATING ARMY OF CUBA IN THE PROVINCE OF
SANTIAGO DE CUBA
MAJOR GEN. CALIXTO GARCIA, COMMANDER
NORTH ATLANTIC FLEET, U. S. NAVY
REAR ADMIRAL WM. T. SAMPSON, U.S.N.
2ND SQUADRON COM. WM. SCHLEY, U.S.N.
ERECTED BY THE GOVERNMENT OF THE UNITED STATES
OF AMERICA

The Fort of El Viso at El Caney may be visited, but the more rewarding excursion is San Juan Hill, where, upon a fragmentary brick tower, topping the eminence, we read the following:

At this site the American troops under Gen. Wm. R. Shafter and the Cubans under Gen. Calixto Garcia engaged for the last time the battle-scarred army which upheld in Cuba the government of Spain. The possession of this hill gave victory to the allied armies, compelled the Spaniards to furl their flags and depart from the Western Hemisphere. Thus on this sacred battlefield Roosevelt and Wood contributed to mark the 1st of July, 1898, as the date on which the sun of liberty first shed its rays on Cuban soil.

The participants in the war are commemorated in bronze: a boyish Rough Rider, hat in hand; a loosely-clad *"mambi"* (Cuban soldier) and even —manifesting time's healing power—a handsome bas-relief to the fallen soldiers of Spain.

The Cubans called the highway that leads to the top of Mount Boniato, "Wood's Folly." "A highway where no man wants to go," they said of it. Now that tourists flock to it in automobiles this feat of engineering no longer receives condemnation. The panorama from the summit includes the range of the Sierra Maestra across an inimitable foreground: the glowing tile-roofed Santiago and a blue wisp of distant Caribbean—pierced by the cloudlike mountains of Jamaica.

El Morro (that is to say, "the promontory") is even more dramatically placed than other castles of the name at Havana and San Juan. It commands the narrow entrance to the bay, over five miles from Santiago. The fortress was reconstructed in 1664 after attack by Morgan. Here Hobson was detained after the sinking of the *Merrimac*. It was through this channel that Admiral Cervera's fleet passed to meet its Waterloo. Peaceful as was the scene on the day of our visit, the presence of the queenly *Danmark*, a Danish square-rigged training ship, turned our thoughts to European strife.

El Cobre, in the hills near Santiago, is the Lourdes of Cuba. The comparison with Lourdes was emphasized as we drove from Cobre toward Balamo. The mountains are at all times strikingly similar to the Pyrenean range and especially is this so on the approach to Balamo, where Turquino lifts his head eight thousand feet above the plain—an altitude unmatched in the West Indies save in the Dominican Republic.

Santa Clara, a modern town, well-paved because the birth- and one-time dwelling-place of the unscrupulous dictator Machado, has little to recommend it to lovers of the picturesque except that it acts as a base for the excursion to Trinidád—their chief objective in all Cuba. Departure is made, before the dawn, from the Plaza Vidal, where the Central Hotel's windows overlook a statue to the patriot Marta Abreu, wife of de Estevez, the first to be a vice-president of Cuba. The señora used her fortune to foster the Revolution and in founding a theater whose profits were doled out to the poor. (In Havana there is a monument to America Arias, wife of José Miguel Gomez and mother of Mariano Gomez, both presidents of Cuba. How many statues erected to women can be found, I wonder, in the United States?)

Imagine us at 6 A.M. rattling through the darkness to catch the train to Cumbre, on which hot coffee will be served, and then, while stars still shine, changing to the one-track line over which we shall travel till 9:30 A.M. to reach our destination: for highway there is none to Trinidád. We could see our breath in the short train that jolted prodigiously from station to station. Officers, in rough cloth overcoats, khaki breasts gleaming with medals and service stripes, shared our congested quarters. One, who might have stepped

from a Zuloaga canvas, rose frequently to slam
the door against the ice-cold blasts. Other fellow-
travelers were two handsome middle-aged mulattoes—one in green suit with pink velvet brocade
scarf wrapped around her pearl-encircled neck,
the other jauntily hatted, nose-veiled, with snood
covering gray hair, gold hoops in her ears, and
crimson polish on her finger-nails. Returning with
many bags (perhaps from Martinique?) they were
greeted at every station and even hailed by friends
in a passing train, as ours waited on a siding. Still
another type was a countryman with two fighting-
cocks, concealed but protesting. In a stumbling
mixture of English and Spanish this lank and sun-
tanned individual made clear to us that metal
spurs are now forbidden, yet one cock is always
killed at a fight ... yes, sometimes both.

Wagons piled with mahogany were drawn up
at stations. Our train rattled on. Forests were
traversed, wooded ravines, mountainous farmlands where zebu cattle grazed; the Agabama
River—reflecting bamboo—was crossed on a daring trestle. Yznaga was passed with its pagoda
tower, built according to tradition in a boastful
spirit to outdo the farmer with the deepest well;
the palm-spangled San Luis Valley with ruins of
pre-revolutionary sugar-mills.

"Tri ni dád!" shouted the guard, as though to
emphasize the fact that this was not the island
Trinidad in the British West Indies.

Trinidád : Archaic wooden casements

Like the other Trinidad the place connotes India. There are the zebu calves, the goats, the dusty compound of the rectangular barracks—the railroad station. The Hotel Canada is the most nearly modern note in all the town, but it stops short of being strident or off key. Painful as are the bumps over cobbles (laid a century ago by prisoners and slaves) if one essays to crawl in an automobile, the stones are scarcely less agonizing than to the feet. Yet discomforts are forgotten in the glamour of the place—suggestive of medieval Cordova or the mountain fastnesses of Aragon... Biescas, Torla, Jaca. Moorish walls, cut by archaic wooden casements, protruding eaves shadowing narrow thoroughfares, venders burdened with baskets on shoulder-poles—Chinese fashion—are commonplaces.

The one-time wealth of Trinidarios caused the town's loot by pirates. Grandees of Spain vied with one another in building domiciles worthy of comparison with mansions in Toledo. Mahogany doors were brass-studded. Patios, enclosed with double-storied arches, bloomed with tropical vines, reaching to intricate grilled galleries, as they do to-day. At least one of the houses is still lived in by the descendants of its founder.

"Have you heard," our innkeeper—a roistering fellow who could have given Sancho Panza points —asked us, "of the millionaire Guillermo Bécquer? He lived here centuries ago and he swore that he was rich enough to build a finer house than his friends Cantero and Iznaga. He began to pave the floors with mosaics, but folks said he couldn't afford to finish the job. Angered by the talk, he did away with mosaics and laid golden coins, onzas (ever hear of them?) bearing the King's portrait. The Governor ordered their removal, it being a crime to 'tread upon the King.' The old wives had it that the builder only said this to save his face. Said the gossips, 'Yes, he's broke.' Incensed at the talk Bécquer demanded permission to pave his mansion with coins on edge!"

The oldest of Trinidád's churches is La Popa on the hillside of La Vigia. It dates back to the time of the town's foundation by Don Diego Velázquez in 1514. Serrano Square was constructed by Cortés, who fitted out his expedition at Trinidád for the conquest of Mexico. On the outskirts of the city, on the banks of the Guarabo, a historic ceiba is pointed out. Here Cortés moored his ships! It was only yesterday, as life crawls by in Trinidád, the forgotten town ... the forgotten town, Trinidád.

Señorita
de Cuba

Kingston ‡ The Coronation Market

Rose Hall

CHAPTER III

TEMPESTUOUS JAMAICA

Lᴇsᴛ my title offend those to whom Jamaica is sacrosanct, let me hasten to admit that it might readily appear to be, indeed it did to Tomlinson, as his boat "crawled over the blue floor in which that sea mountain is set," the most beautiful island in the world. Timing plays a not unimportant rôle in any dramatic presentation.

The month of our arrival was January. Although definitely not the hurricane season, the winds rose to an almost alarming degree. Tongues wagged to inform the new-comer that this was the thirty-fourth anniversary of the "great earthquake." A sudden cold wave evoked an editorial on the similarity of these weather conditions and those that preceded and coincided with the aforementioned cataclysm. Perhaps owing to the circumstance that men of African descent are still sensitive to threatened disturbances of nature, the inhabitants of Jamaica—or at least the leaders of the apathetic racial majority—were seemingly in league with nature's forces, making of their otherwise idyllic island one of the lesser storm centers in an angry and tortured world. How then, for me, could Jamaica rival those fairest of fair tropical islands Trinidad and Tobago . . . basking imperishably in my mind's eye in springtime, peace, and sunlight? To the average American, Jamaica is, next to the Bahamas, the most accessible portion of the British West Indies, and therefore it gives him the pleasurable shock of his introduction to luxuriantly tropical vegetation. It was mere chance—the Leeward Islands having headed our list—that brought us to Jamaica at the tail end of our British West Indian tour.

Columbus, ever with an eye to the dramatic, could hardly have impressed the island better on his patron's mind than by the illustration of its contours given at court when, in order to describe them, he crumpled a sheet of parchment and threw it at the feet of Isabella. His discovery of the island, known to the Arawaks who possessed it as Xaymaca—that is to say, the well-watered, the isle of springs and over-flowing rivers—was on May 3, 1494. Although he called it San Jago, the place reverted to its original name. No less dramatically was the navigator to impress the Indians, not, it is true, upon his second voyage, but upon his fourth and last expedition to the New World, when he was to spend a year upon the island. Seeking refuge from tempestuous seas he put ashore, near St. Ann's Bay, in June, 1503. His two remaining vessels proving unseaworthy, the Admiral sent emissaries in a canoe to the Spanish governor of Española, imploring the aid which was not to reach him until a year had elapsed. In the interim, knowing the time of an eclipse of the moon, Columbus announced to the Indians that, "in consequence of their refusal to supply his wants the moon would be hidden in darkness." The Arawaks, terrified, begged the White Man to intercede for them with his God.

The death of Columbus occurred in the year following his stay in Jamaica. It remained for his son and heir, Diego, established as governor of adjacent Española, to claim rights in Jamaica by sending settlers who became the founders of San Jago de la Vega. The British have been in possession of Jamaica since May 11, 1655—the date when, with surprisingly little resistance, the Spanish surrendered to Cromwell's forces under command of General Venables and Admiral Penn.

Bidding farewell to our home in the environs of the city founded by Admiral Penn's son, we approached this largest of British West Indian islands after quite another fashion than the Admiral's. Flying from Miami, on our third visit to the Antilles, we were to swoop upon Jamaica from

the air. Of memorable flights by Pan-American
Clipper this one was outstanding. Vis-à-vis to us
in the plane were two men, the younger obviously
a German, who had just returned from China,
where he had seen cities laid waste. Unwilling to
talk of war, he busied himself with correspond-
ence, plying me with questions as to the spelling
of such words as "armament," "ingenuity,"
"Caribbean"—fortunately not beyond my depth.
The German's neighbor announced that he had
flown over a hundred thousand miles in South
America alone, in the interests of business—in his
case, glass. He was quick to obtain the pilot's signature and assured us that he possessed a certificate for having crossed the equator. He was, he
said, a subscriber to the Pan-American Airway's
Magazine, *New Horizons,* and always marks the
names of hostesses and pilots known to him. At
bouillon time he commented upon the synthetic
white cups and saucers which he resents but does
not fear as rivals to his ware, remembering the
reaction of housewives to milk containers other
than glass.

The best part of our flight was at ten thousand
feet, from which height we gazed up at unfathomable blue and down first upon mounds of cirrus
cloud with holes of distant water—over which
drifted scudding wisps of mist—then, completely
detached from things mundane, upon an ocean of
churning white cloud-billows among which sleuth-

hound shadows seemed to stalk their prey, while apparently arctic ranges of cloud-mountains rose on the borders of this earth-obliterating sea.

At lower altitude our plane sped, bumpily, over the green, tree-covered hills of Jamaica's Surrey. High-perched ranch-houses caught the eye, flares of red-orange *immortelles,* connoting the probable growth of coffee beneath their branching shade, until, suddenly, we found ourselves sailing low over the flat corrugated iron roofs of the unimpressive town which bears little resemblance to the city Kingston might have been save for devastating fires and the 1907 earthquake.

I cherish the memory of arrival (fresh from a northern winter) at the Pan-American Airport— a gleaming shell seen from the water, banked with flaming poinsettias above which, like sparks from a fitful bonfire, radiated a myriad of glistening butterflies. The ecstasy was heightened on arrival at the Myrtle Bank Hotel upon the bay, with palm-fringed swimming-pool, with bandstand on a grassy lawn beside which we dined. Of a morning, a black boy swept the white blossoms of thunbergia from our path beneath the trellis, where pendant-flowered stems formed fairy swings. Here swagger officers of His Majesty's Navy, obviously proud of their ''figgers,'' clad in khaki shirts and shorts, rubbed shoulders with civil engineers from the U. S. A.

From the windows of our room I never tired

of watching the lurid sky at dawn, a background
for the swaying coco-palms, while, at sunset, it
was again tropically canary. Characteristic of this
view are the red-headed vultures, called locally
John Crows, graceful only in flight, decorating the
palm tops. These sinister birds were my Illustrator's outstanding impression of Kingston, visited
in boyhood. He gave a sigh of relief at their en-
during presence in an otherwise changed world.
By moonlight outside our rattling venetians, the
trunks of royal palms were whitened, giving them
the appearance of the columns of a colonial por-
tico. The sea breeze, so we were told, which blows
by day is known as "the doctor." For ourselves
we were to unearth the fact that the land breeze,
prevailing at night, is dubbed "the undertaker"!
Its fever-producing qualities were probably nulli-
fied by the fact that the American Management
(United Fruit Company) has actually provided
window screens in lieu of the next-to-ubiquitous
bed canopies.

Kingston possesses certain characteristics that
are superlatively good. The first to be recorded by
all ways of reckoning must be its harbor, sixth of
the world in point of size and considered one of
the best, outdistancing all others in the West Indies. Second I should list the view, from the harbor, of the Blue Mountain Range—culminating in
the highest peak to be found in the British West
Indies. Third, from my point of view, is the

Myrtle Bank Hotel, one of the few superlative establishments to be found in the Antilles. Little or nothing else need detain the traveler in Kingston —certainly not its hot and humid climate—but the hotel is a convenient base for excursions. Although the historically minded may care to visit the Jamaica Institute, a sufficient view of Jamaica's best—the Public Buildings and Victoria Garden, with its statue of the late queen and its pair of gigantic banyans—will be obtained when driving along King Street en route to the rewarding suburbs of Half-Way Tree and Constant Spring. In order to augment my own impressions I turn to a list of "Places of Interest, etc., and Amusements in Kingston," enumerated by the Tourist Bureau, and find, in addition to the aforesaid and "Cinema Houses," a number of monuments and parish churches (artistically of indifferent merit) and the following items: "The Strangers' Burial Ground, The Baptist Ground, The Wesleyan Methodist Cemetery, Spring Path Burial Ground, Jewish Cemetery, May Pen Cemetery (Spanish Town Road)"! As the *Revels in Jamaica*, by Richardson Wright, so admirably tells of plays and players of more than a century ago, so too, obviously, much implied by the name Kingston lies beyond recall. Markets in the open air are with better judgment included on the list. At the mere mention of the word, my Illustrator, with more than his usual vehemence, bursts into speech.

"Remember the Coronation Market—how they cursed me when they saw my kodak?...worse than the Orient. One grizzly black man muttered to a woman, who had deigned to speak to me, 'Wot you doin', traffickin' wid de enemy?' "

Another point of indubitable interest is Headquarters House, one of the few buildings that escaped devastation in 1907. It is related that four merchants made a wager, in the eighteenth century, as to which could erect the handsomest dwelling. Headquarters House (so named when acquired by the War Office) was one of the four mansions and was at first called for its builder, Hibbert's House. Here the Legislative Council has met since 1870, when Kingston instead of Spanish Town became the seat of government, and here are the offices of the colonial secretary.

The colonial secretaryship was filled during our introductory sojourn by the Hon. A. W. G. H. Grantham, C. M. G., O. B. E., M. C., who at the very moment we chose to present our credentials was at the airport seeing off the governor, His Excellency, Sir Arthur Richards, K. C. M. G., called to London to discuss certain local and imperial problems. The Honorable Mr. Grantham was, therefore, called upon to administer the Government of Jamaica until His Excellency's return. Despite this fact he and his vivacious American wife received us at Vale Royal, the official residence of the Colonial Secretary and one of the

best preserved of Jamaican "Great Houses." Here
Nelson once slept. From the walls of the banquet-
ing hall a portrait of Sir William Grantham, adviser to Victoria, clad in judicial wig and scarlet
robes, regarded with apparent approval our host,
his grandson, an approval we were immediately to
share. We confess that, in other quarters, we had
been looked upon askance for the reason that, on
so short acquaintance, we should dare to express
any opinion whatsoever on Jamaica. Our host,
with the alertness and tact of the true diplomat,
instantly remarked that the length of stay was not
important in comparison to possession of the
trained eye.

The governor of Jamaica does not hold any
sinecure, and still less does the recently appointed
"Labour Adviser." Hurricanes and cloudbursts
led to such serious conditions on the island that,
in 1935, £2,000,000 was lent for development. Despite this fact, by 1938 the growth of unemployment, bad living conditions, and low wages caused
discontent, focusing in riots.

"If we consider the West Indies as a whole," I
quote the up-to-date *Jamaica Today,* "people of
African origin are in a large majority. The future
of the island depends in great measure on these
and their future depends in great measure on
themselves. Up to recent years many people from
Jamaica sought wider opportunity in the neighboring countries, particularly in Panama, in

Canada, in the United States, and in Cuba. To-day these countries have restricted immigration. The Jamaican peasant is essentially a kindly peace-loving person. For years he has been disregarded or neglected, and there have been no sustained attempts beyond those of the church to educate him in social health.... Tuberculosis and other diseases claim far too many victims. These evils are aggravated by bad housing conditions, by ignorance and by superstition.''

The year 1938 saw the creation of labor unions in Jamaica and the formation, by the politically minded, of the People's National Party. Rival leaders, Bustamente and Manley, presenting a united front, are vocal in demanding not merely an extension of the representative form of government (the ''moderate step in advance'' offered as a result of the visit of a Commission from the Colonial Office in 1921, rejected by the colony), but ''immediate self-government.'' This the editor of *The Gleaner* interprets as boiling down to a demand for self-government in internal affairs—such as is enjoyed to-day by the ''three Bs'' ... not in this case Bach, Beethoven, and Brahms, but Barbados, Bermuda, and the Bahamas. Dominion status would, at the moment, seem an impractical pipe dream, in view of the present state of, or rather lack of, intellectual development.

In the neighborhood of Vale Royal, with its tidy English lawn and well-groomed trees, is King's

House, on the Liguanea Plain, official residence of
the Governor. As though to atone for the monotony of the capital, the suburbs of Kingston—
Half-Way Tree, Saint Andrew, Constant Spring—
blossom with riotous bougainvillea, plumbago,
alamanda....

"Hotter than hell" was the description given us
of Port Royal, to-day a mere village, on the Palisadoes—that spit of sand partly enclosing Kingston's harbor and now a base of the Royal Air
Force. Prior to the earthquake of 1692, Port Royal
was said to have been "the finest town in the West
Indies, and the richest spot in the Universe." Not
only was it considered the richest but also, according to the chronicler, the "Wickedest city of the
world." Buccaneers—of many nations, preying
upon ships sailing from the Spanish Main—found
its harbor well-adapted for their nefarious traffic.
Originally carrying on an illicit provision trade
—resented by the settlers—they received their
name from their habit of preserving meat on
boucans or barbecues. Their proclaimed policy of
opposition to Spain led Jamaican authorities to
wink at other activities. Here one of the most notorious of their number, plunderer of Porto Bello
in 1668, of Old Panama in 1671, was to lord it as
leader of the band and eventually to become Sir
Henry Morgan, Lieutenant Governor of Jamaica.
A funeral sermon was preached for him in Christ
Church and his bones lie not in Davy Jones' locker

but, as appropriately, among the dunes and cacti of the Palisadoes.

The destruction by earthquake of the opulent but riotously unholy community of Port Royal was, in popular belief, occasioned by its sins. As the town sank beneath the sea thousands met their doom.

Reached across the harbor from Kingston—in the olden days all water was ferried to fill the peninsula's cisterns—or, in our era, by the modern road, created a few years ago by convict labor, Port Royal offers no relics of the earliest period, though many reminders of the time when Nelson (he was not yet of age) paced the "quarterdeck" of Fort Charles.

My Illustrator and I found our way to the officers' quarters of the garrison and then to the old naval dockyard, where disintegrating sheds speak of mighty ships careened prior to the age of steam.

Next we were conducted, via the churchwarden's, to St. Peter's, to be shown what the verger assured us was Morgan's gift: the Communion plate, consisting of two patens, a covered cup, and superlatively fine flagon. Experts believe that the latter was made in the colonies at approximately the same date, 1743, as the organ loft—massively carved in a style typically Jamaican. Perhaps, in some cases, the usual order was reversed. The flippantly minded call attention to the whistle in this tankard's handle and remark that its original

use was to summon the barmaid! On the other
hand: "The drinking shops," it has been said,
"were filled with cups of gold and silver embel-
lished with flashing gems torn from half a hundred cathedrals."

Most noteworthy of monuments at Port Royal,
however, is the fort, christened for Charles II and
"which" (according to the report prepared by the
Institute of Jamaica) "is believed to occupy the
site of the Main Sea Wall of the old Seventeenth
Century Fortifications." Nelson, in command of
the batteries in 1779, thought the arrival of the
French fleet imminent, as he watched from his
"platform beside the sea."

IN THIS PLACE DWELT HORATIO NELSON
YOU WHO TREAD HIS FOOTPRINTS
REMEMBER HIS GLORY.

Fearful, in 1782, that the island was, like the
Bahamas, Tobago, and St. Kitts, to fall to the
enemy, "Port Royal and with her Jamaica went
mad" on the return (after Rodney's victory) of
their fleet with the captured French vessels.

Memories of Kingston pale by comparison with
those of our tour of the island. In company with
coal-black Cyril (what racial claim, we wondered,
may he not have had to the name!) and an admirable Buick, we were to sample all three coun-
ties—Surrey, Middlesex, and Cornwall—as well
as every one of Jamaica's fourteen parishes—

Tom Cringle's Cotton Tree

save only St. Thomas over which we had already
flown. Our first afternoon's drive, three leisurely
hours, was to bring us via Spanish Town across

the island to Ocho Rios in the "Garden Parish" of St. Ann—in my opinion, next to the Blue Mountains, the loveliest (although not the most visited) portion of Jamaica. Two landmarks stand along the highway to Spanish Town—the historic Ferry Inn, mentioned in Lady Nugent's entertaining *Journal,* and also an extravagantly branched and buttressed veteran bearing this adequate inscription:

TOM CRINGLE'S COTTON TREE
(CEIBA, OR SILK COTTON TREE)
THIS ANCIENT TREE IS IMMORTALIZED
IN "TOM CRINGLE'S LOG," A STORY OF
ABSORBING INTEREST RELATING
TO THE WEST INDIES,
WRITTEN BY MICHAEL SCOTT.
GIANT SPECIMENS OF THE
SILK COTTON ARE TO BE FOUND
IN VARIOUS PARTS OF JAMAICA.
THEY ARE OF SOLITARY HABIT
AND SELDOM IF EVER FOUND
IN GROUPS. NOTE THE
TILLANDSIAS AND OTHER
PARASITIC PLANTS WHICH
MAKE A HOST OF THIS
NOBLE TREE. TOM CRINGLE'S
COTTON TREE IS BELIEVED
TO BE THE HAUNT OF
"DUPPIES" GHOSTS.

Spanish Town, the former capital San Jago de la Vega, lives in the memory of the past. Its cathe-

The region of wild and green

hills around Mount Diavolo

dral "thrown downe by ye Dreadfull Hurricane"
was rebuilt in 1714. It shares with the cathedrals
of Havana and Cartagena, says an authority, the
honor of being "one of the three oldest ecclesiastical buildings in the West Indies." (But what of
the one at Trujillo City?) The main place of pilgrimage, however, is the square with its Government Buildings and colonnaded monument to Rodney astonishingly clad in sandals and Greek
tunic. Commemorative of Rodney's victory, the
Battle of the Saints, are two cannon, flanking the
statue, taken from the *Ville de Paris,* the pride of
the French Navy—a vessel given by the city whose
name it bore to Louis XV.

The mountainous region with its sweep of wild
and green hills around Mount Diavolo—the road
winds through villages swarming with dark-
skinned children—does not surpass in interest the
cattle country in the parish of St. Ann, where estates are known as "pens." Moneague has its hotel at over a thousand feet. On every hand steep
pastures with stone walls and long-horned cattle
abound.

Dusk was falling as our car bore us through
Fern Gully, once a river bed. Could the vaunted
banks of the Rio Grande or the Rio Cobre, we
asked each other, surpass this scene from fairyland? Here, in the twilight hush, we could imagine
that furtive rustlings issued from possessors of
the seeds of invisibility. On every cliff ferns

freighted with prodigal spores nodded, waved arms of welcome, formed bowers beneath which our out-of-scale chariot barely passed. We held our breaths, fearing to awaken from a Cinderella dream, but, as we rode, every curve revealed another vista of languishing fronds, festooning in unidentified variety our festive though isolated path.

Arrival at the Shaw Park Estate was no anti-climax. On this visit our hostess (née Pringle) welcomed us to Ocho Rios as graciously as she might have done before the mansion had become a hotel. To our surprise we were ushered into the royal suite, occupied during their visit by the Duke and Duchess of Gloucester. (From the de luxe Tower Isle Hotel, on not distant North Coast, brilliant lights attract not only dancers but immense Sphinx moths, fertilizers of orchids. Collectors for the Institute of Jamaica reap an exotic harvest.)

The Lady of the Manor found us, next morning, admiring the view of bay and Caribbean. She explained that Cuba can rarely be seen from Shaw Park, but when it is visible a storm is sure to follow. It was, she told us, on this estate that Ysassi, the last Spanish governor of Jamaica, pitched his tent, before escaping from the British. His ignominious departure in a canoe to Cuba was made from what is known to-day as Runaway Bay. Without Ysassi's provocation to be a runaway, determination is needed to tear one's self from this haven—appreciated as such, in wartime, by English families with youthful or aged members—for inclination is not to run away but to linger in the hillside garden where flowers of England and the tropics vie. Beneath the shade of a heavily-laden nutmeg tree upon the terrace, four excellent meals a day are served by George, the Hindu, and *kling klings* perch on chairbacks expectantly as crumb-pecking Indian mynas.

St. Ann's Bay—now chief port of the parish—is said to be the Puerto Santa Gloria where Columbus first anchored on his discovery of Jamaica in 1494 and where, in 1503, he beached his storm-beaten caravels—the *Capitana* and *Santiago de Palos*. Dry Harbor and Montego Bay were no less known to him, a fact that lends interest to the coastal drive from St. Ann's to the Parish of St. James.

Guests of Shaw Park are welcome at the Roaring River Private Beach, where fresh water from the hills falls with impetuosity into the Caribbean. The Roaring River Falls—the most picturesque in Jamaica—are situated within a few minutes of the highway. The path leads through a plantation of coconuts. From the sky itself the uproarious waters seem to issue, blazing a precipitous trail amongst vegetation green as jade.

Montego Bay—the popular resort on the north coast—was, to my mind, a base for excursions,

not an end in itself. At the Casa Blanca a pleasure-
seeking clientele fluctuated between the cocktail
bar and the bathing beach. Jazz bellowed from
loud-speakers, enlivening or rendering diners
morose, according to temperament. Waves lashed
angrily, at the time of our arrival, beneath the
balcony we were to know in fair as well as foul
weather—shaking the very foundations, as though
in retribution for the rivalry of tumultuous sound
—while from the street-front, quavering pipes and
a tattoo of drums formed the not inharmonious
accompaniment to the pranks of a turbaned and
false-faced band of serenading "John Canoes,"
gens inconnues.

St. James is, par excellence, the parish of
Jamaican Great Houses. Perhaps nowhere else in
the West Indies did colonial planters attain such
pinnacles of wealth and arrogance. Fortunes were
amassed in rum, in sugar, and in the slave trade,
with as little concern for moral values as in the
days of Morgan's raids upon the Spanish Main.
Not till the abolition of the trade, in 1834, and the
total freeing of the slaves, in 1838, did the most
lavish period of Jamaica's landed gentry decline.

Rose Hall is impregnated with reminders of a
bygone age. Where once hospitality reigned, to-
day windows stare blankly and doors gape idi-
otically awry upon an altered world. The drive-
way—once echoing to the sound of hoofs, high-
pitched laughter, and the gruff jollity of over-

lords—has been destroyed in an effort to keep the public from the risk of falling cornices, for the present owner of the estate has abandoned Rose Hall—perhaps because of its notoriety—and has even hastened its decay by transferring the mahagony balustraded and paneled stair to his residence in Kingston. The deserted mansion is doomed, no less than was its mistress, Annie Palmer (the sinister heroine of de Lisser's historical romance, *The White Witch of Rosehall*), daughter of Ireland, practising the "black arts" of Haiti, put to death, not by obeah but throttled by her slaves. Rose Hall, malevolent even by day, left to bats and the moon by night, can hardly be thought of, by the susceptible, without a tremor. Black men give it a wide berth.

The neighboring Cinnamon Hill remains in a state of preservation. Its reputation depends in part upon its former ownership by the Barretts— Elizabeth was to record her shame at the source of family opulence—and in part upon intrinsic merit. Placed on a hilltop, the sprawling length of stone seems to cower like some timid prehistoric creature. The funnel-shaped valley, dropping to the sea, forms a scoop for hurricanes. Attached to a chamber (erected by a Barrett who would no longer abide under the same roof as his wife—a person of color) is a "hurricane-knifer"... the best-preserved in Jamaica. This stone refuge— perhaps twenty feet in length but not more than

Mangroves thrust their stilt roots
into Mosquito Bay

ten feet within—is pointed like a blade against
the nor'easters. Lighted only by loopholes it was
useful, too, in time of Negro insurrections. The
original Barrett settler, sent out during the Cromwell Rebellion, became established in the Vere district. The Barretts originally owned more than the
present eight thousand acres.

In the region of Falmouth, within easy motoring distance of a beach but set on high land among
the hills and not in the malaria-haunted miasmatic
mangrove swamps along the coast, stands another

Great House, with paneled woodwork intact, with massive jalousies and furniture of the period even to Jamaica-carved four-posters. Formerly a sugar estate, Good Hope is run to-day as a "dude ranch." That rivalry exists between its habitués and the frequenters of the Casa Blanca, at Montego Bay, can not be denied. To those who would ride to their hearts' content, while living in an atmosphere of elegance, among congenial folk who cherish the traditions of Jamaica's past, Good Hope with its 6,500 acres, its herds and coconuts, its gardens where long-tailed humming-birds dart, its jungle trails, its ruins of watermill and church —where in the great days of rum the mahogany pews were converted into puncheons—in a word, to all those to whom nature does not spell boredom, the distractions of Good Hope are sufficient.

Beyond Good Hope lies the heart of the Cockpit Country, inaccessible until the construction of the new road gashing the cliffs to Albert Town, whence it continues to Brown's Town. This remote region takes its name from the punchbowl formation of the ravines between its wooded hills. It is a kingdom in itself, a wilderness of hills and vales, with open vistas of an unmapped and still more mountainous territory ... a land to harbor fugitives, the land of Look Behind. The Maroons— whose kingdom it is, descendants of African slaves deserted by their Spanish masters and fleeing from the British, with ancestors unpacified until the year 1796 (when, after a rebellion, some of their number were deported to Nova Scotia and then to Africa)—dwell to-day, nominally under the guidance of their own ruler but, actually, welcoming the protection of the British.

It was on a day of wind after rain that Cyril, rolling his eyes a trifle more than usual, drove us through the Maroon Country to Brown's Town. Houses, we noted, were rarely seen from the roadway skirting the abysses, although there were occasional huts and hillside plantings of bananas. Here, if anywhere, should obeah still have a hold upon the unschooled and credulous. It was therefore with quickened emotion that I noticed a bunch of twigs dangling from a tall banana plant to which it had been attached. I should have mistaken it for a scarecrow had I not read of the potency of such charms against thieves.

"The West African natives," says H. G. de Lisser, "and particularly those of the Gold Coast (from which part of Africa the larger number of the Jamaican slaves were brought) believe in a number of gods of different classes and unequal power.... One particularly malignant spirit... on the Gold Coast, has no regular priesthood. He is called 'Sasabonsum,' and any individual may put himself in communication with him. Sasabonsum's favorite residence is the ceiba, the giant silk-cotton tree." The votary collects twigs or a stone and prays that the god's power may enter into this receptacle, which, thereby, becomes a suhman and its owner a wizard or obeahman. Priests of the other gods may sell charms or even "put death upon a man," but "the obeahmen's chief function is to propitiate gods, to unbewitch." ... They are, in the words of de Lisser "not so much a terror as a fraud."

From Brown's Town in St. Ann's the owners of the Huntley Park Hotel conducted us to The Retreat, once the favorite residence of the Barretts, where one of their number still lies in a rural grave. The tiny school-house, the place in which children of slaves were taught, stands near a Ficus Benjamin, each a survivor from the Barretts' day, as is the winsome mansion—whose ancient barbecue (cemented with molasses) is still heaped with drying coffee beans. The traditional ghost has not walked of late, although "the priest's" ground-floor room, with rattling jalousies, seems to tempt nocturnal if not unearthly visitation.

Market folk on the roads leading to Montego Bay were an unfailing diversion. While the men cultivate their vegetable patches or toil in the cane-fields, the women, with heaped baskets balanced incredibly on heads, repair to market. The roads, especially of a Saturday, were rarely free from stragglers. Some bore milk cans, others yams, bananas, and all conceivable tropical fruits. Often a rolled goatskin—the flesh having been consumed —was conspicuously on its way to the tanner.

Women in white, bearing cakes fresh from the oven, were bridesmaids who, Cyril demonstrated, dare not look behind, even at the honk of a horn, fearing to bring ill fortune on the bride.

On a Sunday we took the coast drive to Green Island, via Lucea. To landward the fat peeling trunks of red birches marred the way with their stout forms, resembling distorted nudes by ultra-modern painters, nudes hugging to their ponderous breasts not normal infants but obscenely bulging ants' nests. Refreshing, it was, to turn our eyes toward a Winslow Homer sea. Waves lashed the pitted rocks and danced, in fretted line, along the horizon. Yet, even on the sea side, sordid huts often jarred the harmony of wave and rock and cocopalm, while mangroves encroached from malodorous banks, thrusting their stilt roots into the waters of Mosquito Bay.

Inland from Montego our road of departure skirted the Cockpit Country until we came—by way of fragrant logwoods (paradise of the famed Jamaica honey-bee) and Lacovia with its grove, converting the thoroughfare into an allée of interlaced bamboo—at last to Mandeville. The reputation of this place is derived from its situation, at an altitude of some two thousand feet, in what has, to the sun-wearied eyes of Scottish settlers, an appearance of the Highlands.

Rainfall at Mandeville but adds emphasis to the cheer to be found at the Manchester—Mr.

Evelyn's admirable hotel. Our own special reason for an unseasonable stay, despite the cold and downpour, was to view the paintings of our friend the late John McLure Hamilton and to converse with Justice-of-the-Peace Howe, who is moving heaven and earth to have the collection hung in the reading-room of the proposed new Library. It was to Mandeville that Hamilton, a son of Philadelphia, long a resident of London, came to pass his last days with his son George, an authority on Mars. The latter established residence at Mandeville while assisting William H. Pickering, an astronomer sent out by Harvard.

On a morning when the arch of a rainbow spanned the African tulip tree aflame at our threshold we set forth to call on the owner of a Great House (in Trelawny) who was sojourning near Mandeville. Having come out from England at the age of twenty-one, this distinguished gentleman—always in sugar and planning to produce three thousand tons during the current year—reminisced of the changes observed during a long lifetime. When he first came out, said he, the native women would curtsy as he drove his buggy along the road, later on they would bow—a mere nod of the head, still later a stare and now (not on his own estate, where he has done much to benefit his employees) when his car passes, as likely as not, curses. Two years ago his cane-fields were burned, at a total loss to him of about £5,000, counting loss of crop, damage to soil, cost of replanting, and number of years for recovery. The fire was probably the act of a man who did not get a job and whose mentality could not in any case have grasped the consequences. Our sympathy was all with our friend, and yet ... and yet ... on reading the Kingston *Gleaner* next day we did not feel the argument that prædial thieves should be publicly flogged struck a responding chord in our bosoms. It has been stated that for many years after emancipation there was a lamentable lack of interest in the people's welfare on the part of local planters. Housing conditions were conducive to disease; more than half the population is still illiterate. The unrest in Jamaica to-day is no doubt an inheritance from century-long abuses bearing a compound interest of hatred.

The Blue Mountains tempt new-comers to Kingston. Not only do the eyes seek, on days when its cloud-cap is lifted, the peak that gives its name to the range (as well as to the world's most delicious coffee)—Blue Mountain, 7,388 feet above the sea—but, at half the height, the settlement at Newcastle, twinkling in sunlight, seeming to beckon.

Newcastle, Hardware Gap, descent to Port Antonio and return to Kingston via Castleton Gardens ... such was our program against which man and weather conspired. Cyril, whose eyes rolled at the suggestion, had not made the trip for years.

"Too long," he said, but meant, we surmised, imagining the road, "too hard."

Head-lines emphasized the floods. Rains in the night had been torrential. Our departure from Jamaica was set for the morrow. The Automobile Club emphatically advised us not to make the attempt. No word had come from Newcastle.

"Will you telephone?" we pleaded.

The answer to inquiries was reassuring as far as the way up was concerned, but nothing was known of conditions beyond the pass. . . . On the strength of this partial assurance we set forth.

Between Mandeville and Kingston dangerous curves were marked "corner" or "double corner," as the case might be. The road to Newcastle omits the all too obvious. Squatting on banks, precariously, road-menders were already at work— Jamaicans of both sexes—hand-chipping stones to gravel, while other groups were engaged in repairing washouts. Cyril, wide-eyed, commented on the lessened danger of head-on collisions since the battalion of British soldiers had been sent to Palestine. Only a few Canadians were at the cantonment built a century ago for the accommodation of white troops when yellow fever raged below. At a steep curve we came upon a quartermaster tinkering with a stalled car. Seeing that he should have to go down for a tow, would we be so kind as to take his ailing wife up to Newcastle?

The woman proved to be a cockney (three years

out of London) who regaled us, in cheerful con-
versational tones, with details of an operation
upon her breast that she had recently undergone.
When she came out from England first thing she
had read (evidently with pride) in an American
magazine, *True Detective Stories,* was about her
own sister's murder. Kind of made her feel at
home. Now she was on her way to the Hill Station
to recuperate: "They do send us up once in a
while."

She pointed knowingly, far below, to Mona Bar-
racks, rows of model quarters known as Gibraltar
Camp, where the inhabitants of Gibraltar, mostly
Spanish, she said, were lodged. She told us, with
obvious envy, of the up-to-date camp at Kingston
provided for German prisoners ... some from the
Graf Spee scuttled by the *Ajax* and *Achilles* at
Montevideo.

"Can't help feelin' sorry for boys of fifteen or
sixteen, even Germans, now can you?" was her
humane comment.

At Newcastle, having, we hoped, forged a link
in the chain of international fraternity, we bade
our loquacious passenger farewell. Close we were
now to Mount Catherine and but two miles from
the Gap. Below us Kingston appeared more smiling than at closer range, while harbor, sea, and
mountains vied in shades of harmonious blue.

Hardware Gap—with a chill in the air that
caused shudders after the stifling atmosphere of

Ocho Rios ‡ The spectacular banana.

Kingston—was reward enough for the risks encountered. Tree-ferns, with bark-like python skins and whorls of leaves surmounted by gigantic fronds, were, at first glance, mistaken for palms. Aloof above the valley we lingered—reveling in the unique vegetation, oxalis, rain-drenched begonias, dripping ginger lilies. Finding the road still partially flooded but intact we plunged from the hard-won vantage point (the pass stands at an altitude of over 4,000 feet) down Buff River Valley toward sea-level and Port Antonio. Nowhere can the praises of this valley have been sufficiently sung. Here is the most spectacular scenery of the island—comparable to any in the Indies—vistas of mountains, cloud-crested, shimmeringly blue, vegetation so lush, so green, upon the hills, as to put the Cockpit Country to shame, isolated thatched cottages guarding terraces of banana, flaming trees and roadside blossoms, and our way ever in company with that madcap the Buff Bay River—joined by countless cascading comrades, leaping among boulders, endeavoring to bar our passage with all but untraversable fords and landslides of chaotic rocks, a mightier than Pyrenean *gave,* a relatively Norwegian torrent.

Not Port Antonio, with its swollen Rio Grande, unnegotiable at the time by raft, nor the Blue Hole (turned a bilious green) could impress us; though the Titchfield Hotel, with its terrace restaurant, tempted us to sojourn in full view of the double port which has been extravagantly called "the most exquisite harbour on earth."

Castleton Botanic Gardens, long-established in a natural hill setting, in some respects exceed in interest Hope Gardens, which no traveler to Kingston should omit, with its allée of divi-divi and its show of anywhere from two to five hundred orchid blooms—none unremarked by its chief horticulturist. Having been told by the latter on arrival at Castleton to inquire for Mr. Terrelonge, for fifty-four years the director, we had the privilege of this retired veteran's erudition. A whimsical, wizened little man we found him, white of race though of weather-beaten tan. Through paths lined with dracænas and crotons we were led to the pool in the upper garden where Victoria Regina lilies astound the Northerner. A dazzling variety of palms was pointed out, a soaring Norfolk Island pine. I was given a chip from the camphor tree and orchid-like blossoms from the Amherstia nobilis (that Burmese monarch of flowering trees) whose perfection H. F. MacMillan proclaims "is worth crossing the ocean to see."

In the lower garden we were shown a trap-door spider's nest in the ground—the resisting door was pried open for our inspection. The dangerous fellow emerges at night ... and dusk was coming on. For romantic beauty (in my mind's gallery of trees it has few rivals) the palm should go to a certain spreading Spathodea, ancient and gnarled

and unregenerately African ... sprays of terra-
cotta-orchids dangling from a tantalizingly high
notch. Not even my Illustrator's warning that it
would be dark before we got to Kingston could
hasten my departure from Castleton before the
closing of the gates.

The Blue Mountains! Travelers who have penetrated to these fastnesses will never again hear
the word "Jamaica" without a nostalgic pang.

Inland the life of the Haitian is rich in local color

In Port-au-Prince.

CHAPTER IV

HAITIAN REVELATION

HAITI is known as the Pearl of the Antilles...a black pearl, if the physiognomy of its people be taken into consideration. Nowhere in the Caribbean can its tropical beauty be surpassed: the island's variegated wealth of verdure, its lofty mountains and virgin valleys, its bluer-than-Mediterranean harbors; and, moreover—the painter's inspiration—the erect forms of its free-born scions of Africa, its no less proud sons and lovely daughters of Africo-French blood and tradition. Haiti, land of rhythm and aspiration; Haiti, conspicuous flower, blooming in the well-nurtured garden of Pan-Americanism; Haiti, sinning and sinned against; we, of your Sister Republic of the North, must not be among those to cast a stone.

Of all the islands visited, Haiti was the one that,

my Illustrator and I agreed, had been least well
represented to us before our arrival. When we
asked for literary bread we had been given the
stone of gross exaggeration, or, not less unsatis-
factory fare, the prosaic denial of all the built-up
castles of fantasy. It was perhaps the more in-
triguing, with such a wealth of vicious misinforma-
tion, to form our own impressions.

In order the better to appreciate the Haiti of
our day, the traveler should be aware of certain
highlights of Haitian history. It was, of course,
Columbus who discovered this next-to-the-largest
of the Antilles—known to the Indians as Haïti,
meaning "high land." Española was the name
given it by the Navigator; Saint-Domingue that
given it by the French. Nowadays the name Haiti
applies, politically, to the western third, occupied
by the Black Republic; Dominican Republic to the
other pseudo-Spanish two-thirds; while the whole
island is known, geographically, as Hispaniola.

Following the cruelty of the Spanish settlers,
the Indians were rapidly exterminated—as early
as 1505, slaves were introduced. By 1517 a royal
decree authorized the yearly importation of two
thousand Africans. By 1630 the island of Tortuga
—off the north coast of Haiti—had been settled
by French and British adventurers who were to
become notorious under the name of buccaneers.
Both Tortuga and what we know to-day as Haiti
became their hideaway from which they issued

Toussaint Louverture

La couleur de mon corps
nuit-elle à mon honeur et à ma
bravoure?

forth to rob and terrorize the settlers on the Spanish Main. In 1697 their domain was ceded to France, and French it remained, prospering up to the date of the French Revolution. Slavery was abolished in 1793, when the English, profiting by Haiti's internal dissensions, invaded the island but were repulsed by the French with the aid of the man who was to become the national hero—the black general, Toussaint Louverture. The latter adopted a constitutional form of government in 1801, he to become president for life; but, this proviso being distasteful to Bonaparte, Toussaint was arrested by trickery and taken to France, where he was allowed to languish in a cold prison and finally to die from starvation. The Haitian Dessalines, personification of cruelty and revenge, now led his people against the French, who, harried and their ranks decimated by dysentery and yellow fever, finally agreed to evacuate. Haïti, the original name, was restored to the western end of the island and, this in 1804, a republic established ... the first Negro republic in the New World.

On the assassination of Dessalines, Christophe and Pétion—the black tyrant and the melancholy mulatto—reigned, respectively, over the northern and southern portions. In 1822, after the death of both Christophe and Pétion, General Boyer succeeded, subduing the entire island until the revolution of 1844 when the eastern two-thirds de-

clared its political independence under the name
of Republica Dominica. The subsequent history
of the Haitian Republic until recent times—indeed
its prior history as well—has been written in the
blood of its citizens. Some idea of the turbulence
characteristic of the first century of the republic
may be gathered from the following facts. Between
1804 and 1915 the men to hold executive power included two emperors, one king, and twenty-three
presidents. Of this goodly number of executives
one was a suicide, four were killed outright, five
died in office (not necessarily from natural
causes), fifteen were driven into exile, and only
one served to the end of his term. Between the
years 1910-1915 seven dusky presidents flickered
like a primitive newsreel across the ill-illuminated
screen of the somber Haitian stage.

After the assassination of President Sam, in
1915, following the butchery of two hundred
imprisoned political opponents, as is well remembered, United States Marines were landed in Port-
au-Prince to establish order, remaining, for one
reason or another, until August, 1934. Although
political parties vary in their approval or dis-
approval of this so-called "occupation," it is conceded on the island, save by a minority group in
Port-au-Prince, that the country benefited by the
twenty-three million dollars of American money
spent on roads, sanitation, and the extermination
of the terrorists known as *cacos* or bandits. It may

be safely stated that the marines were popular
with the submerged ninety per cent of the population, the blacks, welcoming the cessation of political unrest; whereas the ten per cent mulatto or
other variation of Africo-European strain at
Port-au-Prince was, after the fashion of the politically minded, divided according to party lines.

As our Pan-American plane, like some gigantic
flying fish, feathered the waters of Port-au-Prince,
the far-famed capital of Haiti, we were enraptured
by the beauty of this Mediterranean yet tropical
juxtaposition of austere hills and scintillating
Neapolitan bay. Forgotten, it seemed, were the
ante-marine days of insanitation and obvious
disease. Boulevards, where automobiles abounded,
led to the quarter of the Presidential palace and
that climax of modernity, the Hotel Citadelle. Yet
even before arrival at the hotel, the day being
Saturday, we drove expectantly to the Vallière
Market.

As I hesitated, before following my Illustrator
into the maelstrom beneath the roof, old women,
strange and sinister as blackfaced gipsies, pressed
around our car—not indeed thrusting eager heads
and hands within, as would have been the case
on certain British islands—but, when I showed
no inclination to dispense alms, taking the name
of the Lord in vain. Lurid tales of voodoo seemed
more credible on observation of barbaric physi-
ognomies among the black Africans upon the

Haiti ‡ Vallière Market

market-place. The very buildings themselves, connected by a minareted gateway, erected by a
former Haitian president, bear ear-marks of
North Africa—though they did indeed suggest
to us not only Cairo but, by flaunting roofs and
cupolas, the theatrical pink city of Jaipur. Oriental, too, or rather African, were the fruit sellers
along the curbs, scantily white clad and snugly
turbaned, squatting on low stools behind their
wares or resting, Hindu-fashion, on their
haunches. Of all the markets frequented by a
market-haunting pair, to that at Port-au-Prince,
for being noisiest, we must award the palm. The
din of crowds, without, within, the exotic quality
of Creole voices, added to the illusion that we were
indeed in Africa. Above the human cries was
added the cackle of poultry, the bray of donkeys.
Primary color was flaunted by chemises of every
hue hung like banners at a festival. Mounds of
coarse straw hats were for sale at the equivalent
of a farthing. It was on the street, outside the
stiflingly overcrowded buildings, that we lingered
to observe the unwontedly primitive countrywo-
men threading their way on laden burros through
the hordes that, in African fashion, did not re-
strict themselves to sidewalks. Pineapples were
festooned from backs of beasts of burden—dangling to their very hoofs. A peddler's donkey bore
a pyramid of rush-seated chairs, while an Amazon
balancing on her head a clothes basket of cala-

bashes led a horse almost obliterated by his load
of gourds.

To the Haitian the *gourde*—so the calabash is
called—serves not so much for food as for a handy
receptacle, replacing every variety of pot, pan,
or pail. A tale is told that Henry Christophe, the
black king of Haiti, once requisitioned all the
calabashes in the kingdom and, when this was
done, farmers bringing coffee to seaports were
paid by receiving these coveted articles ... hence
the Haitian coin, once corresponding to a franc
(and stabilized at twenty cents), is called a
"gourde." The gold received from overseas for
Haitian coffee filled the Treasury of the newly
founded nation. Another explanation of the name
is that the Spaniards had in circulation both silver and coins of baser metal—the desirable ones
stamped "gourda."

In a happier era we had stayed at the Rock
Hotel at Gibraltar—high-perched on a cliff overlooking both town and sea. Could it be, I asked
myself, as our car rattled up the steep and treacherous approach, that the Citadelle was Gibraltar
refound? The hotel (as its folder put it) is architecturally "as new as New York"...and has in
addition "the charm which is as old as Haiti."
One explanation of this, at first, puzzling combination may lie in the marriage of the artistic American owner (a recent graduate of a fashionable
New York school, infatuated by the tropics) to

one of the President's Haitian guardsmen. (This gentleman, the officer in charge of the Haitian Air Force, can arrange for a flight over the Citadelle Laferrière at Cap Haïtien. If the trip is made by car the Hostellerie du Roi Christophe is recommended.)

As we entered our ultra-modern bedroom with perpendicular handwoven hangings of Madonna blue and bowls of white oleander around which bees circled, we looked down from our cliff to the distant city, from which rose, as at the market-place, as in India, North Africa, the hum of a hundred, a thousand indistinguishable voices, punctuated by the barking of dogs. Before the dawn was to arise the cacophony of cocks, while, after a late dinner upon the so-Moorish terrace, we were reminded of the opera *Louise* and imagined ourselves beholding the lights of Paris from a terrace of Montmartre. At this hour comparative silence reigned, broken only by an occasional weird cry. But, as though to prove this was no European scene, the dome of a myriad stars—repeating the lights on land and sea—had the unfamiliarity of a sky where a topsy-turvy dipper pointed downward to a relatively fallen North Star. As we stood upon this terrace, high as castle parapet, as darkness deepened we became aware of an intermittent throbbing of innumerable drums. Port-au-Prince was encircled—for even from the water-front came the pulsating sound-waves that envelop the town on a Saturday, the

night of nights for peasant festivals ... sound-
waves so enthralling as to entice to motion the
most sedentary of mortals.

The Palais National of the Haitian president
dominates the Champs de Mars. To its rear are
military barracks, while from its front windows
may be seen the Avenue George Washington, the
Palais de Justice on the Place de l'Indépendence
where, in a single tomb, rest the remains of Dessalines and Pétion—founders of the Haitian Republic. Of the union of this ill-assorted pair it is
said: "They died enemies, may they awaken
friends."

Often, of an evening, the excellent band of the
Garde d'Haïti may be heard in the kiosk on the
parade ground. Near-by is the Musée National
Fondation Stenio Vincent—the newly-created pet
of its founder, president of the republic from the
year 1930 until May 15, 1941. Here may be seen
portraits of Haitian patriots, letters and memen-
toes of inestimable value to Haitian historians,
and, moreover, the extraordinary hills and dales
of the mark or signature of the illiterate black
king, Henry Christophe. Here, as well, is a
wrought-iron anchor from Columbus' flagship the
Santa Maria—wrecked off the north coast of Haiti.

The crown of the Emperor Soulouque, known
as Faustin I, is not on view at the museum, but
may be seen, when the proper strings are pulled,
in an inner chamber of the Banque Nationale de

la République d'Haïti. Magnificent as a crown can well be is this creation made in France, almost a century ago, for the head of a dusky potentate. It is said to contain seven hundred and sixty precious and semi-precious stones and to be valued at half a million dollars. Its apex is formed by a glittering cross, set on an orb of lapis, supported by royal palms, whose radiating gem-studded trunks alternate with imperial eagles.

We were soon to have our first encounter with the Haitian police—only distinguishable from the equally khaki-clad gendarmes by the star upon the breast. Accompanied by Luc, our highly recommended chauffeur, my Illustrator and I betook ourselves to police headquarters to obtain the needful permission for a four-day excursion to Cap Haïtien. As Luc disappeared into the immaculate building we were left upon a balcony where chairs were offered. Becoming interested in watching the arrival of what we were told was American aircraft — four army planes — we ignored the proffered chairs until an officer emerged to request us to be seated, saying: ''It is not orderly to stand.'' Former postmaster Farley, he told us, was arriving, en route to Panama, and was to be entertained by President Vincent.

On our departure, armed with the necessary papers, we met upon the pavement of headquarters the eccentric ''Dr.'' Reser, a former pharmacist with the American marines, to whom we had been given a letter. The sunburned and begoggled doctor immediately invited us to see a voodoo dance in which he was to take part with his patients (he is in charge of the local insane asylum). While this conversation was in process a stern, though smiling, police officer appeared and directed us to move away from headquarters:

"It is," he said, "disorderly to stand"

Luc Frédéric was, despite his color, so French as to make us forget his combined racial strain. He was not alone a skilled mechanician but had been trained in the American agricultural school. The buildings of this school are now used by the Haitian Club—near the Pan-American Airways—whose pool we had noted from high altitude.

The expedition with Luc and the up-to-date Dodge car was to be a high-spot in our West Indies tour. Our start was made of a Sunday morning for the ten-hour drive over the plains and mountains leading to Cap Haïtien. Our first impression along the way was of churchgoers, coming afoot or on donkey-back—a French touch being the wearing of mourning among women, black madras with white dress, and an occasional incongruous widow's veil. The churchgoers were interspersed with other erect females, each balancing a water-filled calabash, or, as the case might be, a basket of milk-cans topped by funnels. Later we were to come upon the masculine section of the population—all on cockfights bent. Strag-

The arid region

glers by twos and threes, each with a cock upon
his arm, were not unusual. Most of the birds were
splendid chanticleers, worthy objects of their
masters' concern. The pits—of which there were
many in the interior—were formed of a circle of
low posts, a stockade on which men sit, while
others, always men, crowd about and boys hang
watchfully from neighboring treetops. Once we
noted a portly dame, chair and table on head, who
stationed herself near a pit to sell *clairing* (white
rum) or perhaps the muddier *tafia*.

On the Artibonite Plain—between hills and the

of Gonaïves

Gulf of Gonâve—the scenery was strangely
Biblical. Often a Holy Family (dark-skinned it is
true, but one soon forgets the distinction) passed,
mother and child riding upon a donkey. The
drought—not to be broken until July—had left
the district devoid of aught but yuccas and spiny
tree-cacti. Arcahaie was passed; Saint-Marc with
its spouting-pipe fountain at which parched children filled their buckets; Gonaïves—famous in
Haitian history. The way from Gonaïves, turning
inland to Plaisance, via Ennery, becomes overwhelmingly rich in local color. Indeed, more po-

tently than *clairing,* it goes to the head of the born traveler.

Darkest Africa is to be found—a startling revelation to one who had never anticipated the seeing of African compounds. No trace of French blood now, nor anywhere to matter save in Port-au-Prince. Crossing the beds of dry rivers we came upon these African villages or rather *cours de famille*—family compounds. Each group of shaggily thatched white- or salmon-plastered huts was fenced apart, each had its roofed threshing floor, its storehouse on mushroom-topped staddles—protection against rodents. Some folk had, for the rearing of seedlings, constructed earth-topped platforms; in trees hung ears of unhusked Indian corn; emaciated boarlike black pigs and goats, their action hampered by collars of poles, enlivened the picture, while pigeons—white, in contrast to their owners—roosted on crude cotes.

Approached by Luc, who addressed them in Creole, although he found at times their northern dialect difficult of comprehension, the natives, though shy, were disposed to be friendly. Couples employed in the rhythmic pounding of grain—rice grown near Gonaïves or the ubiquitous *petit mil* resembling broom corn—would continue the alternate motion of tall pestles in primitive mortars, to the delectation of my Illustrator; or, it might be, nearer the Cape, the grinding of sugar by the historic method of oxen and wheel.

A family compound of central Haiti

Comments ran as follows:

"Man goin' to take my picture. What he goin' to do with it?"

"No good clothes on," said another woman, "but glad to have my picture go to the great city."

Meanwhile a virago from an opposite compound stormed at the other for allowing herself to be photographed, shouting:

"Those Americans will say, 'What poor dirty-looking people, the Haitians,'" and, in sotto voce to her children, who showed curiosity, "Get out of there. It will bring you bad luck."

Good luck, we were told, was sometimes induced by the wearing of patchwork *robes de couleurs* for the youngsters and so-called "penitential" dresses (a term of abstinence goes with the wearing) for adults—white, patched with red and blue, in compliment to certain African deities. When first remarking these noticeable garments we had guessed that their color-scheme had been originally intended to attract the American marines!

The scenery around Plaisance has been called "paradisiacal." It merits a more pleasing word. Beyond Ennery the narrow road roughens—the car frequently hovers on the verge of an abyss. Luc told us that he had made a round from Port-au-Prince to the Cape in twelve hours. The road is dangerous, Luc admitted, doubly so in fog, but some drivers actually prefer to make the lonely trip by night when there is less danger of colliding with another car on rounding a treacherous curve.

The chain of Plaisance was revealed to us, cloud-topped, arid, Andalusian in beauty. Luc had arranged for a stop at the Farm-School of Chatard, on the approach to Plaisance, of which his young brother and godson, Marc Frédéric—a product of Columbia summer school—is director. The agricultural schools of Haiti are an adjunct to the education of the people, sponsored originally by the Americans, and are proving of inestimable worth in the battle against inefficiency and superstition.

Our arrival at the Pension André at Cap Haïtien —despite the color of our hosts—recalled similar experiences in France. The building itself was erected by a French general of a bygone régime. When once we had descended to the salle-à-manger there was always a certain excitement, especially of an evening, as to whether we could find our bedroom on mounting the disintegrating wooden stair, following the oh-so-narrow corridor, turning right to avoid the pitfall of the cul-de-sac. That the expedition to the lower floor—when made at night—was something of an adventure we had been warned by a publisher friend, who, having made it, had preferred, though sober, to finish the night on the sofa in the salon, rather than attempt, in the Stygian darkness, to identify the bedroom shared with his wife.

Dr. André (whose grandfather was French), since the departure of the Americans, is in charge of the Hospital. The oldest building of this buff-and-white arcaded group was, in former days, the barracks; the newest was built by the American Red Cross. Here Sisters of Charity flit upon their errands of mercy. The doctor, in addition to long hours at the hospital, was frequently clad for rounds on horseback to the hill villages.

Madame André (daughter of General La Roche and educated in Paris) adds elegance to the establishment and enlivens the twilight hour with her runs and variations on the piano. Months had passed since the pair had received word from their son, Haitian consul in Belgium, his Flemish wife, and fair-haired child. Although Madame's ground-floor apartment was supplied with the last word in modernity—radio, French-dial telephone, Hotpoint range, and General Electric refrigerator—the mere details of housekeeping were left, one surmised, more or less to run in the traditional groove.

Bells being unknown in the bedrooms, all that was necessary, when a lack of sheets was discovered, was to shout for the omnipresent factotum: Jacques, garçon and even, at a pinch, valet-de-chambre, he who had been trained as cook on the Plantation Dauphin. From our tower window might be seen, by day, branched bougainvillea against an azure sky, while at night, in the direction of the hills, a level half-moon caught the eye. Beyond the red-tiled roofs rose the dominating historic cathedral and the parish house, showing crossed emblems, the red and blue flag of Haiti, the yellow and white of the Church, and the motto: "Catholique Haïtien Toujours!!" In the street, groups of joyous children sang as lustily and acted with the same spirit as those depicted by Boutet de Monvel—despite the darkness of their skin—"Sur le Pont d'Avignon" and such rounds as "Frère Jacques." Yet the ancestors of these self-same playmates had risen in their wrath, under the black general-in-chief, Jean Jacques Dessalines, driving the few surviving Frenchmen, with their women and children, to the parade ground for inhuman torture and execution, and, moreover, slaying every remaining white occupant in a house-to-house visitation.

The history of Cap Haïtien is lurid. It was here that the French prospered; here, too, that they made their last stand. Here it was that Pauline, sister to Napoleon, lived scandalously (the ruins of her palace may be seen) while her husband, General Leclerc, the Governor sent by the Emperor, cajoled the natives and trapped the heroic Toussaint to imprisonment leading to his death in France. The French Revolutionists, having granted freedom to Haitian mulattoes in 1791, reversed their decision in the same year. It was this action that induced the men of color to join the blacks in their insurrection against Napoleon's enforcement of slavery. Under Toussaint all had been freemen. The infuriated populace—under the leadership of Dessalines and, at Cap Haïtien, of the implacable Christophe—retaliated against French cruelty. Leclerc and thousands of his soldiers were to die of yellow fever. Pauline was to return to France and later to marry the Prince Borghese. The war of the races continued under Rochambeau—"unworthy son of a famous sire." The final evacuation of Haiti by the French was accomplished from the Cape, January 1, 1804, under the guns of the British fleet... which saved the remnant of the starved garrison from a worse fate. The aboriginal name of the island, Haïti, was restored, and the tyrant, Dessalines (born in Africa, slave of a slave) became governor and later emperor of half a million blackmen. After the assassination of Dessalines the Spaniards claimed the eastern end of the island, naming it Santo Domingo; while the remainder was ruled by rivals: in the South, Pétion, in the North, Christophe.

That so slight are the vestiges of the "Little Paris of America," the center of French culture in Haiti, a city of fountains—the water introduced by the French from the hills—where once forty thousand white men dwelt...and to-day perhaps a score, is in part due to the earthquake of 1842; in part to the act of the commanding officer, who, rather than see the city fall to the forces of Leclerc, had, before retreat to the hills, ordered his troops to set torches to the town. This commanding officer was Christophe, and he led the way by setting fire to his own dwelling. In 1811 he was to become the self-proclaimed king (of the North) and his wife, the queen; his offspring were to become "princes of the blood"; in addition, he was to create among his dusky subjects three princes of the kingdom, eight dukes, twenty counts, thirty-seven barons, and eleven chevaliers. Among other deeds of this fantastic ruler, the prototype, it is said, of *The Emperor Jones,* possessor of nine palaces and eight châteaux, was the erection of the fabulous Citadelle—constructed as a last refuge against the French... the French who were never to return.

The life of Henry Christophe is unparalleled. Son of black parents, at the age of twelve Christophe sailed as servant to an officer with the 1,500 men sent from Haiti by command of Louis XVI, at Franklin's instigation, to the aid of General Washington.... There were also over 2,000 volunteers from Guadeloupe and Martinique. Later Christophe, illiterate until the day of his death, was to be a waiter in a café in Cap Haïtien and to marry a girl of fifteen, who, at the time, little could foresee the day when she would become a queen!

Our appetite for a sight of Christophe's ruined palace of Sans Souci had been whetted by accounts read of the arrival there of a governess for the Princesses Athenaire and Amethyst. The lady was from Philadelphia. Up to that time no white person had been allowed to approach the palace. The tale of this Quakeress' reception sounds like a page torn from Arabian Nights. His Black Majesty had, as bodyguard, a somber note among gorgeously arrayed courtiers, an ebony Goliath —the Executioner. Bright were the palace walls as the gold of Benares. But, startling to this Quaker maid, was the presence of Christophe's blond mistress. Not jewels offered by the queen could induce the lady to remain.

Rising with the sun, my Illustrator and I were

to cross the Plaine du Nord on the twenty-mile drive to Milot. Vying in splendor with the palaces of French kings, Sans Souci, this day-dream of a slave, is arresting even in ruin. The royal chapel, gutted like the palace by earthquake, has been restored; the grandiose stair and all-but-interminable array of arches dazzle the beholder, who, lifting his eyes to the adjacent hills, needlessly fears the possibility of anti-climax in the objective of the day's excursion—arrival at the Citadelle. Upon the plaza, where mounts awaited, stands a mammoth star-apple (*caimitier*) under which King Christophe was wont to dispense his own and unquestionably original idea of justice.

From the saddle we looked back upon the overgrown sheltered garden-terraces of this strangely situated château, strayed, one would say, from France; scene of the final act of that fantastic drama of Christophe's life, a drama ended by the firing of a golden bullet. Ahead the steep trail mounted—there was, of old, connection by subterranean passage—to the still hidden fortress of the Citadelle Laferrière, so named for the master builder from abroad who had conceived and directed its construction. My Illustrator led upon the mule Patience; I followed, astride a pony, while our mounted guide and grooms afoot kept up, despite the steepness of the way, an interminable chatter of Creole, the drift of which was local gossip, we surmised, judging from such

words as *"blancs," "la jalousie"*...invariably
calling forth guffaws.

The beauty of the trail for the trail's sake is a
well-remembered portion of the day's recollec-
tions: it might have been quite otherwise if shared
with a Grace Line boat-load or rather with those
passengers stalwart enough to undertake such
strenuous exertion. One cheerful tale was told of
a dowager, edging away from the abyss, the path
made slippery by rain, who "lost" her foot as
her horse hurled her against a rocky cliff.

"Lost her footing?" I suggested, endeavoring
to thwart my nag when he veered perilously.

"No, her foot," our guide insisted, but refused
to explain whether the severance had been instantaneous or later by amputation.

Not the famed drive from Maracay to Caracas
can rival the beauty of the vistas of high mountains, the clouds, the lush tropical vegetation, the
foreground of bracken, the lift of mahogany
trunks and sky-aspiring kapoks. Through plantations of bananas, where laborers sang haunting
chanties, through groves of coffee—source of
what wealth Haitians can boast—we pushed expectantly onward. Far below was Sans Souci, its
splendor of poinsettias, its myriad butterflies. Orchid clusters had been passed at half-way tree;
then, as we mounted from tropic to temperate
zone, at the very foot of the sinister fortress
sparkled the mocking familiar faces of dande-

The Citadelle

lions: emblems, we liked to think, even in the welter of our modern world, of the sane, the usual.

"For every stone a human life"...muttered our guide, as we lifted eyes to the masterpiece of the towering fortress—impregnable, no doubt, at

Laferrière

the time of its creation, though never called upon to prove its martial worth.

The Citadelle dominates—from its eminence three thousand feet above sea-level—the near-by hills and vales, the distant Cap Haïtien, the notorious isle Tortuga; and, to eastward, seven mountain ranges.

The Citadelle! Of all West Indian monuments it is the most outstanding, comparable for immensity, design, state of preservation, situation and sheer incredibility of history with any fortress of the world. After long anticipation we were to be, nevertheless, stunned by the impact of our first impression. On approach, perilous as was the final grueling ascent, our attention was focused upon this ship-prowed mass of masonry, cloud-tipped. By no unusual stretch of imagination might an avenging war god part those ominous thunder-filled clouds to launch this embattled warship from its way of hilltop into depth of valley cloud, I thought. Riding beneath its ponderous mass I trembled, as—my head reeling from the tropic heat—the fortress embedded on its hill seemed to lurch as though to topple upon me.

"Stop craning!" shouted my Illustrator.

Having been unguided, my horse had stumbled upon the margin of the vertiginous ascent.

Stretching cramped legs, we dismounted to enter the yawning portal of the dank fort. Here bricks were made, powder, even cannon balls—mounds of them still lie beside the mounted guns—a gun, perhaps for every day of the year ... some weighing many tons, but all, it is said, hauled from the valley by human labor. One, we were told, powerful enough to reach Port-au-Prince, was fired by order of Christophe, but this gun leapt over the wall and was irretrievably lost in the bush below. The breach is shown to-day. The King's room was in the prow of the "ship." At a dizzy height, stand two parallel platforms. Here, we were informed, Christophe forced mutinous soldiers, at the word of command, to "forward, march" into the abyss. It is said that the same path was trodden by the contractor who alone shared with Christophe the secrets of the building. Enough is known of the black Christophe to prove his greatness—of a sort; enough to condemn his morals—judged by any Christian standards (how many in our own world dare be judged by the standards of Christ?); but those who would know more of the Man, Christophe, (L'Homme, as he liked to be called) should read *Black Majesty* by Vandercook, a masterly presentation of the career of this slave-born Haitian king. Especially is the death scene poignant: Christophe, haunted by the ghost of a murdered priest, suffering a stroke in the chapel at Limonade, invalided, menaced by deserting followers, taking his own life at Sans Souci. Having foreseen this day the king had sent $6,000,000 in gold to the Bank of England to the credit of his faithful queen—who, with the aid of friends, was able to smuggle the king's body to the Citadelle. Because of haste it was tossed into a vat of quick lime, and the lady, with her daughters, was able to make her escape to Europe.

When we stood beside the meager tomb in the courtyard we read:

CI-GIT

LE ROI HENRY CHRISTOPHE

NÉ LE 6 OCTOBRE 1767

MORT LE 20 OCTOBRE 1820

DONT LA DEVISE EST

"JE RENAIS DE MES CENDRES"

There is said to be much treasure still buried in a vault beneath the doorstep of a certain tower, we were told, as we lingered, by a gendarme with an eye on convicts at work in an adjacent moat.

"Some years ago," said the lieutenant, "an American came with a permit to dig. Every one knows there is treasure. After three days' search the excavator gave up ... and why? The spirit of Henry Christophe had spoken, saying: 'He for whom it is intended is not yet born.' "

Our departure was made in blistering sunlight. We thought of Dr. André's remark when we had commented on his snug Basque béret: "I am an offspring of the sun. I have no fear."

As our horses stumbled over the rocks of the precipitous downward trail—pitching us, parched and panting, forward on our Mexican saddles— we had the thought of sunstroke uppermost in our minds. It was then, with the valor of desperation, that we welcomed the tropical deluge that, for the last hour of the way, doused us to the skin ... reducing supposedly protected express checks and letters of credit to an almost unrecognizable pulp.

For an expedition to the Plantation Dauphin, police papers, red tape are necessary. Like Milot, the sisal hemp plantation lies near the sea upon the Northern Plain. The golden blossoms of logwood, swarming with bees (the logwood honey of Haiti is renowned) hung, as we passed, upon the treetops like a mist. Haunting was the fragrance, as of lilies. Donkeys, five abreast, strained at loads of the red-hearted wood—to be used as a dye. Primitive carts, drawn by yokes of oxen, creaked in and out of cane-fields.

An extraordinary sight greeted us upon passing between the gate-posts marked, respectively:

HAYTIAN AMERICAN DEVELOPMENT CORPORATION 1927
LE PLANTATION DAUPHIN, S. A. 1936

Outspread before us on the dry and level plain (the plantation measures twenty-two square miles) was a blue-green sea of sword-leafed sisal plants—like so many regimented soldiers. For miles we drove, past native villages of the workers, until at last the factory we were to visit and plantation house where we were to lunch—with Mrs. Robert L. Pettigrew, wife of the American manager who was incidentally consular agent to the Cape—came into view.

Our hostess, a daughter of Georgia, revealed her enjoyment of Haiti in displaying her collection of pre-Columbian relics unearthed in the arid, formerly untilled bush of the plantation: spearheads, skinning knives, grinding stones, pestles and mortars, probably of Carib origin; while, from findings in another section of the estate came fragments of Arawak pottery: bat-handled bowls, an owl pestle, combs and other ornaments of shell and bone and barracuda jaw. The lady warms to her subject and also to that of Saturday evening at the plantation. On that night her husband allows the drums. From the villages, far and near, come many of the four thousand workers on the plantation to profit by this form of individual expression. Fearlessly our lady and her guests mingle with the crowds that, intoxicated by the rhythm of the drums, dance and sway till crack of dawn.

At the shed where the local train unloads we were shown the process of taking the fiber from the leaf tips—not from the sides also, as in henequen grown in Cuba. Here we noted cocks—to be used in fights—tethered within sight of their solicitous masters. Noise, heat, dust, and acrid odor could not destroy the beauty of sweating ebony bodies set in patterns of ceaseless motion. The official who had us in tow emphasized his preference for Haitian rather than Mexican, Spanish, or Indian workers. The Haitians, he assured us, though they get excited at times, do not set things afire, are not vindictive. We inquired as to whether the Haitian worker could raise a family on thirty cents a day—forty-five cents is paid to a foreman—to receive the laconic reply: "Yes, several!"

Sisal is a native of Yucatan, but the largest cultivations are in Africa. The Dauphin Brand Sisal Fibre is of four grades. In contrast to the gleaming white fibers baled in parallel lengths is that made by a secret process converting green waste into tow. Sisal—in the form of pads for inner-spring coiled mattresses and auto-cushion upholstery, binder twine, and rope—is transferred by lighters to ships in the bay, thence to proceed to New York, New Orleans, and Plymouth, Massachusetts. Little do the purchasers of sisal visualize its origin in Haiti!

Fort Liberté, on a bottleneck bay, perhaps twenty miles beyond the plantation and as far from the Dominican border, is a forgotten town, in partial ruin, a remnant of the once prosperous French settlement, Fort Dauphin. The ancient church, the open-air pulpit remain, a few antique houses with niches rifled of their saints. Black babies play in gutters. What has the future, we wonder, to hold for such as these? Our minds revert to the slave-born Henry Christophe.

One episode enlivened our visit. My Illustrator, with a flair for the unusual, brought our car to a sudden halt in time to confront, with his camera, a line of convicts. The desperados cast baleful glances at my impetuous partner, as did their armed guard. Luc, meanwhile, did not reassure me by stating that these fellows in red stripes (unlike the blue-striped minor offenders) were long-termers, in all probability murderers.

Across the Dominican frontier, almost within sight from Fort Liberté, and facing the Haitian village of Ouanaminthe, sleeps the hamlet of Dajabón, scene in 1937 of the "Border Incident," in actuality the most appalling slaughter of innocents of our day, a slaughter if not instigated, at least certainly not prevented by the dictator, Trujillo, and costing his fellow-countrymen a round though inadequate sum—as what sum would not have been?—when considered as an attempt at payment for the barbarous toll of 12,000 priceless human lives.

"The President of the Republic will receive you at his country-place at Kenscoff to-morrow at four" was the news that greeted us on our return to Port-au-Prince. "If he likes you it will be hard to get away," continued our informant. "Remember, although Monsieur Vincent speaks English the conversation will be in the language of the country, French."

Kenscoff (not "Kinscolt," as the resort is listed by Aspinall and his slavish copyists) we had already visited but, on the former occasion, our interest had been on the market-folk to be seen along the route, the burdened *bourriques,*

not on the high-walled villa of the President's
mountain retreat. At Pétionville we had paused
part-way for a view, from the American Club, of
the Cul-de-Sac Valley, where men go for the
shooting. They get ducks, but sometimes malaria
as well.

On our second arrival at Kenscoff the captain
of the guard, conversing affably and with digni-
fied reserve, in English, ushered us into the in-
formal reception room of the president's villa.
While we were admiring the valley view, with
its foreground of hillside garden, President Stenio
Vincent entered, apologizing for causing us the
trouble of coming to Kenscoff, but he had decided
to let nothing interfere with this needed refresh-
ment. A Haitian president, he said, does not have
the assistants of the chief executive of a larger
country. He must do the work himself. His sister,
he regretted, had remained at Port-au-Prince to
entertain his brother, the consul in New York.
Conversation turned to what he was pleased to
call the Musée Nationale, not completing the title,
which is Fondation Stenio Vincent—the President
having been its founder.

"Papa Vincent," as he is affectionately called
—the soul of generosity—is deeply concerned with
both the education through schools and libraries
and the general welfare of the peasants. On Sunday he had made an expedition to Cornillon, in
the section known as Grands-Bois, to open a new

road, where previously had been a mere trail. Thousands of peasants were assembled who had never before seen a president. A high percentage, perhaps the highest anywhere, of the people are landholders, and this is, of course, good socially, although the president admitted, perhaps not of so much importance economically.

Monsieur Vincent stressed his friendship, as Secretary of the Interior, for Mr. Roosevelt, whom he had first known as Assistant Secretary of the Navy. At that time, he said, they had both expressed their desire to retire from politics— Roosevelt to return to the practice of the law. Vincent has visited the United States more than once. Last time he found it necessary to cancel his return by air in order to have a restful voyage to recover from American hospitality. His formal visit to Washington, in April, 1934, was returned by President Roosevelt, aboard the *Houston,* a gesture not forgotten by Haitians.

More than an hour having passed and there being no sign of dismissal, I expressed a desire to watch the ceremony of lowering the flag—announced by a bugler and for which the guard was assembling. We sauntered to the veranda, overlooking terraces of saucer-sized roses and a coffee *pepinière.* Mountains concealed the actual setting of the sun. The officer in charge consulted his watch. Again the bugle blew. Again we stood, and stood, and stood. Time, we thought, was no re-

spector of the great. Perhaps the watch could
bear a little shaking? For the third time the bugle
sounded, and now the blue and red flag was slowly
lowered, not one, as at the palace, bearing the
official L'Abre de la Liberté—a "wild" or royal
palm.

Farewells were lingeringly taken, the evening
had grown chill: how different at this altitude was
the temperature from that at Port-au-Prince
where the thermometer (according to Ober)
"hangs around the nineties." As a gracious aid
to the enjoyment of our stay, the President arranged that we should visit the historic Fort at
Port-au-Prince—for the time-being closed to the
public—where the officers were to treat us like
royalty.

President Vincent, we read, is of the National-
ist Party—not traditionally as coöperative with
the Americans as that of the Liberals, the party
of his successor Elie Lescot. Colonel Paul Magloire
—elected President, in 1950, to succeed President
Estimé ousted by a military junta—has, in 1951,
taken steps with President Trujillo of the Dominican Republic to facilitate an agreement to re-
inforce the 1928 Havana Convention on rights and
duties of states in civil uprisings.

The International Exposition held in the winter
of 1949-50, the 200th Anniversary of the founding
of Port-au-Prince, attracted throngs. On the Boulevard Harry Truman, facing Gonâve Bay, are still

to be found the Haitian Museum, the Pavillon d'Ameublement and the Théâtre de Verdure.

One of our outstanding impressions of life in Haiti was a soirée given in our honor by Madame Suzanne Comhaire-Sylvain, whose scholarly sister we had met at Bryn Mawr College. The party was held in the family mansion at Peu-de-Chose. The father of our hostess, George Sylvain, an intimate during his lifetime of President Vincent, had been ambassador to France, as well as an author crowned by the French Academy. (His translation of La Fontaine into Creole is justly famous.) His mantle has fallen upon his daughter Suzanne, who, as well as being an author of note, an authority on Creole, is founder and dean of the École des Lettres of Port-au-Prince and professor of philology and anthropology, also Inspector of the schools of Port-au-Prince. Her record in *Who's Who in Latin America* is too long to list; let us only note that she was educated in Paris and is married to Dr. Jean Comhaire of Belgium —author, and owner of the Librairie Caravelle at Port-au-Prince. The Sylvain family may be cited as an example to prove the truth of Captain Craige's statement, in his enthralling book *Cannibal Cousins*, that certain families of the Haitian élite have produced extraordinarily brilliant minds for successive generations.

It was at this hospitable house, while sweet wine of Italy was being served, that we were to meet the historian Dantès Bellegarde, former Haitian delegate to the League of Nations and, of late, popular lecturer at Atlanta. This affable gentleman told us, laughingly, that it had been discovered that he was related to Dumas. After the discussion of the delight of European travel, the conversation was to turn, most unfortunately, to the subject of the treatment of Haitians visiting the United States. . . . Jim Crow cars, refusal of admission to many hotels and restaurants. Our hostess, a sensitive young woman, said, for herself, she would never care to face the ordeal. We were apologetic, explaining that changes were bound to come with the education of the Negro.

"But," said Madame, "it will take a hundred years . . . and where shall we be?"

In conservative families of the Haitian élite, customs are modeled on French patterns. Mourning, worn by children as well as by elders, is so strict that, after the death of an uncle, no member of the household may touch the piano for three months. A former music student told us that after the death of three uncles and, finally, of her father she turned to sociology and the study of the law! It was this same young woman who was to whet our curiosity on the subject of zombies. She knew a doctor who decided to investigate the truth of whether in actuality these beings return from death. He consulted an old man of the mountains, who was said to possess a knowledge of herbs handed down from African forebears. A test was made upon the doctor's cat, who was given a white powder and seemed to die.

"Do not bury the cat," said the old man, "but keep it in the cellar. After three days I shall return."

In the meantime the doctor, by means of injections, did his best to restore the animal, but to no avail. At the appointed time the old man of the mountains reappeared. The cat was seemingly dead and cold, but not decomposed. Once more it was given a powder, after which it immediately revived and, as though demented, fled from the room.

"Certainly," said my friend, "there are zombies."

"Zombies," said a skeptical American, long a resident of Port-au-Prince, "are people who have forgotten their identity ... so there are many zombies in the United States. Those who say otherwise can never give proof. Expert doctors say there is no medicinal plant grown on the island unknown elsewhere. Idle tales ... superstition."

Like religion and morality (in Haiti and elsewhere too often divorced) these contradictory statements seem to run in diverging grooves without possibility of meeting. Sensational tales of magic abound, such as those of a well-known author whose only knowledge, we were told, consisted of a truck ride between boat calls at Cap

Haïtien and Port-au-Prince; and those of another who practised voodoo until driven temporarily insane; and, to a lesser degree, those of a third who has both eyes open for the gruesome. According to these tale-bearers a zombie is a resuscitated being in whom a living death has been produced and interment made during a cataleptic trance. The voodoo seer, by means of an antidote, revives his patient who, thereafter, is brainless and soulless, but able to perform physical work for a master. It is said that the Haitian Criminal Code contains a clause appertaining to the administering of such drugs, that the giver shall be guilty of murder whether or not his victim dies. True zombies, on the other hand, are said to be those that die and rise again from the dead. They are, we were given to understand, of less frequent occurrence; although countryfolk from time to time, we noticed, decorate a fence post with the skull of a donkey . . . to fend off evil spirits.

Haitians are by some considered to be a moral people because of rather general adherence to their own standards. In the upper classes marriage is the rule, but its expense often deters the impoverished. The poor man nevertheless goes to the mother of the girl and asks for her hand, showing his ability to support her, and a feast is given in honor of the occasion. Other families are, however, frequently raised, simultaneously, with full knowledge of the "wife." Although the majority of the people call themselves Catholics, ninety per cent of the population consists of illiterate peasants, half of whom probably combine the worship of their nature gods with that of the Christian God. Household altars or shrines combine pictures of the saints and fetishes to whom, as in Africa, a little meal or rice is offered.

Did you see a voodoo dance? is the question inevitably asked. The answer is that, on the arrival of a ship, so-called voodoo dances are staged for the benefit of tourists. That if, as may be, the purely religious dance, for which the Pethro drum is pounded, is still on occasion given, it is not apt to be within hearing of foreign ears nor are its bloody sacrifices apt to be viewed by foreign eyes—though the most that traditionally might be seen, in our era, would be a slaughtered ram and not the "goat without horns," or human sacrifice.

The Congo dance, or Saturday night *bamboche,* is another matter: for this the Rada tom-toms throb, beaten, with stick or hand, with extraordinary virtuosity. Although it is in the African tradition that dancing is for the gods, the religious significance, in this case, is secondary and the phallic rites do not inevitably follow.

Haiti Singing is the title of a book. Another might well be *Haiti Dancing.* Song and dance, with semi-religious import—they ought not to be divided—are the outstanding Haitian demonstra-

Rada

tions. Perhaps because of this very outlet the native blacks more than others in the West Indies are embodiments of cheerfulness—an almost Chinese mirthfulness, coupled, also, with an equally Chinese dearth of worldly possessions.

"To-day in the Haitian hills," writes the author

of *Haiti Singing,* "the old music fills the air, the old customs go on, and ancient deities are abroad at night.... Vodoun is strong, it cannot die easily, and this is one thing missionaries do not seem to understand. You cannot readily destroy something with such deep and genuine roots.... The *houngan* [priest] is the intellectualizing agency of a tremendous emotional force."

European dancing is considered immoral by the conservative Haitian. It is well to remember this and to keep an open mind when attending Haitian folk-dances. Although *méringues*—a form tracing its origin to the minuets danced by the élite in Haiti during the French régime—are to be seen, the Rada forms are those of true African origin. To the throb of the Rada drums—three in number—the *chacha* or rattle of the mistress of the dance (who also leads the singing), shoulders, hips, abdomens, every muscle of the supple bodies of the dancers vibrate. Lawyers, engineers, girls of refinement take part, garbed in extravagantly brilliant color, in such a group as that organized by Madame Lathon, under the patronage of Monsieur Lescot. Only the dance group of Shan Kar is to my mind comparable with these barefoot Haitians. Both are bound by an underlying religious tradition.

One dance, I remember, demonstrated the rhythmic drying of coffee beans, shaken by the girls in shallow baskets—the men forming a vital background; another was called Carnival King. But, for the most, the gods were represented: the god of travelers, the lame god, the god of twins, girls (symbolic of purity) clustered about the central figure of a god, and finally, the dramatic climax of the undulating, sinuous dance—becoming more and more ecstatic—Damballa, the all-powerful snake god. One with the dancers were the drummers and their drums, pulsating as though audible heartbeats of Mother Haiti.

The "staccato pounding of Pethro drums" is more rarely heard; and still less frequently heard, by whites, is the roar of the bass Arada drums—often nine feet long and calling for two players —sounding from village to village.

Familiarity with African ways in Haiti gives double poignancy to a former news item on the Emperor of Ethiopia. When the sound of the royal war drums reverberated among the hills, the Ethiopian tribesmen knew, beyond shadow of a doubt, that the Lion of Judah had returned.

May the leaders of Haiti nevermore need to sound the call to arms.

Ciudad Trujillo : † †
Ruins of the Church of St. Nicholas de Bari.

The ALCAZAR: Ciudad Trujillo

CHAPTER V

THE CRADLE OF THE NEW WORLD

"As MAY in Cordova!" were the words Columbus
applied to that shining island of the West, with
hills and dales vibrant with sunlight, seeming, on
that sixth day of December, 1492, to be calling
aloud for the name the discoverer was to give it,
Española, Little Spain. Long known as Santo Domingo, the island of Hispaniola is to-day divided,
as we have seen, between the French-speaking Republic of Haiti, on the west, and, on the east, the
Spanish-speaking Dominican Republic.

On the left bank of the Ozama, the Spaniards laid
—on Sunday, August 4, 1496, the feast day of San
Domingo de Guzman, founder of the Dominican
order—the first stones of Santo Domingo. The
name of the patron of the city was, as well, that
of the Spanish word for Sunday, and also that
of the father of Columbus. After the destructive
hurricane of 1502, the budding capital was recon-

structed, under Governor Ovando, upon the opposite shore. It had the distinction of being the first city in the Western Hemisphere founded by immigrants from the Old World. Its site was characteristically chosen on the strength of gold discovered, upon the banks of the Rio Jaina, at near-by San Cristóbal. Here later was to be reshipped the riches destined for the King of Spain; while the man through whose genius the New World's treasure had been unlocked was, after arrest and imprisonment, permitted to languish and die in penury, on Ascension Day, May 20, 1506, at Valladolid.

The tale of Columbus' relations with a city whose conception was his own inspiration, is incredible even in a land where the inconceivable often becomes the rule. Although the Admiral was entrusted with authority to govern the island in the name of Ferdinand and Isabella, in reality, it was necessary for him to travel to Spain to defend his honor, leaving his son, Don Diego Colón, as his representative and as mayor of the city of Santo Domingo. Although exonerated of the charges brought against him, Columbus was again to be accused by his enemies who obtained a Royal Decree for the Admiral's dispossession. Bobadilla was named to supplant the Discoverer as governor, and one of his first actions was to imprison Columbus, the latter's son Diego, and his brother Bartolomew. The Admiral was, as every school-

boy knows, sent to Spain in chains and, although
he was given his freedom by the king—who held
a reception in his honor—Ovando, not Columbus,
was sent as governor of Española. It was, be it
remembered, during the régime of Ovando that
Columbus, on his fourth and final voyage to the
world of his Discovery, although threatened by
forecasted hurricane, was refused permission to
land at Santo Domingo. It gives the reader of history at least a passing sense of satisfaction, on
pursuing the record, to learn that, although Columbus reached Puerto Hermoso, and later the Jamaican shore and Cuba, continuing to the "Straits
of Darien," the city of Santo Domingo was destroyed by the predicted tornado, including
twenty-one government ships; moreover, among
those who forfeited their lives was the Admiral's
arch-enemy, the former governor, Francisco de
Bobadilla.

Santo Domingo can, and does, boast of the
possession of the first stone church, university,
and fortress in the New World. The church, that
of San Nicholas de Bari, was constructed by
Ovando, in 1503, as a means to obtain coveted dis-
pensations. Its building was by enslaved Indians.
Despite this fact, the unholy reason of its coming
into being, and its ruined condition, St. Nicholas
is, to my mind, the most pleasing structure to be
seen in the Capital. After the fashion of the time
it offered asylum in the form of an iron ring to

which a pursued man might cling, and thereby avoid arrest. It is said that not even the powerful dared to violate this privilege of sanctuary. The Tower of Homage dates from the same period, a fortress now restored beyond recognition. It is believed to be here that Columbus was imprisoned by Governor Ovando.

The Alcázar, an imposing ruin, rises abruptly from the harbor's edge. Here from 1509 to 1524 dwelt the Viceroy Don Diego Colón (son of Columbus), second Admiral of the Indies, and his high-born lady, María de Toledo, niece of Ferdinand. Here was born their son Luis (one of seven children) who was to become third Admiral of the Indies. So sumptuous was this fortified dwelling that its construction was delayed for months on the accusation that Don Diego was building not a residence but a fortress. It was only on the testimony of the King's own engineer, sent from Spain, that work was permitted to continue. In the throne room were the Arms of Castile, later to be captured by Drake.

"The wall that defied Drake still encircles the town itself a spectacle of bygone magnificence and present squalor," wrote Sir Frederick Treves, early in our century. It was on January 10, 1586, that Drake and his privateersmen ravished the town. Santo Domingo was entered by strategy, looted, and held for a month by the piratical crew who departed at length on receiving payment of

25,000 ducats, the townsmen forfeiting, to boot, a total of eighty cannon.

It was from the city founded by Columbus that Balboa set forth to view the Pacific, Cortés to the conquest of Mexico, Pizarro to Peru, Velázquez to Cuba, and Ponce de León to his quest for the Fountain of Youth and his ultimate discovery of Florida.

In the year 1511 Santo Domingo's jurisdiction over the Antilles was complete; while by the ordinances of 1528, its rule was extended to include Central, North, and South America.

The Pope, to whose hands the heathen were said to be entrusted by God, had granted to Spain, in the year 1493, by right of this authority, "the possession of all lands lying to the west of a meridian drawn one hundred leagues westward of the Azores and to Portugal all lands lying to the east."... On these grounds all but Spanish comers to the New World were considered outlaws. The introduction of African slaves, as early as 1505, by the Spaniards was made without forethought of the extraordinary transformation thus to be engendered in the racial strain of the islands and, by consequent infusions of the same blood, eventually, of the continents of the Western Hemisphere. At Santo Domingo, Hawkins was to conduct sensational barter, this in the year 1562, exchanging slaves for the coveted treasure and fabulous spice.

"A web of confusion," the author of *Caribbee Cruise* calls the name of the second largest of the West Indian islands. Haiti, Española, Spagnolla, Hispaniola, Santo Domingo, which shall it be?

"Now that we have got it quite clear in our minds about Santo Domingo [not the island but the first city of our civilization in the New World] there is no such place." ... Not the least nefarious acts of dictators are their changing of time-hallowed traditional names.

By the hurricane of September 3, 1930, about a fortnight after Trujillo became President of Dominican Republic, Santo Domingo was swept to oblivion, and, in its stead, Trujillo City rises. Of all the monuments that miraculously escaped total destruction, in addition to those already mentioned, are two city gates, the Jesuit Convent—used as Treasury offices—the church of the former Dominican Convent, and the ruined San Francisco, the Santa Barbara Fortress, and, foremost of all for its associations, the Cathedral—incorporating the church, built in 1514, of Santa María de Travestere—elevated to the rank of Basilica in our century, where the treasured relics of Columbus are entombed.

To give the devil his due it must be recorded that Trujillo vetoed the change of name when a law to that effect was passed by Congress. During his absence on account of health, in 1936, the new law was promulgated "owing," writes a local authority, airing his knowledge of English, "to an expontaneous demonstration of gratitude!"

Unlike Havana, where surprising taste has been displayed in keeping the historic city intact, while building new quarters in modern fashions, Trujillo City has almost unfailingly obliterated the old in the name of restoration. To such an extent is this true that were it not for the sentimental respect Americans owe to the bones of Columbus, and the interest they very naturally manifest in sites connected with his name, there would be small reason to touch by boat or plane at the Dominican Republic—a country as yet unprepared, save to a limited extent at the capital, to meet the requirements of the average tourist, although offering asylum to about 2,000 Spanish loyalists and to many thousands (the total may reach 100,000) Jewish and other European refugees. Save for a few salvaged relics, Santo Domingo is so dead and buried as almost to justify the giving of a new name to the city that has risen under the direction of the dictator Trujillo.

To have even an inkling of the problems to be faced in the Dominican Republic it is necessary to glance at a few pages of history—beginning with the foundation of the Republic in 1844 and leading up to what was officially known as The Military Government of the United States in Santo Domingo. During the period of the American occupa-

tion—from 1916 to 1924—laws were made by the
Military governor, an American admiral, and administered by members of our navy and marines
without aid of native officials, although, save at
American headquarters, the flag of the Dominican
Republic continued to fly. By some the occupation
is cited as an example of intervention to protect
American investors; by others it was considered
necessary, indeed obligatory, in the name not
alone of interest but of humanity. The story is dis-
passionately told, in two ample volumes (a history
of the years 1844 to 1924) entitled *Naboth's
Vineyard* by Sumner Welles—sent by President
Wilson as a special commissioner to the Dominican Republic.

The most rapid glance at these pages reveals
a scarlet warp and woof of criminal assault and
assassination. The "Wherever you" order from
Heureaux to his soldiers led to the resignation of
Colonel Vásquez ("Wherever you go, you will
understand your soldiers are to consider as their
property all horses, cows, chickens—and women
—that they may find."), and later to the plot
whereby Cáceres, on July 25, 1899, shot Heureaux: his own administration was to be cut short
by an assassin's bullet. Insurrections and flights to
Cuba follow in quick succession. The theme of
civil war being the same, whether power lay, for
the moment, in the hands of Jiménez, Vásquez,
or Cáceres as president, whether the parties were

known as Jimenistas, Velasquitas, or Horacistas, or, later, reorganized as Partido Liberal, Progresita, or Nacional.

Not until the inauguration on July 12, 1924, of General Vásquez as president, accompanied by the lowering of the American flag from the fort at the mouth of the Ozama and the raising of the Dominican standard, may the new era of independence be said to have dawned.

"The benefits resulting from the Military occupation of the Dominican Republic, so far as the national interests of the United States are concerned, have been of infinitesimal importance when compared to the suspicions, fears, and hatreds to which the Occupation gave rise throughout the American Continent," writes Mr. Welles, and goes on to speak of the hostility created in the hearts of a number of Dominicans.

Since the days of President Grant's attempt at annexation, especially since the official high-sounding phrases of President Wilson, who nevertheless sent a ward politician as minister, Dominicans have had cause for suspicion of American motives. Yet the poverty of the country requires the introduction of foreign capital. It is to the interest of the United States that loans should be financed to keep our neighbors from wallowing in the slough of poverty (loans such as the $1,500,000 borrowed from the Export-Import Bank for a slaughterhouse and refrigerating plant for meat to be shipped across the Mona Channel to Puerto Rico) ; and, moreover, that there should be no misappropriation of funds, which might, as before, lead to the necessity of imposing military occupation by the United States. Judging from the highways, hotel, and other modern structures rising at the capital, we thought there was little danger of repetition of the former disastrous situation.

The recent blot on the escutcheon of the Dominican Republic is of an altogether different nature, and Trujillo's modernization of his native land can not, to my mind, whitewash the stain of the most blood-curdling massacre of modern times— "the Border Incident," so-called by Dominicans, already referred to in the Haitian chapter. True, the rancor of the Haitian occupation of 1822 to 1844 was a remembered thorn, but the fact remains that although no war excited human passions, hundreds, nay, thousands of Haitians were slain, with no chance for flight or self-defense. The order went forth, this in the year 1937, that all Haitians were to be repatriated. Trucks were loaded with these workers (humble, dark-skinned folk), trucks driven not to the border but to corrals where the unfortunates—men, women, and children—were brutally attacked by soldiers armed with machetes. Lest eye-witnesses may be thought to exaggerate, let the size of the indemnity speak for itself. The indemnity paid by Dominican Republic for the affair—which extended not alone along the border but, premeditatedly, wherever Haitians dwelt—was a round sum of $750,000.

Flying from Port-au-Prince on the western, Haitian, end of the island which Dominican Republic and Haiti share, my Illustrator and I had an opportunity to observe the arid, sparsely settled, mountainous country that lies between the capitals of these lands. We were to look down upon the Haitian lake of Fondo, and, later, upon that curious phenomenon, the salt Lago Enriquillo on the Dominican side of the border. Landing was made at San Pedro de Macoris, from which town we drove at dusk to Trujillo City.

Perhaps on no other lap of our voyage by air did we feel so far from home as upon that somewhat inauspicious arrival. Fresh from the wonders of Haitian scenery we were oppressed by the towering cane which walled the narrow highway, alternating only with swamps from which dank odors emanated. Lickety-split our car careened onward for hours, all but out of control because of the spasmodic coughing of our non-English-speaking chauffeur. Fearing that he was in the last stages of a deep-seated consumption and might pass away en route, we were able to glean in our non-West-Indian Spanish that it was merely the influenza, that every one at Trujillo City had suffered for months. The bit of information was not altogether comforting; nor was the fact that, at one point, the man was forced to alight at a wayside bar to fortify himself with grog.

That influenza was prevalent was only too apparent on arrival at the Hotel Fausto. Coughs warranted, it seemed, to turn their owners wrong side out, rose from surrounding bungalows, and anguished shouts for "Em'ly," the faithful Indian-looking maid who administered lime, rum, and honey. To our surprise this factotum greeted us in cockney accents.

"To get on in the world," said she, "you 'ave to speak Henglish."

Although night had settled upon the city, incessant hammering announced the erection of a new bungalow to accommodate an influx of delegates to the Dominican Republic Settlement Association, providing new homes for European refugees. (Twenty-five thousand acres of land for this purpose were the personal gift of General Trujillo.)

"Why Fausto?" we asked our prosperous-looking landlord, whose irrelevant reply was: "Have you not heard of the opera Faust?"

The connection was never clearly established in our minds, but it did indeed seem to us that there was a subtly Mephistophelian turn beneath the surface of the most obvious transactions in the Dominican Republic. Let me hasten to praise the quality of food and of beds at the Hotel

Fausto, the netted windows, the hot as well as cold water of our individual shower.

A yellow-faced "nigger" of the type familiar in caricatures, derby hat cocked awry, served as chauffeur to the hotel taxi. He informed my Illustrator of the ban on photography of the picturesque. Any driver permitting foreigners to take pictures of market folk, beasts of burden with their high-pooped saddles, thatched huts, would be fined fifty dollars, and, for the second offense, the tourist would be fined five hundred dollars and six months in jail. Only the modern phase of life may, in the future, be shown beyond the borders of the Republic. Rumors had reached headquarters of the sort of thing amateurs had been displaying on their silver screens. On announcement of this ultimatum, my Illustrator grunted his relief that our stay was to be brief.

Like a refreshing fountain in the desert was the overflowing babble, in well-chosen English, of one Manuel Quesada (a Puerto Rican), guide to the city and more especially to the Cathedral. Quesada was to tell us the nicest story we had heard of Mr. "Charlie" Schwab. It was in 1910 that Schwab had employed Quesada as guide for the island, after which cards were exchanged at Christmas. Twenty years later, following the cyclone of 1930—which in a ten-mile area killed forty-five thousand human beings as well as wounding ten thousand others, the loss in dollars being estimated at some forty-two million—Quesada received a message from Schwab to which the guide replied: "Everything lost but life, thanks." Next day, by cable, five hundred dollars was placed to his credit ... a credit that saved him, his young teacher-wife and infant son, from ruin.

Quesada was to tell us the reason for the acute and especial coughing of chauffeurs. They had been called upon a few days before—some five hundred cars had made the trip—to travel through clouds of swirling dust to the little town of Higüey, 170 kilometers to the east, where, annually on January twenty-first, the fête of the Virgin of La Altagracia is celebrated.

Remarking our lack of enthusiasm for such reconstructed piles as the freshly-plastered Homage Tower, on which is mounted an anti-aircraft gun —an edifice without any visible links in the chain of its history to connect it with the days of Columbus and Drake—our mild response to such sights as the sun-baked boulevard named for George Washington and disporting a pseudo-Washington monument dedicated to Trujillo, our cicerone led us, by way of the rewarding ruins of San Nicholas, San Francisco, and the Alcázar of Columbus, without further delay to the Cathedral.

The Cathedral, when all is told, is the sole magnet that draws the average American to Trujillo City. Be not disturbed, my fellow-countrymen, if

you have already, as I had, been shown the burial
place of Columbus in Seville and the chapel in
Havana where the supposed bones of Columbus
rested a while—en route, as it proved, to Spain.
Pay no heed to all this and accustom yourself to
the thought that Columbus, according to the most
authentic modern scholars, indeed rests where he
would be, in the chief city of his brave New World.

The story has often been told of how Doña
María de Toledo traveled from Spain, in 1544,
with the relics of her husband and those of the
Admiral, her father-in-law, in accordance with the
latter's expressed desire. Here they were rever-
ently interred in the Cathedral. After Spain's loss
of the Dominican Republic, and then of Cuba, it
was thought fitting that the leaden casket, dis-
interred from the Cathedral and supposed to contain the relics, should be sent to Havana and later
to Seville. Sensational, then, was the discovery,
in 1877, of a second casket—farther from the high
altar and nearer to the outer wall—marked in
the language of the day with the recognizable
name of Cristóval Colón—the other casket having,
evidently, been that of Columbus' son. Owing to
the danger of deliberate destruction of the relics
by invaders, the markings of the tombs had been
obliterated in a bygone time of stress, after which
their resting-place had been forgotten. Not only
is the Cathedral, begun in 1514 and still unfin-
ished, a place of burial for the dead, but it has

The Cathedral of Trujillo City

where the relics of Columbus are entombed

on occasion housed the living. Drake used the
edifice as barracks, taking the bells and burning
the files. William Penn's father came with the
notorious Venables to destroy the city in 1655
but, owing to panic among his men, was repulsed.
After the hurricane of 1930, over two thousand
people found shelter within these high-arched
walls until such time as the million and a half
dollars sent by the American Red Cross had provided them with new dwellings.

Secretary of State Hull has presented Trujillo
with a crystal case in which the bones of Columbus rest in a vacuum, in order that the tomb may
be opened without jeopardizing the remains. The
dates on which the relics are exposed are September 10th—the day of their discovery in 1877—and
October 12th, the date of the discovery of the
New World. The casket may not be unlocked except in the presence of the mayor, the secretary
for foreign affairs, and the archbishop, each of
whom possesses a key needful to the unlocking.
The costly structure of the tomb is guarded by
the Lions of Castile.

History, secular as well as religious, centers in
the Cathedral. Two of its three Dominican arch-
bishops (the others were of Spanish or Italian
origin), Monseñor de Meriño and Monseñor Nouel,
have been elected president of the Republic. The
Chapel of Immortals contains the remains of the
three national heroes, Duarte, Sanchez, and Mella,

leaders of the revolt of February 26, 1844, by which the Haitians, who had occupied the entire island for twenty-two years, were ejected to their side of the border and the Dominican Republic established.

Duarte Day happened to fall on the Sunday we spent at Trujillo City. After attending mass in the Cathedral, where the white-winged head-dresses of nuns recently arrived from France graced the nave, we drove to the Convento Dominico, built in 1508. Near-by, students piled their wreaths at the foot of the monument to Duarte. Quesada, who had accompanied us, lamented the fact that we could not see the Good Friday ceremony when, toward midnight, electric lights are extinguished and thousands of candle-bearers form the procession known as "searching for the Lord."

Of an afternoon we drove through hoary surviving gates of the one-time walled city, past the Plaza and Hospital of the saintly Padre Bellini, past the cement mold of the until-recently-living ceiba tree on the dock where Columbus is said to have moored his ship, past the vessel of that modern yachtsman Trujillo—a vessel on which the Generalissimo has traveled to France and, on more than one occasion, to the United States—past the ultra-modern Jaragua Hotel, and past the model playground named Ramfis Park for Trujillo's then twelve-year old son who, at this tender age, wore the uniform and drew the salary of a general.

In the residential section a villa bearing a garish sign in electric bulbs attracted our attention, a sign which read: "Dios y Trujillo." This house, it was explained, belonged to the widow of President Jacinto B. Peynado, who—feeling that he owed everything, including his house, to the Generalissimo—had had this tribute erected and who, a few months before, had died murmuring the name, "Trujillo, Trujillo."

The Generalissimo was absent in the United States, supposedly on pleasure bent, but, it was whispered, sotto voce, really for an operation. As we drove past the residence of the Dictator on the outskirts of the town, police in blue linen and soldiers in khaki and rough-rider hats—especially strict, we were told, during the master's absence—kept our car in motion. Officers stopped us en route as we persevered to visit Trujillo's country estate, the Hacienda Fundación, beyond San Cristóbal. We were fortunate in arriving in time to watch the milking of the famous herd of cattle. Aside from the amusement of counting "Spanish Bayonets" in cottage gardens, their yucca-like leaves "blooming" with egg-shells ("an old custom, to amuse one's self ... perhaps for luck," we were told), our chief impression was of the flaming bloom of *immortelles* towering against a midsummer blue (and this in January)

**Blooming
with egg-shells**

and foothills lush with banana and coco-palms—
leading the eye, as sunset neared, to the cloud-
crowned Central Range.

To end on a note of Columbus, rather than of
Trujillo, our final drive was to take us across the

Ozama, its widened and dredged mouth now known as the port of Trujillo City: Santo Domingo, since the days of steam, had depended upon landings made from the open sea. On this farther shore, as well as a partly-ruined chapel associated in the popular mind with the Mariner, is the chosen site of the Columbus Memorial Lighthouse which, it was hoped, would be erected by 1944—the centenary of the founding of the Dominican Republic. Work was begun in 1947 on the first unit of the project planned to extend for almost a mile, to serve as a guide to navigators by sea or by air and to which the bones of the Discoverer will eventually be transferred. The architect has created a symbol for Columbus in the long form of a double cross—"a gigantic cross incrusted in the ground." As resolved by the Inter-American Conference for the Maintenance of Peace (Buenos Aires, 1936), "the erection of Columbus's Commemorative Lighthouse [with its twenty-one rays] will be the symbol of the fraternity and union of America."

La Cuña, the Cradle ... at no other spot—crime-stained though it be—could this poetic symbol be so fittingly erected. The words of Shelley come to mind:

> Most wretched men
> Are cradled into poetry by wrong;
> They learn in suffering what they teach in song.

Columbus
The Discoverer

El Morro of Puerto Rico

SAN JUAN♦ Sally-port of San Cristobal Castle

CHAPTER VI

INCOMPARABLE PUERTO RICO

OLD Spain, modern America meet on the incomparable island of Puerto Rico. Is it not in part owing to this union of opposites that there begins to emerge the as yet diaphanous and shadowy vision of an eagerly awaited heir—a Pan-American—in whose hands may rest the future well-being of our battered world? Geographically, politically, intellectually, there seems no adequate reason to contradict the ardent plea put forth by the advocates of the University of Puerto Rico that theirs is a unique opportunity for the reconciliation of varying viewpoints, for the fostering of human advancement, through the cradling of both cultures common to dwellers on our Western Hemisphere.

Paradoxes abound in Puerto Rico. I should almost say that because of them the island holds its unparalleled position. To the seeker after modernity there is San Juan—Miami transferred to a tropical isle; there are, nevertheless, indestructible Morro and other remnants of medieval Spain.

The traveler who prefers the protection, in these troublous times, the security his own flag gives, should be attracted to Puerto Rico, but he will, none the less, have opportunity to study the language and surviving customs of Old Castile. According to temperament he may be, at first encounter, stunned by the insistence of the one or yet of the other. To the philosophically minded, the problem presented will but enhance the interest. Apparent as are the failings of both civilizations, obvious to the most casual visitor on arrival upon these shores—on longer acquaintance it can not be denied that the divergent virtues of both emerge.

In contrast to the ephemeral fascination of certain smaller islands, the charm of Puerto Rico becomes the more binding in direct ratio to the length of stay. Her faults are not of her own making, but stem from the mistakes of her settlers. No more fertile soil offers for another Holy Experiment... for the flowering of a true Democracy.

Although for the time being the highway encircling Puerto Rico is being widened, if not for military reasons at least to afford the safety jeopardized by an increase in traffic—and with this widening comes the destruction of thousands of flamboyants that have delighted the eyes alike of traveler and native—yet the new-comer is reassured to find not only the phenomenally rapid growth of these trees, well-suited to their habitat, but to discover the undisturbed peace of the interior hinterland.

Spain, I have said, was in the habit of losing colonies. Columbus, it seems, was in the habit of crumbling a parchment to throw at the feet of Spain's queen. His telling way of demonstrating the mountainous quality of the island was recounted at Jamaica, and again, with still greater justification, at Puerto Rico. That this island, the Boriquen of the Arawaks, was discovered by the Admiral on his second voyage (on November 19, 1493), when he watered his ships at Aquadilla, is well known. . . . Ponce de León, a member of the expedition, was to guard such memories that, fifteen years later, he asked and obtained leave to settle there. The site of the city of San Juan was to be called Puertorico—the Rich Port—which name was later, incongruously, to change places with that given by Columbus to the island: San Juan Bautista. Ponce, appointed governor by the king of Spain in 1509, was to be superseded by Diego, son of Christopher Columbus. For almost four hundred years, for better or for worse, the Spaniards controlled the fortunes of what has, since 1898, become a territorial possession of the United States, Rights of citizenship were granted to the inhabitants by act of the Congress of the United States in 1917.

Democratic ways have moved into El Morro and made themselves at home. Of a morning the place is open for the inspection of visitors. No guide awaits, no sentries challenge—a refreshing exception to the general rule. The traveler is reassured by soldiers encountered along the way that everything is open, to poke about at will. Sounds of Spanish records and snatches of conversation remind the new arrival from the North that "our boys" garrisoned here are, in this case, speakers of Spanish.

El Morro of Puerto Rico, seen after the formidable Cuban strongholds bearing the name at Havana and at Santiago, is in no sense an anticlimax. Fertile imagination could not well conceive a more astonishing construction than this Leviathan baring its jaws seaward with bone of surf in its teeth. Three tiers of batteries face, with medieval bravado, the restless open sea. Not Drake, in his last battle, could board the place. Misled by the deceptive appearance of Morro from the water, the Admiral brought his fleet within range of guns which were to roar in the direction of his flagship, killing two captains at the Admiral's own table; while, on the following night, a retaliatory foray, in the dark, resulted in the burning of one

Spanish man-of-war but the subsequent sinking of nine British boats with a loss of four hundred men.

Another futile effort to capture Morro for Britain was made by Sir Ralph Abercromby, who landed troops at Santurce and besieged the capital in 1797, two months after Chacon's surrender to Abercromby of the island of Trinidad.

Sampson was to bombard the castle in May, 1898, retiring without inflicting noticeable damage. Here, off El Morro, in July, the United States fleet was to display its strength. After the suspension of hostilities on August 16th, an American cruiser was to enter the harbor; while on October 18th of the same year, Spain was to withdraw her troops from San Juan, relinquishing her last foothold in the New World.

After conversation with Lieutenant Colonel Mariano Vassalo (who prefers to remain a chaplain rather than to accept a proffered bishopric and who speaks with especial pride of the men of the 65th Infantry now stationed on the outskirts of the town at Camp Buchanan), we surmised that the fine morale of the troops may in part be attributed to the influence of this intelligent and agile priest.

Begun in the year 1539, El Morro shares its ancient honors with the fortress of San Cristóbal, its junior by two centuries, and the less imposing San Gerónimo at entrance to Condado Bay. A

mighty sea-wall links Morro to its partner Cristóbal, hewn from the solid rock. In antiquity second
only in the New World to Santo Domingo, the still
partially walled city of San Juan, of which Morro
forms the tip or wedge, looks its age, despite the
vandalism of uncommonly brutal restorations and
certain unwarranted demolitions. Balconies and
Spanish miradores add luster to the diversely
painted dwellings, remnants of Spanish enterprise, low-lying, as though fearing to poke their
heads above the protecting walls.

On the Plaza San José stands a full-sized
statue of Ponce de León, cast from English cannon captured from Abercromby's forces in 1797.
The neighboring church of San José, rewarding
because of its antiquity, has been robbed for no
apparent reason of the bones of Ponce de León,
which now rest less happily—or so it seems to me
—within the precincts of the Cathedral. The inscription on the tomb informs the curious of the
fact that Juan Ponce de León was buried in Santo
Tomas de Aquinos (to-day San José) in 1559,
and transferred to the present tomb in A.D. 1. 909.

"Nineteen hundred and nine, I suppose!" was
my comment, but my Illustrator was unconvinced.

Finally a youthful curate corroborated my
assumption, apologizing that workmen are "Such-
know-nothings"; but apparently not assuming for
the powers that be any responsibility in failing
to rectify the initial error.

The Casa Blanca, oldest continuously inhabited dwelling-place in the Western Hemisphere, residence of the commander of the Military Department of Puerto Rico, owes its origin to Juan Troche, son-in-law of the Conquistador. Set in gardens hospitably easy of access to the visitor —as indeed are the spacious chambers of the mansion—on the other side of the Water Gate (or chief gate to the walled city and, like Casa Blanca, overlooking ramparts on the Caribbean) is the governor's seventeenth-century habitation, La Fortaleza. Two gateless apertures in the remnants of the city wall remain—that of Santa Rosa, where cripples cluster at the entrance to the old Spanish cemetery, while carefree youth strums its guitars, in the face of death, disease, poverty, and the filth of the adjoining squatter's village clinging to the sea-wall—surpassed in depravity only by that slum of slums, at the aperture of San José, masquerading ghoulishly under the nomenclature of La Perla.

Modern San Juan—beyond the precincts of the walled town's islet—need not be described to those acquainted with Miami. The Caribe-Hilton Hotel dominates at San Gerónimo Point. Suburbs, similar though second to those of Havana, have sprung up in the region of Santurce. In the de luxe Hotel Condado, on a spit of land between the lagoon (or bay) and the Atlantic, the two cultures of Puerto Rico conflict. Built, in 1919, by

Warren and Wetmore in adaptation of Spanish-mission style, with airy windswept rooms and loggias, this outstanding hotel need not fear the competition of even such a fashionable rival as the Caribe-Hilton, the latest word architecturally.

My Illustrator and I, on return from our motor tour, thought of settling at the Palace Hotel in the old town, but were discouraged by the following conversation. A clerk threw open the doors of an attractive suite. Our inquiries as to the price were shouted against the caroling of an adjacent prima donna.

"Does she sing all day?" I asked, and was forced to repeat the inquiry.

"Yes, Señora," was the reply, "all day."

"Does she sing all night?" I bellowed, facetiously.

"Yes, Señora, at the restaurant."

As in Havana the chief focus of interest in the city lies in the Parque Central, so, in San Juan, the same may be said of the Plaza Baldorioty de Castro—better known by its former name of Plaza de Armas. The square is bordered on two sides by shops. Its western end is dominated by the Treasury Building in Spanish Renaissance of a century ago, rich in hand-wrought iron balconies. But the glory of the Ayuntamiento (a reproduction of the Casa del Rey in Madrid) is no more. True, its towers and arcade remain, but instead of the knowing restoration, for which its antiquity called aloud, it has been crassly replastered beyond recognition by the ignorant cohorts of the W.P.A.

Doubly were we to regret the passing of the Plaza de Armas after hours spent with Professor and Mrs. Rafael Ramirez de Arrellano at Rio Piedras.

"In the old days," said this distinguished professor of history in the University of Puerto Rico, bringing out an old print, "the center of the plaza was of tile, and there were four statues representing the seasons."

"Yes," chimed in his motherly American wife, "when I first came to Puerto Rico as a teacher I remember the rows of rocking chairs rented to dowagers—chaperones were a necessity in those days!—the young people parading up and down. Thursday and Sunday evenings were concert nights. One end was for upper class; the other, with free benches, used by servants and the military. By and by, when there was no money for musicians, we had army bands. Can you picture the square as it was—flanked with old gnarled trees?"

"Oh, why was it destroyed?" I almost sobbed.

"You must not reproach the Americans," said the professor. "They get more blame than they deserve. It was in ninety-seven, the year before they came, that the people, disillusioned, turned against things Spanish. Having obtained autonomy, it was to be Puerto Rico for the Puerto Ricans. They made a party of tearing down the old city walls. Young people, even girls, dressed as workers with picks, started the job, leaving the brunt for dynamiters. Then, in 1928, came the hurricane that took the trees."

Like most upper class Puerto Ricans, Professor Ramirez is proud of his Spanish descent...he comes of an old family of San Germán and treasures heirlooms. Their own happy union leads this pair to predict the increasing understanding brought about by international marriage. Señora Ramirez told us how refreshingly white she found the islanders, having been accustomed to the one white to ten black ratio in her native state of Mississippi.

"Is there," I asked, "a prejudice against learning English? We found many more people who could speak it in the Scandinavian countries than we do here."

"No," I was reassured, "except, among certain politicians, against its being taught in the schools. The teachers are themselves often woefully ignorant. There is no money for books... as in Spain, there is more graft here than ever in the United States."

The Professor spoke of the thirty-eighth anniversary of the founding of the University of Puerto Rico—we had been shown the admirable buildings—where he has taught for twenty years.

He expressed the heartfelt wish that he could live to see certain reforms come true, especially as regards vocational training.

On the grounds of the University stands an impressive monument to Eugenio Maria de Hostos, the centenary of whose birth was celebrated in 1939. Goldberg wrote of him in *An Anthology of Spanish-American Poetry:*

> Yet to Spanish America and—as one day will be discovered—the world, Puerto Rico gave the imposing figure of Eugene Maria de Hostos, an investigator, a thinker, critic, sociologist and man of action, who is one of the crests of the continent's culture. Literally he overflowed the banks of his "tight little isle" into the numerous nations of the same speech and traditions, carrying wherever he went the message of toleration, progress, freedom, and a deep comprehension of human frailties and potentialities.

Our budding friendship with Adolpho de Hostos, official historian of the island, distinguished son of a distinguished father, was perhaps the high light of our stay in San Juan. At his villa we were allowed to browse over the contents of a bookcase filled with volumes by or on the senior de Hostos, a bookcase topped by a monumental head of this patriot. Not second in interest were cases of exquisitely mounted pre-Columbian relics. These museum pieces have been excavated, over a lifetime, by Adolpho de Hostos, chiefly in kitchen-middens on the south coast of

Puerto Rico, but some in Dominican Republic and others in Central America. Especially notable was a necklace of three hundred and five stone beads, probably Arawak, with cavities (suggestive of those in teeth!) where feathers had been inserted. There are only a half dozen of this type in existence, so we could imagine our friend's emotion when he heard that one of this kind had been unearthed on the south coast and carried, by a countryman, into the mountains. De Hostos walked miles inland to obtain it ... finding at last the *jíbaro's* hut and demanding the treasure so sternly that the native was fearful of keeping it.

A rack contained stone "collars" sculptured to represent, perhaps, linked branches—these to be found only on the island and at Dominican Republic—and probably symbols used in religious ceremonials. Oddest of all, we thought, were the worn, sinister-looking black stones, no bigger than fat limas—"sucked" (so they said) by medicine-men from a patient's painful limb and asserted by them to have been the cause of the trouble.

Even to-day in the environs of modern San Juan, superstitions are rife among the colored. Our American friends who have a bungalow—across the bay in the "rain belt" that freakishly includes the stretch of water but not the capital —for years employed a cook who was accused by a man worker about the place of being a witch. A stronger sorcerer sent poisoned meal which was put in the woman's bed, but the cook ignored it. Finally one day the domestic had to pass the other witch's cottage. The latter rushed at her with a machete shouting: "This is what will happen if you don't leave. Some one from this village should have your place and not you from San Juan."

The terrified darky, having no spells to meet this situation, took French leave.

At the house of these friends we had admired "string" rugs, dyed in subtle shades, popular on tiled floors though used by the natives in lieu of saddles; the blue and chartreuse parrakeets; hibiscus of glorious red—the special quality of the unhybridized variety.

"But why the geese?" I queried, our host having expatiated on their evil tempers.

"To give the alarm!" he answered. "They're wonderful watchdogs!"

It was through the advice of this friend that we redoubled our precautions never to drink unboiled water.

"Some do for years," said he, "but you never get over a bad case of amœbic dysentery. A man goes home to the States. You merely say 'The tropics has got him.'"

Our tour around the island led us westward from the capital to Vegas Baja, where we were shown hand-tufted sculptured rugs in the process of creation. One piece, with a design of musical instruments, had been exhibited at the Metropoli-

tan Museum, and others were on their way to
Sloane's. At the Ingenio (Central) Rio Llano at
Camuy we were to observe a new note—in lieu of
carts, red Studebaker trucks laden with cane. The
city of Aquadilla on the west coast claims to be
acknowledged as the landing-place of Columbus,
while the near-by town of Aguada puts forth an
equal claim. Both places have erected commemorative crosses.

Neither Mayagüez, the third, nor Ponce, the second city of Puerto Rico, have as much appeal to
the traveler as the mountainous interior of the
island. To us Mayagüez was chiefly of interest as
the birthplace of Eugenio Maria de Hostos and as
headquarters of the needlework industry second
only, in giving employment to islanders, to the
manufacture of sugar. The craft shop of Saint
Andrew's Mission tempts the connoisseur of the
drawn-work characteristically Puerto Rican. At
Hormigueras the high-perched shrine of Nostra
Señora de Monserrate has been compared to
Sainte Anne de Beaupré, but of greater interest
is the weather-beaten Porta Coeli, at San Germán,
said to be the oldest Christian church in the New
World.

The town of San Germán was originally a port
on the southern coast, but, after frequent sacking
by the French, the survivors of the destroyed
settlement moved inland to this "new" site in the
hills. The year was 1570. The place retains a

The oldest Christian church in the New World

savor of Old Spain—much to the delight of Spanish refugees now on the faculty of the Polytechnic Institute of Puerto Rico. This school, about to celebrate its thirtieth anniversary, has, of late years, become an outstanding non-sectarian, co-educational, liberal arts college, due in part to the activities of its president, Jarvis S. Morris who, during the past year, has delivered forty lectures in the United States on the problems of Puerto Rico.

Our stay at Costello Hall, the Guest House of the Institute, was stimulating in its contacts with members of the faculty. Especially congenial was the distinguished painter—his canvases sometime on view at the Carnegie International Exhibitions —Señor Cristóbal Ruiz, lately of Jaen, Spain. He has found this haven after a year on the faculty at Columbia University, where both he and his French wife considered the language and climate of New York severe handicaps. Mrs. Morris drove us to the hilltop residence, Casa María, where Captain Heylman has assembled every variety of cactus to be found on the island. The view of the wide valley—beyond which rises the Sierra Gorda Range—was illuminated by torches of *boucare,* aflame with bloom, patches, it seemed, snipped from a sunset sky ... the *bois immortel* (Erythrina) of French and English colonies.

Ponce—known as a stronghold of liberalism as well as an industrial center—baking in sunlight on its parched plain, did not detain us longer than for a drive up to the residential El Vigía and down to the Playa with its busy docks and swarming United States marines. By the time of our arrival in Ponce we had given up hope of controlling the irrepressible habit of our chauffeur, Miguel, to point out the flagrantly obvious, after the fashion of certain lecturers with slides.

"Very nice drug-store," Miguel would keep up a running comment, "sugar central, see Señora;

very nice bananas, Señor; very nice movies...
you see picture Charlie Chaplin?''

"Miguel," I snapped at him, "if I wanted to see
American movies and ten-cent stores I'd go right
back to San Juan and fly to New York."

The modernity, the banality of Puerto Rican
cities—San Juan, Ponce, Mayagüez—is forgotten
upon leaving the sugar-fringe of the coastal plain
to venture upon that high-ridged plateau of the
interior, across which uneven dais nature has
thrown a sculptured mantle of green. El Semil,
Barranquitas, Cidra, Cayey, Aibonito—echoing
the last-named the traveler does not fail to exclaim: "Ah, how beautiful!"

El Semil, once a far-famed coffee hacienda, was
devastated by the San Felipe hurricane of 1928.
The road from Ponce, via Juana Diaz, mounts in
the direction of the Toro Negro Range. Dangerously steep and curved it is on approach to El
Semil but enlivened for miles on end with crotons
and hibiscus. The glory of the way and not the
rather unprepossessing "dude ranch" to be found
at the journey's end rewards the adventurous.

How well I remember, on the day of our visit to
El Semil, the caressing gestures of the ranch
owner's wife, as she fondled the newly-bundled
vanilla beans culled on the plantation... reveling
in their insipidly sweet-smelling stickiness.

Coamo Springs Hotel at the Baños de Coamo
offered us the hospitality so associated with such

institutions the world over. I could with ease have imagined myself again in a rocking-chair at Bedford, Pennsylvania (even the New York paper was supplied!) had it not been for the chatter of caged monkeys, the exceptionally interesting planting of diverse varieties of long-established tropical trees, and the fact that our attentive host was formerly of Barcelona.

Miguel, surprisingly, waxed eloquent on politics as we drove through the village of Coamo where, on the plaza, we remarked benches, marked as usual with the names of donors. One was decorated with the emblem of the Popular Party, the head of a handsome *jibaro* or countryman, wearing the characteristically fray-edged farmer's hat. Miguel was a Republican, but his party had not done well, he admitted, for the people. The Socialists had, therefore, transferred their support to the new Popular Party—a sort of New Deal. No one wants to belong to Spain, he assured us, and few, nowadays, are Nationalists—only crazy ones. Statehood, said he, would bring us justice. We don't have a fair deal now; no rich man goes to jail. There is a law, he said, that corporations shall not own more than five hundred acres—but they get around that ... they give it to their families. Talk turned to the first Caribbean Festival, soon to be held in Puerto Rico.

The Asociación Azucarera Coöperativa Lafayette, owned by the Puerto Rico Reconstruction Administration, is one of the experiments upon which Mr. Roosevelt's New Deal may pride itself. Ten thousand acres of once absentee-owned land have been turned over to coöperative groups whose members will, it is hoped, eventually be able to acquire the property. There is a modern sugar factory with capacity to grind twenty-five thousand tons daily. P.R.R.A. has, in addition, established concrete houses for workers, gardens, playgrounds, a hospital, as part of the rural rehabilitation program. In the face of all this modernity it is appropriate to hear that it was on this very plantation—he erected a three-mile line for his own use—that Morse made some of his preliminary telegraphic experiments in 1849. The hacienda, La Enriqueta, was at that time the home of his father-in-law, but the house has been swept away by hurricane.

High-perched in the heart of the most beautiful region of the island, Aibonito shares with Barranquitas popularity as a refuge from the heat of the plains. Tasteful villas are set in bowers of scarlet—the very roadsides seem about to burst into flame, so intense the orange-vermilion of leaf and blossom flaunted from tree, vine, and shrub. The long dark pods of flamboyant recall, in winter, last year's bloom, while newly-fledged West Indian almonds sing with color.

Barranquitas gave us a bit of amusement which it was, at the time, necessary to conceal. With a flourish Miguel, the politically minded, brought the car to a standstill before a very ordinary frame house, not in the gracious environs but in the heart of the once barely accessible town. (It is the Americans who have completed this stretch of highway.)

"Birthplace of Luis Muñoz Rivera!" announced Miguel...in a tone that could have been appropriately used at Mount Vernon to announce: "Birthplace of George Washington."

In order not to permit the pause to grow awkward we sprang from the car and entered this house of death. Alas! that the accent is not, as yet, on the birth. The walls of the downstairs rooms were covered with mortuary bead wreaths, salvaged at time of the funeral. Cheap chromos of

In the cane field

the deceased returned our startled stares. A death-mask held the place of honor between the well-worn last shoes (actually as characterful as those of Chaplin!) and the rope (to my frivolous mind suggestive of hanging!) with which the coffin had been lowered. Let not those who have not laughter well under control penetrate to the nether regions, where honors are shared by the last-used car (a Rolls-Royce), the death-bed (a hospital cot), and, crowning glory, the hospital bathtub! An under-takerish sort of individual—I could almost swear he wore a frock coat—expatiated on the patriotic significance of this shrine, reminding us that from birth to death (1859 to 1916) the life of this man was of importance to his fellow-citizens. As editor of *La Democracia* he had fought the corruption of the Spanish régime, we were told; had in 1897, when autonomy was won, become President of the Spanish Liberal Party; had headed the cabinet under General Brooke, the first governor under the American rule; and had for years been Resident Commissioner in Washington. It was with sighs of relief, however, stifling giggles, that we with-drew from this macabre setting to drive in search of the key and at last to stand within the digni-fied enclosed plot of the tomb—to which, on July 17th—the holiday commemorative of Muñoz Ri-vera's birth—thousands repair.

On the Jájome Highway near Cayey is perched the summer residence of the Governor of Puerto

Rico. Formerly a lodge of road-workers, the villa stands on this stretch of the famous King's Road or Spanish Military Highway which crosses the island from San Juan to Guayama, as well as via Aibonito to Ponce.

The day we passed the governor's residence, leaden clouds at first concealed and later revealed the golden glories of the setting sun, sinking in unheralded splendor into the distant sea. The composition of high valley, cañon, and mountain range caused my Illustrator to remark that this view was to his mind far more pictorial, more majestic than the vaunted vistas on roads to Caracas. As evening fell we turned into the hospitable Treasure Island Camps, built by an American some ten years ago and run effectively to-day by the youthful Mrs. Héctor Gandía, whose husband (a graduate in agricultural engineering of Louisiana State College) administers the adjoining four hundred acres in pineapples—the Treasure Island Plantations of Cidra.

Not the royal suite at Ocho Rios in Jamaica could surpass in charm the simple cabin known as Honeymoon Cottage at Treasure Island. The mantle of stillness was hardly disturbed by the wafted sound of a native string orchestra playing, and singing, the latest Puerto Rican dance tunes in the central palm-thatched pavilion—a pavilion with roof and mighty blackened tree-posts reminiscent of Japan. The only raised voices were the peeps—"bo-peeps," I thought until corrected —of tiny frogs (encountered also at Guadeloupe and Barbados), tireless as katydids, known here as coquís from their reiterated syllables, "co-quí, co-quí, co-quí."

Distant cabins were concealed, we found on waking next day, by blossoming mangoes, a screen of that dusty-pink African vine, so popular in Puerto Rico, known as Congea tormentosa. Yellow-breasted *reinitas* (little queens!) hopped confidently upon the chairs at our breakfast table, chirping for crumbs, while we awaited pineapple—served every day of the year. We found ourselves in a bower of thunbergia and fragrant jasmine in a mood still under the spell of our early morning prowl. We had been tempted by the insistent cooing of doves and had followed a trail down the steep hillside and through the still dripping woodland to the bamboo thicket. The water of the swimming-hole was muddy from the rains, the brook rushed uproariously past ferns—even tree-ferns —to find calm beneath gigantic clumps of arched bamboo. Rays of the newly-risen sun pierced between the glistening stems. Little wonder, we thought, that owners of private planes fly frequently from the hurly-burly of San Juan to the landing field at Treasure Island.

Cidra, Cayey, Caguas—tobacco lands surround the three, hillside domains in the mountainous interior in contrast to the flat plantations found in

Along the old Spanish Military Road

Cuba. Puerto Rican industries, growing a tobacco suitable for cigars, have suffered since the vogue for cigarettes has lessened the demand for their product. Of especial interest is the La Plata Valley Resettlement near Cayey. The P.R.R.A., owner of the land, has divided the tracts into four hundred and sixty-one farms, often terraced hillsides with barns and concrete hurricane-proof houses, for rental to landless farmers who are supplied with seeds, plants, and live stock.

There could hardly be a better way to gain an impression of Puerto Rican landscape than to make the run—the round trip in an afternoon—between Caguas and San Juan. Caguas, fourth city of the island, busy center for sugar-cane and tobacco, has a plaza—dominated after the fashion of Spanish lands by its church—where, of an evening, the people not only congregate according to custom, but parade, the men and women headed in opposite directions.

Along this Route 1—the old Spanish Military Road—may be seen the best that the interior offers ... a best unseen on the more frequented coast roads. Here are plantations of sugar; a central where laden ox-carts assemble; cattle farms; *bucare,* splendid in bloom—red, terra-cotta, ocher, or, as may be, blossoming flamboyant. Bananas clothe the hills, immense stretches of bamboo line the roadside ... a paintable country indeed, with foregrounds of intimate, highly-cultivated knolls;

the local color of *jíbaros* with their ponies grouped about charcoal fires, where whole pigs roast upon the spit; the view of the cloud-reaching Toro Negro Range and unobstructed glimpses of the peak known as "the anvil." ... El Yunque, the anvil, the most popular peak in Puerto Rico, in the Caribbean National Forest of Luquillo.

On our visit to Luquillo we rejoiced to hear that three-fourths of the virgin timber of the island is now part of the Caribbean National Forest, dating from a Presidential Proclamation of 1935. Luquillo, which is included in this reservation, had already been established as a national preserve by the proclamation of another Roosevelt in 1903. The devastation of virgin woodlands has been largely the work of the charcoal burners—anathema to tree lovers.

An influx of the populace—marines, scouts, and lassies of all ages and complexions—disturbed the customary peace of the central picnic ground at noon, for we had chosen a holiday ... not Muñoz Rivera's but the no less popular Washington's Birthday.

At the entrance to the vast and mountainous region of the park we were especially impressed by a hitherto unobserved palm—the Palma de Sierra, coarser and more rugged in growth than the familiar royal—alternating with Ceropia peltata, the conspicuous trumpet tree whose immense silver-lined leaves play so showy a part in West

Indian foliage. Luquillo is one of the famous "rain forests" of the world. Without going farther afoot than along the Rio la Miña Trail, we observed the gorgeous red blossoms of epiphytes (non-parasitic airplants) enlivening the tropical tree trunks, festooned with lianas and large-leafed jungle vines. But of all accessible paths Big Tree Trail is my favorite—although to follow it makes the pedestrian feel that he has the stature of an ant, not even the significance of a tree-climbing snail. Checkered is the sunlight even at noonday, so deep the woods. So moist their surfaces, the boulders, as at Fontainebleau, are moss-grown, feathered with tiny ferns. In the stillness the falling of a dried leaf startles, as does the scuttling of a lizard. The clarion whistle of birds enthralls. Not in girth are these "big trees" most notable but in the reach of their sun-aspiring crests.

The monarch, handsomest by far, is the Laurel Sabino or Magnolia Spendens. The Tabonuco or Candle Tree (which burns when touched by a match) provided (somewhat dangerously, I thought) wood for the restaurant tables, we were told by a forester. Guama supplies wood for charcoal—we had noted stacked bags of the fuel along the trails; Roble blanco is a desirable lumber; while Ausubo is valuable for both furniture and construction. . . .

"Is this," my Illustrator demands, "a book on forestry?"

With a scathing look in his direction and a last word, despite the interruption, that more than three hundred tree species have been identified in the Caribbean National Forest, I somewhat hastily close my chapter.

Vega Baja

Charlotte Amalie

St.Thomas.

CHAPTER VII

UNCLE SAM'S VIRGINS

THE exemplary Virgins of the United States possess most of the virtues and few of the vices of tropical islands. Their beauty and climate, as well as the welcome given to Americans as fellow citizens, the absence of revolutionary uprisings, dangerous snakes, fevers and the like, are obvious. Many times my Illustrator and I have landed upon their shores. Our latest arrival was by the Furness Line's indomitable *Fort Townshend*. For swifter return, we preferred flight by air. I remember our first arrival at St. Thomas by Bull Line steamer.

Charlotte Amalie, seen from the harbor, delectable from my Painter's point of view, combined an unanticipated wedlock of Danish primness and Mediterranean abandon. The tropical note was, we thought, only slightly stressed, owing in all probability to a Southern European dryness. The hills, rising abruptly behind the town, were, as at Gibraltar, patched with gray catchments by which means rainfall is coaxed to fill the cisterns of the parched town. Spreading across three spurs of the mountainous ridge, Charlotte Amalie won, at first sight, our allegiance. The balance of Blackbeard's and Bluebeard's towers on the heights, the Catholic church, commanding a hillock above Frenchtown, added to the creation of an intensely European whole.

What attractions the one and only town of the island has to offer are, we were soon to find, limited. Passing a British ship loading with bauxite for Canada, we drove directly to the Grand Hotel, on Emancipation Park, facing the harbor. Danish management added to the charm and efficiency of this admirable establishment. From our bedroom windows we were able to see Bluebeard's Hotel—far from the sing-song of native life—with not a pang of envy. Could we not from our dining terrace feel ourselves onlookers at the spectacle of Charlotte Amalie's history in the making? To market, to church, to the docks, to the Virgin Islands Coöperative the natives passed—chattering melodiously to companions and, if alone, to themselves or to the nearest passer-by. Here, too, were turned impassioned pages in the uninhibited drama of Charlotte Amalie's unblushing existence.

Columbus, we had read, passing the clustered islands, of which St. Thomas, St. John, and St.

Croix are by far the most important, had, without
landing, charted the group as the Virgins—a name
derived from the myriad virgins (eleven thousand,
to be exact) of Saint Ursula. It was in 1666 that
the Danes took possession of St. Thomas to make
an uninterrupted stay, save for two brief British
interludes, until its purchase (with St. John, St.
Croix, and lesser fry) by the United States. The
round sum of $25,000,000 paid for their unprofit-
able property must have appealed to the thrifty
Danes. However, Uncle Sam not only benefited by
acquiring a naval coaling station at St. Thomas,
but, the year being 1917, forestalled the danger of
the island's becoming a base for the enemy.

The drain upon the paternal treasury has been
as constant a dribble as though the Virgin Islanders had been able to drill their way into the coin-
filled hold of the American Ship of State. . . . Gold
robbery was, perhaps, a lesson learned in former
days from the piratical frequenters of St. Thomas.
Emulating the Caribs the buccaneers used the harbor as a base for sea raids. Blackbeard is said to
have dwelt at the lookout that bears his name under the alias of James Thatch, doing business as
a merchant prince—entertaining some of his fourteen "wives," the "princesses" from whom Princess Street derives its name—until recognized by
a Danish captain. That a French adventurer,
Edouard de la Barbe Bleu, and his jealous Spanish paramour, crossed the threshold of Blue-

BLUEBEARD

beard's Tower seems to rest on baseless legend, despite my Illustrator's effort to give body and substance to the tale. This fortified tower was built by the Danes in 1689. The heyday of the harbor's prosperity was, in all likelihood, from the middle of the seventeenth to the middle of the eighteenth century.

My ignorance of what was meant by the Triangle Trade caused amusement in St. Thomas. It appears that, in Colonial times, the triangle—by means of which our esteemed ancestors gained wealth with their sailing ships—was formed of New England, Africa, West Indies. In Africa, Co-

lonial calicoes were bartered for slaves for the
Indies, whence rum was picked up to be carried
north to lessen, for its users, the rigors of New
England winters. The firm of A. H. Riise, established in 1838 by a Danish chemist, has won over
fifty gold medals and diplomas for rum, not to
mention the bay rum for which St. Thomas is
famous.

Seated luxuriously in the governor's automobile we were shown the salient beauties of the
island. Mounting the almost perpendicular streets
and hills back of the town, we came to the pass
and took the St. Peter Mountain Road, which will,
when completed by local C.C.C. boys, bear President Roosevelt's name. From the high cliff, known
as Drake's Seat, we beheld Magen's Bay, where
pelicans congregated, dropping like plummets into the blue waters. It was from this view of the
islets and the channel, known now by his name,
that Drake is said to have profited when pursued
by buccaneers. From a near-by cliff no less a person than Governor Cramer had recently fallen, an
accident which had cost him broken ribs and collar bone, and from which he was, at the time, re-
cuperating in Antigua.

From the Charlotte Amalie side of the island we
caught glimpses of the popular bathing beaches
and Lindbergh Bay, where the aviator had landed
in the *Spirit of St. Louis*—returning homeward
from his goodwill flight to Mexico and Central
America.

In contrast to the well-groomed quarters erected
for the Americans were the tumble-down dwellings in squalid Frenchtown. The governor, we
were told, has no means of helping those not citizens of the United States. These French aliens
came originally from Normandy to the French
island of St. Barthe, shared with the Swedes, but,
to lessen their chances of starvation, they immigrated, perhaps a century ago, to their present
refuge. Surprisingly, they have kept pure their
racial strain, though intermarriage within their
own ranks has somewhat sapped vitality. The men
are still, however, enterprising fishermen and the
women expert weavers of hats and baskets. Cha-
chas, of doubtful derivation, is the nickname by
which these folk are called. With French thrift
they are said to inhabit forlorn shacks in order to
avoid taxation.

Americans enamoured of life on the French and
Italian Riviera have now flocked homeward. Mr.
Arthur Fairchild, though likewise enamoured,
made the decision to live under his own flag when,
in 1918—after years of search in Italy—he came
upon the ideal site and the dwelling, since that
date his home. The century-old house, Louisenhof,
at that time disintegrating on a cleft in the ridge
that forms the back-drop for St. Thomas, commands a two-way view—on the one side the so-
nearly Mediterranean town and sea; on the other,
Magen's Bay and the sterner Atlantic.

There was quite a little ceremony connected with meeting this elusive bachelor, connoisseur, philanthropist, Fairchild of Stockbridge, Massachusetts, and one-time broker of New York. No telephone disturbs the medieval atmosphere, no highway approaches the grilled gate with tempting bell-pull, but only a steep path up which a pack-donkey scrambled daily with market produce and with mail. Happy were the recipients of a missive from Mr. Fairchild naming an hour when he would be "at home." Never did he receive when cruise ships were in port.

The texture of the Fairchild mansion charmed my Illustrator, in sunshine scintillating as mosaic, combining glints of brick (once used as ballast in the days of sailing-ships) with native stone, "blue bit," in varying stages of ocher, gray, and ultramarine. A Brazilian Rose dropped golden blossoms from stark branches to retaining wall of the court, as we entered the precincts sacred to the best Mediterranean tradition in gardening and architectural arts. Pergola, loggia, courtilla, aloe, cactus, cypress gave illusion of Italy. Journeying with his architect, Mr. Fairchild had traveled with camera and measuring rod to Amalfi. Masculine were the massive furnishings of the drawing-room —its northern windows provided with emergency shutters to withstand the hurricane.

An amiable divergence of opinion existed between our host and the Honorable Mr. Lovett, acting governor of the Virgin Islands, as to the origin of the unmistakably Southern European arch so noticeable on the terraced and arcaded streets of the capital. Our host, following his penchant, preferred to call the arch Italian, while Mr. Lovett believed it to have been brought—as elsewhere in the Indies and on the Main—from Mediterranean Spain.

No less did they differ on what the first considered somewhat too radical new laws. The latest divorce laws might startle these gentlemen. It would seem fantastic to them that certain hotels at St. Thomas give special rates to honeymooners or, with impartiality, to the disillusioned for the six-week period required to obtain divorce!

Governor Lovett was a Bostonian, whose elegance of manner and appearance suggested Henry James and whose New England accent, he told us, had not been considered an asset when he had served as Professor of Literature in the University of Chicago. We were to see the gentleman in action on the President's Birthday. On that long anticipated day—a public holiday in St. Thomas —the ballroom of the Grand Hotel, with its adjoining supper terrace, was the scene of a fantastic transformation. From a poster behind the cocktail bar the face of Roosevelt looked down benignly. The use of palms and shaded lights was lavish, the "swing" band of the best. Mr. Lovett, the soul of dignity despite the jaunty angle of his paper cap, with the wife of Dr. Lanclos, led the grand march. Several hundred guests participated —only the élite of the island had been invited to subscribe to the Presidential Ball. In one respect, however, this party bore no resemblance to any that we had ever attended. The girls (for most were young) were spiritedly dressy; the men—a few in dinner jackets—wore, like the governor, tropical suits; couples whirled by in kaleidoscopic sequence; but the one astounding difference was borne home as they passed . . . a few were white, a few were black, but the vast majority were colored.

The modesty of the dresses, the grace of the dancers, were outstanding. Sailors and marines in white or khaki uniforms were seen with dusky partners, here and there a handsome "bronze" youth had chosen a paleface. The chief event of the evening was competitive exhibition dancing. Three couples, it was obvious from the first, were in the running—oddly enough representing the two races and the combined racial strain. The couple of African hue, a jaunty youth, an angular girl wearing a monkey-jacket of brilliant red, displayed agility without grace. The white couple, a spare sun-tanned damsel and an American marine, were the popular favorites from the start, she in a white halter frock, he handling her after the fashion of a cave man—twirling her dizzily, throwing her, panting, from him with the ferocity of an apache. The third, the colored couple, number thirteen,

won our approbation. The youth, noticeably the
tallest and most loose-boned dancer on the floor,
was inexhaustible. Ingeniously, when temporarily
robbed of his partner, the belle of the ball, not
content to try another, he performed a pas seul,
with, in lieu of lady, a good-luck "bird" with waving "plumage" concocted from elongated bal-
loons. His partner was full-blown, in ankle-length
voluminous net the color of a saffron tea-rose. She
was winsome; she was alluring; she could when
pursued shimmy enticingly; she could pout; with
the facility of a ballerina she could improvise a
tantalizing solo; she could relent and nestle cap-
tivatingly close. His was an infinite variety of step
and gesture, hers was a lyric beauty of poetic line.

Overpowering, to northerners, became the heat,
the dust, the scents used by the dancers. We sought
the terrace where, beneath the stars, we watched
the ballroom lights grow dim, grow alternately
red or green. The climax came when these divergent racial strains (singing is second nature to a
Virgin Islander) took up the to-night not banal
but fervent refrain: "Happy birthday, Mr. Roosevelt, happy birthday to you!"

Since the days of Governor Pearson—when Mr.
Roosevelt paid a visit to the islands, driving to the
then government-owned Bluebeard's Hotel—up to
and including the régime of the new Governor
most of the islanders have been ardent American
citizens. Hard times made a changed allegiance

not unwelcome. The humorous features of the transferred affections are depicted in the frothy yet subtly profound *Star-Spangled Virgin;* while another rewarding character study is Struthers Burt's *Entertaining the Islanders.*

A few years ago, the Danish crown prince and his princess paused at St. Thomas, visiting the Virgin Islands Coöperative (The Native Shop) and paying their respects to the statue of Christian VIII in Emancipation Park and, on the waterfront, the toylike fortress, built by the Danes in 1671, a splash of red-hot color in a setting of palm and screw pine. Streets, even to-day, after the fashion of Denmark, are known as Gade. A gem of architectural survival, Hotel "1829" on Kongens Gade, commands the same breath-taking view as that upon which Government House looks down.

From the more arid end of St. Thomas, the motor yacht *Flamingo* makes tri-weekly trips, four miles eastward, to the island of St. John—taken by the Danes in 1684 and settled by them in 1716. Former Governor Pearson has written: "Many Americans do not realize that they own a tropical paradise in the Caribbean just 1,400 miles from home." From the point of view of the few habitués it is a matter of prayer that the many do not soon make the discovery.

Our excursion between Red Hook, St. Thomas, and Caneel Bay, St. John, was made by motor-launch on a day when the famed waters startled by their color. In this "tropical paradise" (unlike the ultramarine waters off Paradise Beach in the Bahamas), pure cobalt reigns... "blue-blue" as if the sky had let fall not "a flower from its cerulean wall" but shimmering patches to float upon the billowy mantle of the sea. The white fringe of coral beaches gleamed in sunlight, frayed, indented borders of the close-woven texture of the island's cloak of green. Hills were untracked except by trails; dales unpeopled save by a handful of pioneers.

In other portions of the island, we were to learn on landing, several hundred natives wrest a living from gathering the leaves of the wild bay tree (Pimenta acris) to form the bay oil mixed with white rum that has given St. Thomas added fame. There are, too, fishermen; cultivators of yam and plantain; feminine weavers of fine baskets sent, as are the products of St. Croix's home industries, to the Virgin Island Coöperative at St. Thomas. A native needs but a strong right arm, a machete, a goat and donkey...though sojourners at the Caneel Bay Plantation may afford the luxury of a horse. No wheeled traffic mars the peace of roadless St. John.

After dipping cautiously into the blue of a cove (would our skins be dyed to a similar shade?) swimming beyond coral beaches and avoiding branched fragments, my Illustrator and I sunbaked, and attired ourselves under a sheltering sea-side grape. With feeling of well-being we strolled lunchward at last beneath the semi-shade of tamarind and palm.

At the "Commissary" store, sizzling in sunshine beside the dock, we encountered a botanist, with wife and boys, a resident of St. John since August. He was nostalgic at the thought of leaving for New York, after having classified some hundred and fifty trees, leaving others yet unidentified—among them a virulent poisonous one that had forced him to take a fortnight's interlude. My inquisitive eye, running over the labels of familiar American brands upon the shelves, was drawn to the word Copenhagen: Esprit de Valdemar—the old Danish Cologne, cherished for over a century by travelers to Scandinavia.

The pearl-earringed and silk-slacked mulattress in charge of the Caneel Bay Settlement—a half dozen red-roofed bungalows owned by the Virgin Island Tourist Company, on a thousand-acre former sugar estate—had orders from the Grand Hotel, St. Thomas, of the same ownership. We were to eat our picnic lunch in the shade and breeze of the director's bungalow. A boy was called to carry our basket and Prosperity cooler. The mulattress would herself conduct us. As, scorched by the noonday sun, glancing at ruins of a historic mill, we puffed up the steep hillside, our leader tossed over her shoulder a remark that Mr. Rasmussen, of the Grand Hotel, had said:

"Authors should know each other." There was an author at St. John.

"Really," I answered, doubtful of the wisdom, and too hot for enthusiasm.

Arrived, supposedly, at our destination we followed our native up the steps, pushing open the screen-door to a cottage. Our guide muttered names as a man in a flowered bathrobe rose from a table littered with breakfast dishes. The boy, hesitating as to where to put the lunch and thermos, was assisted by the gentleman of the bathrobe, who murmured he would clear the coffee cups.

"Please don't trouble. There is no hurry," we assured him. "You are the director?"

"The director?" he echoed. "I am Francis Hackett."

Francis Hackett! It would have given me no less a shock had he said "Francis the First"! Francis Hackett—the man who had, in his own words, been "enslaved" for ten years of work on two biographies, *Henry VIII* and *Francis the First*, and whose *I Chose Denmark* had set the literary world agog. But Mr. Hackett is an Irishman from Kilkenny. The stage was set for laughter. He suggested that, when he would be dressed, after our meal at the true director's, we should meet again on the beach. It was, then, with a gentleman, "dressed" airily in sunburn, trunks, and eye glasses, that we compared the beach with the Danish one at Hornbæk and discussed affairs of world and nation. With his literary Danish wife, Signe Toksvig, Hackett finds peace beside the sea.

Hotels and shops not to be found, as yet, at St. John are abundant at St. Thomas and St. Croix. To those who visit St. Thomas to "take the cure," as they put it (that is to obtain divorce on grounds of incompatibility), its more sophisticated attractions appeal. St. Croix, dear to artists, offers Continentals (American residents not born on the Islands) peace of mind. Idyllic as is the Hotel-on-the-Cay, with its palm-fringed beaches yet it is outdone by the fabulous scale of St. Thomas's Virgin Isle Hotel—unsurpassed on the Islands, rivaled only by Bluebeard's Castle with its inimitable view of the harbor. The Buccaneer Hotel, St. Croix, balances the Hotel Flamboyant, St. Thomas. Near Truman Air Field, St. Thomas, is the Caribbean Hotel, with noted Calypso band. The distinguished Lockhart owners of the Grand doubtless realize the unique worth to the public of a traditionally famous restaurant in unparalleled setting.

St. Croix, an island three times the size of St. Thomas and far more fertile, was considered a richer prize in bygone days. Spain, Holland, England, France, even the Knights of Malta have been its owners. Sold by France in 1764 to a Danish company and later passing to the Crown, with St. Thomas and St. John it is now the scene of one of Uncle Sam's most interesting experiments. Sugar, cattle, rum tell the whole story. "Old St. Croix"

Rum has been distilled and bottled on the Virgin Islands since 1838 and connoisseurs assert that it is unequaled.

Coral reefs almost completely close the miniature harbor of Christiansted to larger craft than yachts and schooners. Cruise ships go to Frederiksted. On a tiny isle rises the stately Danish Mansion, once the Governor's summer residence, now the delectable Hotel-on-the-Cay.

Christiansted! Pentheny's!—the two are synonymous. Inconceivable that the one should exist without the other. The description "pension hotel" had in no wise prepared us for the place. Having come ashore in the rowboat of the "Grand Duke," an elderly Negro, we were at once confronted by the picture-book town: the strawberry-red Danish fortress overlooking the dock; the inimitable King Street, with wealth of balcony and Mediterranean arcade, hardware store where Alexander Hamilton once was clerk, Government House—one of the most stately of West Indian mansions—and, finally, Pentheny's, the house that was to be our temporary abode. Later we were to see the interior of the governor's house, furnished, alas! in modern taste. The King of Denmark has taken to Copenhagen the furniture from the galleried ballroom; the rest, sold at auction with other mahogany of impoverished owners has found its way ... we shall see where.

The great mansion that to-day is Pentheny's

In Christiansted

was in probability constructed as the private *hôtel* for a family of French aristocrats. Every detail of its balconied and arcaded street-front, the refinement of pedimented windows, its spacious court, point to this conclusion. The salon, *au premier,* masquerading to-day as "sitting-room," contains antiques worthy of listing: one immense rug—made in a lamented St. Thomas factory, one secretary bookcase, one tall-topped desk, one chest of drawers, one ornate piano, one oval table, two drop-leaf tables, five tilt-top tables, six round tables, two huge sofas (the cane-seated curved one tracing its origin to Government House), five enormous mahogany cane-seated rocking-chairs and four ditto armchairs, not to mention twenty-five side chairs! The sunlight peeps in discreetly through Venetian blinds, brightening the faces of the portraits of Cornelius Pentheny's ancestors; while at night, bell-glass hall "lanthorns" glow from the arched doorways; and dozens of candles, in unblinking wonder, stare upon this grandeur, like gleaming eyes of imprisoned sprites peering from the depths of hurricane shades.

It is around the spacious board, however, in the adjoining dining-room that wit and information flow. At the head of the table sits the hostess, the silver-haired Norwegian mother (diligent as Dorcas); at her side, when affairs of shipping and ship-building permit, her son "Mr. Cornelius"—

owner of the house and of the seven schooners riding in the harbor. This husky seaman—of combined Scandinavian and Scotch stock—like his father and grandfather before him carried the mail, latterly by motor-boat, to St. Thomas, until the job was taken over by the *Catherine*. Nowadays his boats bring oil and gasoline from Puerto Rico.

What types we found at table! Conversation was no less a cause for lingering than the all-too-bountiful supply of fish-pudding, cheese soufflé, chicken stuffed with raisins...luscious fruits. Chosen, perhaps, for size, my Illustrator sat opposite his hostess—with four and a half yards of damask between, and dishes of royal Copenhagen that might have been the envy of a queen. To my right was a youthful Georgian, just over an attack of Dengue or "breakbone" fever, working for the Virgin Island Agricultural Experiment Station, telling me with an embellishing drawl his latest problems:

"I said to a fellow, who wanted aid, 'We gave you seed, chickens, goat, horse and cart last month. Why do you need help?' He had eaten all but the horse and cart!

"This very morning I found a native, a man weighing over two hundred pounds, sobbing in my office. 'What's wrong, John?' I asked. His answer was: 'You gotta help me, suh. My wife's moved in and she won't go 'way'!"

Other table companions were a consultant for the remodeling of the post-office; a world-traveled Bostonian—a dilettante, forsaking Bermuda owing to war conditions, enlivening our meals with anecdote; a veteran salesman, deaf but avid for world news by radio; and, at the time of the ceremonies of Governor Harwood's inauguration, Mr. De Castro, acting administrator of St. Croix; the esteemed Judge Moore; the commander of the Coast Guard in these waters. After the popular Hastie, De Castro was to become Governor.

Mrs. Roosevelt had registered at Pentheny's on her fleeting visit to the island.

Not Frederiksted, on the west coast, where steamers land their passengers from open roadstead, lesser than Christiansted in architectural interest, could detain us long, nor could the sunparched beach beyond with its seaside cottages and Country Club (branch of the New York Yacht Club, though minus yachts!) built by Mr. Canady of Toledo, Ohio, who has also invested in two thousand acres of hill country with the thought of future development.

The glory of St. Croix lay in her Great Houses —now pitifully in ruins. Habitable mansions, dating from the old days, may, however, be found. In the region of Frederiksted there was Sprat's Hall, leased by a Cape Cod painter; Judge Noll's place, Butler's Bay, with an approach of too-stout-to-be-shapely guinea tamarinds. From the coastal highway near Sprat's branches Mahogany Road, living up to its name better than many a decayed manor, leading in the direction of woodlands from which the passer-by scents charcoal kilns; and the Jolly Hill Experiment Station—where moisture-loving pineapples and oranges are raised.

A Pennsylvanian was to show us, at her son's estate Anquilla, where old slave quarters are intact, Indian relics unearthed under conditions of drought that would have caused a less valiant digger to falter... carefully restored fragments of Siboney, Arawak, Carib. I fancy from the conversation that the most laborious excavation or farm overseeing was more to the lady's taste than helping with the census, a job that she had been prevailed upon to undertake.

The natives, we were told on all sides, are openly unmoral. A young woman in domestic service may have several small children by different fathers, who probably support them.

"I'se not a bad girl," said such a one. "When I leave a man I leave him."

Often mere children go to older men who, better than youths, can offer them support; while middle-aged women, who know how to get along by *praging* (pilfering), are called, and literally are, the "keepers" of young men.

Lindquist, a mechanic at the aviation field, was, on some days, our efficient driver, contradicting, for the most part, the information imparted on other occasions by his black substitute. For example, Watch Houses, pointed out by the latter as places where slave mothers used to leave their babies when working in the cane-fields, were, according to the former, ancient shelters for munitions and gendarmes who, in slave days, had alternated in eight-hour shifts. Insurrections were not unknown at St. Croix. Indeed it was by means of the revolt of July 2, 1848—when conch shells blew and bells rang to the terror of estate owners —that the Negroes obtained freedom for themselves and for those of the other Danish islands. The news was carried to St. Thomas by the schooner *Vigilant* and proclaimed "at the drumhead."

Sugar-lands once produced St. Croix fortunes —reaped when conditions were advantageous, forfeited in times of drought and unfavorable world market. Compare the figures of a boom year, 1920, $4,086,671 with those of 1931—after the failure of the West Indian Sugar Company—$118,000. Governor Cramer wrote in his last Report: "The rise of cane cultivation acreage after 1933 from 4,505 acres to 6,500 acres in 1940 is almost entirely attributable to the expenditure of Federal funds..." Mr. Ickes reports as follows: "For several centuries St. Croix rum has been world famous. The asset of that reputation gave hope that the unprofitable production of sugar could be supplemented by the profitable production of rum to the end that the former 18,000 cane acres might again be put into cultivation and employment be afforded to its agricultural population." P.W.A. and W.P.A. and the Farm Security Administration have all benefited small holders. The growing of "Colono" cane, that raised by these farmers, is encouraged, while a Government-fostered non-profit corporation, The Virgin Islands Company, founded in 1934, produced 80 per cent of the island's rum. During cane-cutting, Gold Label Government Rum is made, while between seasons the White Label brand is manufactured from molasses.

The names of the estates have been retained even when their Great Houses have fallen to ruin, their sites identified only by melancholy stone water-towers and fragmentary sugar-mills. Old maps show regular outlines to the plantations, but, after an influx of Irish immigrants, about 1800, the plots began to show vagaries, as these Irishmen, prone to bet on cards and horses, gambled away squares of acres to their neighbors. Anna's Hope, Peter's Rest, Strawberry—more colorful than its name—Freidenborg with its ancient tombs of the Markoes (those resident on the island fallen from their high estate), the provocative trio, Upper Love, Lower Love, Jealousy; Adventure, Bethlehem—with its modern processing equipment—Golden Grove—forsaken by the President of the Virgin Islands Company—indicating a section of

St. Croix :
Melancholy mills and towers

the gamut, border the Central Highway. At La Grange the ardent Gertrude Atherton, who had unearthed, while engaged upon the writing of a romantic life of Alexander Hamilton in *The Conqueror*, the certificate of her hero's mother's death, has erected a monument to the lady. Rachel Levine, for such was her name, died here while visiting her brothers.

On the east end of the island Cramer's Park lies in a district famous for wild cattle and deer, yet notorious for its manchineels—the "greene apples" of St. Croix that proved fatal to Sir Walter Raleigh's seamen. Shoy Beach has won an evil name since a drowning, and no Negro will point the way; but Vagthus with its lonely dunes (called by Americans Watch Ho!) presents little danger to the wary, constantly mindful of undertow.

The climax of our stay might have been considered the ceremonies attendant upon the local inauguration of the new Governor of the Virgin Islands, for which the arcades along King Street, including those of the stately Pentheny "Hotel," were arched with triumphal palm. It did give us a pleasurable start to recognize the Honorable Mr. Lovett from St. Thomas, and, seated beside the governor's lady, Cornelius Pentheny, unexceptionably garbed in a dark coat, in his joint capacity as man of property and member of the Municipal Council. Also the climax could well have been the serenade led of an evening by Michael

(Sipple to his familiars), caretaker of the Lim-
pricht Garden on which our bedrooms gave. A big
black fellow was Michael, with furrowed brow and
battered panama. His scratch band produced such
numbers as "Mamma Hold Baby," "You Walk
with Me," and "Listen to the Mocking Bird," by
means of one tin can (used as a drum and tuned
to accompany Michael's singing), a gourd, guitars
and triangle, and a growling bass, quavering as
the note from a conch shell, with superhuman effort conjured from the salvaged exhaust pipe of
an automobile. Yet not the scratchy band—although preferable to the reiterated playing of a
record, in the wine-shop by a deserted benedict,
of "It does not matter now"—was the week's high
point. It came, unexpectedly, on the eve of parting, when our husky host asked us to see the
schooner he was, with his own hands, building of
native cedar, using the natural elbows of wood.
This had been done in the fabulous wrecked *Vigilant* of which our host had been the owner and
for which this boat, of the same length, would be
named. Each of his schooners, he explained, plying to San Juan, was in the habit of taking a half-
dozen carrier pigeons. Would we care to visit the
loft where a hundred and twenty-five pairs were
installed? We would indeed.

It is, then, to the picture of the swarthy "Mr.
Cornelius" that my mind leaps at mention of St.
Croix. A gallant Cruzian he, decidedly not the

ascetic—rather, the stalwart seafaring man; yet,
aflutter with circling, cooing favorites, by the sin-
cerity of his devotion to feathered brethren he was
assuredly akin to the saintly Francis of Assisi,
who, remote from this island of St. Croix, bore
the banner of the Holy Cross.

The French Village

Antigua: St. John, the Capital

CHAPTER VIII

THE LEEWARD ISLANDS

COLUMBUS, among other laurels in his wreath, wore the discovery of all the islands of the British West Indies, save only one, Barbados, where the honor of precedence is given to the Portuguese. There is a tradition that the admiral bestowed his own name on the island of Saint Christopher because of a fancied resemblance in the form of its upstanding mountain to the figure of the saint bearing the infant Jesus. Assuredly, the staff of the patron of travelers and gardeners, thrust into such fertile stoneless ground, would have blossomed without benefit of miracle.

Mariners of Spain, of France, of Holland, and of England have contested for centuries—even as statesmen contest to-day—the ownership of the West Indies. Certain members of the group belonging to Great Britain—especially St. Kitts of the Leeward Islands, and Barbados—pride them-

selves upon being, with the exception of Newfoundland, the pioneer Colony of the British Empire. Fateful have been the tides of conquest, of
unalleviated hatred, of exaltation, and of relative
despair, which can only be likened to turbulent
forces of nature that periodically sweep over the
archipelago—earthquakes, volcanic eruptions, hurricanes. Nowhere, perhaps, can be found more
forcible proof of the triumph of the creative spirit.
After the thunder is heard the still small voice.

History records other thunders besides that
from natural causes. It is with pride that the descendants of West Indian families inform the visitor, who, it is assumed, is without all previous
knowledge of events, that the Battle of the Saints
—when cannon roared off Dominica between the
British fleet commanded by Rodney and the
French fleet commanded by de Grasse—no less
than Trafalgar decided the might-made right of
Britannia to rule the wave. That her dominion
(now diminished) over the sea has brought peace,
if not prosperity, to her West Indian possessions
is undisputed. Unfortunate economic and social
conditions have, however, led to the appointment
of a West Indies Royal Commission. Federal
Union of British islands in the Caribbean has been
recommended, but, as yet, the colonies are not prepared to acknowledge its advantages. The British
Government—let Americans who would "take
over" the islands in lieu of payment of war debts

note—has agreed to appropriate £1,400,000 per annum for ten years. This will meet the emergency caused, primarily, by the uncertainty of the sugar market, on the stability of which the prosperity of the islands, by and large, depends.

"Columbus is welcome to his caravels and 'Sam' Morison to his voyage in the footsteps of Columbus!" exclaimed my Illustrator.

"The Lady Liners are good enough for me, *Lady Drake, Lady Nelson, Lady Hawkins, Lady Somers, Lady Rodney,* their names are music to my ears!" I echoed his thought, standing beside him on the deck of a Canadian National Steamship. (The *Lady Nelson,* sunk by German submarine at St. Lucia, was salvaged. It and the *Lady Rodney* are the only survivors of this former fleet.)

"I thought we were arriving at Saint Christopher this morning," I told him, "but the pronunciation of the names of these islands must be learnt on the spot. To say Saint Christopher is unheard of. The island we are approaching is St. Kitts."

Since sunrise we had been searching the horizon for our first glimpses of the Leeward group. St. Martin had been passed; then St. Barts, with glints of surf on distant beaches; the dim mound of Saba. At eight o'clock a superb cone loomed to starboard, Statia—a Fujiyama island. At eight-thirty came the inevitable call to breakfast, and Lady Liner collations are not lightly to be foregone.

St. Kitts to port! Silvery flying-fish fringed the waves. Mount Misery's summit was capped with cloud. Was our ship actually in motion? we asked each other, or was this twenty-three mile coast-line a passing panorama staged for the delectation of eager passengers? Yellow-green cane-fields contrasted with the Caribbean blue of the water. At higher levels vegetables prospered on fertile terraces. Now and again spindling coconut-palms, in loose formation, straggled to the water's edge. Wooded heights mounted skyward. A tropical fragrance mingled with the breath of the sea. Close to Brimstone Hill we passed, the lowering Gibraltar of the Indies. Despite its formidable appearance, the fort never proved its mettle; indeed, in 1782, it capitulated to the French.

Basseterre, the capital, where we were to make our landing, was perhaps a less interesting town —for all its nine thousand inhabitants—than we had imagined, for it had been reconstructed in 1867 after a disastrous fire. Jaunty fishing-boats scudded by. We caught glimpses of ebony black crews, of maroon-lined hulls. Launches clustered to leeward. We were to choose the canvas-topped *Queen Elizabeth,* although we had at our disposal the *Queen Mary* or the *Normandie.* One boat was filled with singers, and the song that I recall was "King Edward and his Love." Divers demanded attention. As we stepped ashore shakers of weighted gourds besieged us. Negroes, exceed-

BasseTerre: St.Kitts.

ingly forlorn, pressed about us—venders of baskets, beggars calling for pennies.

"Mother of the Antilles" is the proud title borne by St. Kitts, it having been from this base that British colonists set forth to people other islands. Barbados, it is true, had nominally been settled, but not in fact until four years after the arrival at St. Christopher of Captain Thomas Warner, of the King's Body Guard, accompanied by his wife, son, and fourteen companions, on January 28, 1623. The landing took place at what is to-day the town of Old Road.

It was at the time of Warner's return from a voyage to England, the following year, that a French pinnace, under the Sieur d'Esnambuc, crept into port. The ship was badly damaged, only thirty of the crew had survived an encounter with a Spanish galleon. Permission was given for these Frenchmen—the settlers of Basseterre—to remain at the ends of the island. In England Warner had obtained from Charles I full power to "govern, rule and order" the islands of St. Christopher, Nevis, Barbuda, and Montserrat. The aid of the French was welcomed to combat the menace of the belligerent aborigines.

An Indian woman, Barbe, by name, at one time warned the Englishmen and Frenchmen of an imminent rising of the Caribs. The natives had rallied braves of other islands to join in what they intended to be the massacre of the white man. It is said that two thousand Caribs lost their lives at Bloody Point, while—despite manchineel-poisoned arrows—no more than a hundred of the French and English forces met death. It was not until 1629 that the Indians were driven from St. Christopher, their chief's son carried to England to become a member of the household of Merriefield, a wealthy merchant, and the financial backer of Warner. The latter was knighted at Hampton

Court in September, 1629. In October of the same year, a fleet of thirty-five Spanish galleons and fourteen armed merchantmen, en route to Brazil, paused at Basseterre. The French made a quick decision to change their place of residence. They were later to return from their refuge on the island of Antigua. Six hundred Englishmen, captured by the Spaniards, were transported to the mines of South America.

D'Esnambuc had aroused the interest of Cardinal Richelieu, and with his aid the French West Indian Company was formed. It was from St. Kitts that Martinique was colonized in 1635. Warner's son had set forth in 1632 to settle Montserrat. In 1636 Negro slaves were introduced to replace the Indians. Following the death of Warner, who governed the island for twenty-five years—there were twelve thousand English inhabitants at the time of his demise—the Bailly de Poincy governed for twenty-one years, until his death at the age of seventy-seven. He dwelt regally at his Château de la Fontaine. Indeed, when the king sent a younger man to replace him, this gentleman was not permitted to land, but was greeted thus: "The people of St. Christopher will have no other Governor than Monsieur de Poincy and will take no orders from the King of France." In view of his record in the colonization of other islands de Poincy was not supplanted.

Because of a glut on the English market, at one

time Warner and de Poincy decreed the destruction of all tobacco plants. The order has a modern sound.

Brimstone Hill, according to the Caribs, was the summit of Mount Misery blown off and deposited beside the sea. In reality the hill consists of a core of volcanic rock, covered by limestone, in which coral formation is discernible. A sulphurous vapor drifts, at times, from what is, to all appearances, the old crater of the supposedly extinct Mount Misery. The natives of St. Kitts, we thought, had more than enough misery from various causes without need of volcanic eruptions. They are among the most impoverished of West Indians, despite the fact that the Carib name for St. Kitts signified "the Fertile Island."

It was with mingled feelings that we had stepped ashore on what the author of *Caribbee Cruise* has called "the least happy of the islands." Squalor was unfortunately apparent; disease; yes, misery; yet, withal, the insidious lure of the tropics was overwhelming. Years had passed since our own last sojourn near the equator. Never before had we voyaged so far southward on our own hemisphere. The unprecedented and the unforgotten balanced the scales of remembrance.

The objective of our first shore excursion was, ostensibly, the visit to the fortress of Brimstone Hill. The vegetation and native life seen along the way were, to us, still more rewarding. Frangi-pani trees rained fragrance upon our unsuspecting heads, until, glancing upward, we were intoxicated by the waxen loveliness of rosy petals. High over-head white cedars swung pendant bells; banyans we recognized; spreading bread-fruit trees, heavily laden; majestic flamboyants—some in leaf, and others, after the way of their kind, naught but gnarled gray trunks and a splendor of scarlet. Flamboyant, Royal Poinciana; by mention of either of its names the remembered tree flames in-to life. In Florida it bore the proud title of Ponce de León, but at St. Kitts it is said to have been the discovery, and to be the namesake, of the local hero, the Bailly de Poincy.

Black men, wielding machetes, toiled in the blazing sun of the cane-fields. We could well believe, watching the play of muscles, that this was indeed among the hardest physical tasks performed by man. The rickety railway of St. Kitts carried not passengers but cane. Donkeys, too, were laden with the same burden; cane formed the thatch of roofs; pressed cane was baled for fuel; cane was spread upon the fields as fertilizer. North of Basseterre, beside the sea, stands the up-to-date Central Sugar Factory—to which Nevis also sends its cane—manufacturing twice as much sugar to the ton as by the obsolete mus-covado process.

Huddled beneath the sparse shade of palms or peering from shaggy-roofed huts, women in slinky

cottons and pickaninnies in a state of nature
watched our passing car.

"The world's worst hovels!" I exclaimed, for-
getting, for the nonce, Havana and San Juan.
"The Bhils in India live better than this, and so
do the blacks of Haiti. In China there are the
famine sufferers." ...

"For picturesqueness give me Penang," murmured my Illustrator ... to whom housing conditions are of little import.

Sir Francis Drake (for whose Lady a liner
was christened) himself had once come to Basse-
terre "to refresh our sick people, and to cleanse
and air our ships"; the Scottish mother of Browning's father was originally from St. Kitts and
loathed the system of slavery as much as did the
poet's wife, moreover, it was from St. Kitts that
the impressionable Miss Swartz hailed, that "rich
wooly-haired mulatto" who was the pupil, in
French, of Becky Sharp. More real to us to-day
than the majority of living native sons was another Kittefonian of fiction, Conrad's *Nigger of
the Narcissus*.

A clergyman landed in St. Christopher three
years after its original settlement. In 1672, however, the Governor, Sir Charles Wheeler, informed
the King of England that ten thousand Christians
were served by only two ministers, "both scandalous livers and one a notable schismatic." Six
years later the Bishop of London sent six preach-

ers of the gospel to the Leeward Islands, each to be paid—"besides the perquisites of marriages and funeral sermons"—£100 a year or 16,000 pounds of sugar.

Brimstone's fortifications were constructed by slave labor—such as has darkened the pages of the history of St. Kitts. Owners contributed one out of each eighty slaves. The fabulous wealth of sugar-planters rested, obviously, upon an unstable base. When the abolition of slavery was accomplished, in 1834, plantations were abandoned. In 1850 Portuguese laborers were introduced into the island. The commerce of Basseterre, if not of the entire island, is said to be in the hands of their descendants.

Nevis presents an altogether different picture, although a channel of only two miles separates the islands; and monkeys, introduced into St. Kitts by the French, are said by the natives to have their own submarine passage. Is it then lethargy that prevents the people of an island owned by a few families from migrating to Nevis, where plots of land are available? The more intelligent aspect of the inhabitants is noticeable to the most unobservant on his arrival at the capital of Nevis, Charlestown by name.

Unlike St. Kitts, Nevis still flaunts some remnants of the tattered ensign of her not altogether inglorious past. Hamilton and Nelson are the names most often on the lips; but vestiges in

tangible stone perpetuate a sense of continuity
with other days. Arrivals are driven at once to
reopened Bath House, dating from the eighteenth
century. The chronicles of Captain John Smith
narrate that more than twenty years before, this
navigator had remained "a good time" on this
little isle "to water and refresh my men." Here
members of the crew were "scalded" by "dew
from the trees"—rain from the poisonous manchineels which still lift their twisted trunks near
the Bath Springs. "Here we found a great poole,
wherein bathing themselves, they found much
ease ... they were cured in two or three days."
The mineral spring and thermal waters (admirable for the cure of gout and rheumatism) made
Nevis the center of gaiety in the West Indies ...
the "Tunbridge Wells of the Caribbees." Forty
thousand pounds were spent on the Bath House
and Pump Room. The water is said, by a noted an-
alyst, to resemble that of Wildbad Springs of
Württemberg.

It was to Nevis that the dandy Christopher
Jeaffreson (excerpts from whose letters I have
quoted) repaired, clad in an outfit to procure
which he had written as follows to his sister in
London:

"I praye you send me an embroidered and fashionable waist-belt and let everything be modish
and creditable, for the better sort in these islands
are great gallants."

Needless to add, the gentleman sought the hand of a fair lady (one Miss Frances Russell, sister to the wife of the Captain General of St. Kitts-Nevis), a young person aged fifteen (Christopher was thirty-one and a widower) whose marriage portion was £1,500 and four Negroes. Mistress Frances, however, gave her aspiring suitor "brisque denyall."

The trade wind was blowing as our boat put in to the modest capital of Charlestown. As we entered the bay the ruins of the house where Alexander Hamilton was born, on January 11, 1757, were pointed out. The father of Hamilton was a well born Scottish merchant of St. Kitts, his mother's forebears were French Huguenots. The family was to migrate to St. Croix. Wrapping ourselves in coats against breeze and showers, we stepped aboard the launch *Maylily* (pronounced by the steersman "Mé li li"). Pelicans, drollest of birds, perched upon and dived from near-by rowboats.

No sooner had we put foot ashore than we were escorted by a helmeted policeman, whose face was as black as his linen uniform was white, to what he called Charlie Pem's (Charles Pemberton's) car, driven by William. The combination was ideal. The dark-faced chauffeur was a joy to look upon —tan suit, blue shirt, green felt hat—and every word he spoke was gentle as a caress. Beggars there were none; but we were greeted as "Mom-

mer" and "Popper," in friendly fashion, by natives of uncertain age—obviously greater than
our own. One was an ebony black woman, draped
in plum color, with a plaid bandana turban and
coral necklace; another an Amazon balancing on
her head a huge basket filled with cups and saucers. Bandana shades were echoed by the roadside
in bougainvillea, allamanda, and corallita vines,
while patches of orange dodder caught the sunshine.

Nevis has been described as "little more than
a single volcanic cone which rises to a height of
3,596 feet," also as a "dapper" island. I find
dapper far too prim an adjective. *The Gorgeous
Isle,* Gertrude Atherton's name for it, comes
nearer my impression.

The island was included in a grant by the Earl
of Carlisle in 1672 and, the following year, was
settled by Englishmen from St. Kitts. Its first
capital was destroyed by earthquake, and the
island has known ravages at the hands of the
French. In 1706 thousands of slaves were taken
by them as booty—Nevis being the slave mart of
the Leeward Islands. The name Nevis (*nieve,* the
Spanish word for snow) was given by Columbus
because of the mountain's cloud-wreathed summit.

Our way led to Montpelier House—of which
only the globular stone gate-posts date from the
time of the marriage of Trafalgar's hero.

ON THIS SITE STOOD
MONTPELIER HOUSE
WHEREIN ON THE 11 DAY OF MARCH 1787
HORATIO NELSON
OF IMMORTAL MEMORY
THEN CAPTAIN OF H. M. S. BOREAS
WAS MARRIED TO
FRANCES HERBERT NISBET.

Prince William Henry, Duke of Clarence (afterwards William IV), Admiral in command of the West India Station, stood as best man. Montpelier House was in those days the home of Governor Herbert, uncle of the bride—the widow Fanny Nisbet (aged twenty-two) whom her faithless husband was to desert for that bewildering beauty, Lady Hamilton.

An unpretentious dwelling stands to-day on the old foundation. A blooming mango towers above the stone walls so characteristic of Nevis, that, in contrast to stoneless St. Kitts, give the rugged island an almost Breton appearance. A mere stone's throw away rises the windmill of the old estate—a substantial tower also reminiscent of Brittany. It is owned by an Englishman who lives in the successor to Montpelier House. We were fortunate to find this sugar-mill in action and to have its owner explain to us the traditional muscovado process. The structure stood upon a knoll overlooking a bluer-than-Breton sea. When, owing to a shift in the breeze the sails ceased to revolve,

Nevis ‡ The Montpelier sugar-mill

a dozen or more darkies, straining like mules on a towpath, turned the wings to windward. A centenarian black man who stood guard at the doorway ushered us into the stifling interior, where we watched canes fed, one at a time, to be crushed between cylinders, the juice jutting forth as though joyously liberated from an imprisoning body. The smell of boiling liquid issued from an adjacent building—a smell connoting fermentation. Donkeys frisked upon the slippery chaff, where, upon our approach, my Illustrator, to the accompaniment of guffaws from onlookers, had ignominiously fallen.

The historic Fig Tree Village Church of St. John, stands like its prototypes in England, among the graves of former parishioners. Many ancient carven tombs enhance the interior of this modest building but its renown, nowadays, seems to depend upon the fact that here the register recording the marriage of Nelson and Fanny Nisbet is displayed.

On a tour of the island of Nevis, walls, stone gate-posts, remnants of mills and of estate houses continue on every hand. Widely scattered are the schools and churches, signs of comparative prosperity. William, our driver, showed us his own abode, idyllic from the painter's point of view, with its setting of palms and flowering trees and its view, across the sheen of water, to Saba and

St. Kitts. Later we passed coconut groves, with yellowing palms heavily laden. Zebus grazed where only zebus could find pasturage. Razor-backed hogs delayed our passage, as did arbitrary donkeys, ridden by men astride sacks, long legs dangling. The village of Newcastle is famed for its terra cotta. Scrawny women poked roadside bonfires where water jars were baking.

My remembrance of Charlestown is chiefly of its fire-bell attached to an immense sandbox tree —a bell, I noted, made in Baltimore. Upon it was posted the following:

"THE CLOSED SEASON FOR COTTON IN NEVIS
IS FROM JUNE 15TH TO SEPTEMBER 15TH.
ALL COTTON AND OKRA PLANTS
MUST BE COMPLETELY DESTROYED
BY BURNING BEFORE JUNE 15TH.
NO COTTON MAY BE PLANTED BEFORE SEPTEMBER 16TH."

The signature of the Agricultural Superintendent was attached.

A tall silver image of Saint Christopher graced the hood of a car drawn up beside the pier. Was its Catholic owner, we wondered, a nostalgic citizen of St. Kitts?

The islands of the West Indies are formed from the peaks of a partly submerged chain, called by geologists the Caribbean Andes. This range of towering volcanoes is said to have connected the

North and South American continents. The claim
is substantiated by prehistoric fossils and the similarity of Indian tribes. The Lesser Antilles, lying
in the path of the trade winds, were known to the
Spaniards as the Windward Islands. By an arbitrary ruling of the British, the name Leeward has,
inappropriately, been applied to the northernmost
half of the Windward group, and to that alone,
while only the southernmost retain the old name of
Windward. During the winter and early spring
the "trades" blow with undeviating regularity, as
air flows from both north and south to replace that
rising from the torrid regions of the Equator.

Antigua is the capital of the Leeward Islands,
that is to say, the dwelling-place of the governor-
general. It is odd to our ears, in this connection,
that in 1721, and again in 1752, the captain-gen-
eral sworn in at Antigua to govern the Leeward
Islands had been "promoted" (for such is the
word used) respectively from the governorships
of Maryland and of Pennsylvania. Antigua (pronounced An tee ga) is, to my mind, less attractive
than its neighbors because, unlike them, only partially hilly. The island was named by Columbus
for the church of St. Mary of Antigua at Seville.
The Admiral did not tarry here, owing to the
presence of Caribs and the absence of drinking
water. Edward, the son of Sir Thomas Warner,
with a contingent of British soldiers, took Antigua

from the Indians. In 1640 a raiding Carib chieftain abducted the wife and child of the Governor. The distracted Englishman formed a party to pursue the offenders to their island of Dominica. Although he was successful in his quest and brought his family once more in safety to their own hearth, a deranged mind caused the unhappy husband to accuse his spouse of having left him of her own volition. The tantalizing tale, as many in more modern times, stops short of the hoped-for happy ending. Murder, fire, hurricane, and pestilence have played major rôles on Antigua's stage. Never, save for a brief occupation by the French in 1666, has Antigua flown other than the British flag.

A Norwegian freighter was anchored outside the bar at the entrance to St. John's harbor, but our own landing-place was at the harbor's end—St. John, the capital. Here we immediately boarded a motor for English Harbor, with its Dockyard associated with Nelson. The Captain of the *Boreas* was stationed at the Leeward Islands from 1784 to 1787, and was to call there on his way to Trafalgar, picking up the *Spartiate* and leaving the *Northumberland*.

Our road led between sunbaked cane-fields with, now and again, redeeming glimpses of distant hills and turquoise sea. At the suburb of All Saints a notice "Beware the train" warned of a grade crossing, but the absurd officious locomotive that delayed our car, after the way of the Indies, hauled not passengers but cane. Pickaninnies decked with bougainvillea danced by the roadside, calling for pennies. At St. John, venders of bead necklaces and shell chains had thronged about us, but were told firmly by our chauffeur that he, too, had chains to sell.

English Harbor gave us the feeling that it was an old print come to life. As a monument to the hero of Trafalgar it is unique. In these blue basins Nelson had careened and refilled ships. Docks, barracks, and yards all are preserved. Clarence House, once the residence of Prince William, Duke of Clarence, and the youthful Fitz Clarences, is conspicuous between English and Falmouth Harbors. It is, nowadays, the country-seat of the governor-general. Prince George (George V) visited English Harbor on Christmas, in '83— as midshipman aboard the *Canada*. A sailor, announced the local guide, was ordered to paint the greetings still preserved on the ancient storehouse wall.

"Some, who don't know," said the guide, condescendingly "would tell you it was painted by the Prince. The old spout outside the door is marked '1850, V.R.' That, of course, stands for Victoria Rex.". . . The remark gave an opening to gigglers of the party, who, doubtless, had seen Helen Hayes' play in New York.

In the Admiral's House a picture is shown of His Honor John Peterson of St. Vincent, brother to that unfortunate Colonel shot in a duel at the Dockyard by Lord Camelford in 1798 ... a premature death later to be avenged in England. Two figureheads from wrecks are affectionately dubbed Queen Elizabeth and Queen Victoria. A tree of immense girth shelters the Admiral's House. Its trunk was rougher to the touch than a pebble-dashed wall and, in addition, was viciously spiked with thorns. The spread of the branches, curious fruit, pendant red-purple flowers gave me a lasting impression of the extraordinary characteristics of the sandbox. Lofty manchineels grow on the path to Clarence House, while others, bearing poisonous fruit, were passed even in the neighborhood of huts ... not thatched but sporting instead that bane of artists the world over, corrugated iron roofs.

St. John boasts a cathedral of the name, but more entertaining is the open-air market. Bananas, yams, soursops, crude salt, savagely red meat piled the counters, beneath every one of which were stretched prostrate forms. At first glance we feared these blackfaced crones were beggars, but no, the aged merely sought refuge from the pitiless sun. Bandanas or fruit-piled baskets protected many heads, even "stove-pipe hats" formed of the locally-baked terra cotta

Montserrat

ovens, carried home in this way, like as not ex-
tinguishing the features. Black-skinned throngs
surged in and out of the market gates and jostled
to High Street, mounting garishly-painted omni-
buses.

How little did we realize that fate was to bring
us again to Antigua. On our last trip talk turned to
the hurricane damage to buildings at Nelson's

Dockyard, also to the de-activated U. S. bases and Coolidge Field, the American influx to Exchange Bay and the delightful Antigua Beach Hotel.

Montserrat is known as the "Emerald Isle of the West." At first we were inclined to believe that the name was given because Montserrat, which has flown the British and French flags by turns, was in Cromwell's day settled by the Irish, of whom there were at one time three thousand. However the intrinsic characteristic of the island —the glory of its verdure—well merits the appellation. An acrid odor of sulphur emanates from the crater of the dominant peak, Soufrière. Wooded hills may be seen from the ship, hedged orchards of citrus fruits: limes and papaya are, next to Sea Island cotton, Montserrat's chief cultivations.

When our boat dropped anchor in the roadstead of Plymouth, capital of Montserrat, passengers amused themselves by tossing coppers into the water to be dived for by black "boys"—who turned the white soles of their feet upward at sight of the smallest coin. We noted with amusement that certain woolly heads were red, proof of the Irish occupation, if any were needed beyond the brogue spoken by the inhabitants.

"Howdy!" their din of voices rose to us, "Look, pity sakes!" "Look, love of Mike!"

Our shipmates, on landing, headed for the Montserrat Club, telling us there was "nothing to see

here." My Illustrator and I employed, as chauffeur, the genteel George. The village of Harris
was our first objective. The gorges, as well as the
donkeys, passed upon the mountain road, reminded us of Ronda. The Bhil-like villages were,
however, more reminiscent of India than of Spain.
The shadows lengthened. It was cooler on the
heights. Reilly's, a plantation house, was passed,
set in an Eden of vegetation. Another estate, that
of Reilly's father, was appropriately named Paradise. Black amazons proudly bore burdens on
bandana-wound heads. Beneath silk-cotton trees,
dusky figures squatted, hand-pressing limes.
George, pointing a brown hand upward, remarked:
"We use silk for pillows. You call kapok."

Fishermen were mounting homeward, burdened
with lobsters—a variety resembling the French
langouste. To Park Hill Village we drove and to
Isle Beach, where black men busied themselves
with nets. My Illustrator remarked that the roads
were good, but not too good. In other words, Montserrat is as yet unexploited.

Crops of Sea Island cotton, hedged against the
wind, alternated with ravines luxuriant with jungle vegetation...a foretaste of Dominica and
Trinidad. Bread-fruit trees amazed us by their
grandeur. Leafless flamboyants stunned us with
splendor of florescence. Immense tamarinds towered over us. Calabashes groaned with fruit.

A black Amazon of Montserrat

Black-eyed thunbergias wreathed the hedges. More lonely, wilder, more mountainous than its neighbors, less visited, and therefore more imaginatively dominating is Montserrat.

It being a Saturday, we were puzzled at the Sunday cleanliness of many natives until we came upon groups returning with hymnals from a church of Seventh Day Adventists. The majority at Montserrat, however, like the Irish before them, are partial to the Catholic faith. It was a shock, on our return to Plymouth, to see other crowds massed about the entrance to the Realto, advertised as a "talking theater." "Pitt seats" read one sign, another, "Five pennies changed for movies," and over all beamed the much-magnified countenance of Clark Gable.

Turning our backs on this less congenial scene, we stepped into the dory *Wally* and were rowed toward our looming liner. The sun had set. Already electric lights gleamed along the rail of the swaying steps we were to mount. Ashore darkness was spreading over the land, pricked by occasional twinkles. When night casts its mantle upon the lesser islands, the natives sleep. Thoughts of Columbus came to mind, how he had named Montserrat for the mountain of the Holy Grail in Catalonia, of how unchanged, in all essentials, the island was since the time it had received its name.

"The most spectacular of the Leewards," said

my Illustrator. "No wonder Columbus thought
he had reached the East Indies."

Behind my companion, low on the horizon—previously unseen by us since our voyage to Singapore—hung, luminously, the Southern Cross.

ARMS
of the
Leeward Islands

1787
March 11
Horatio Nelson
Esquire
Captain of his Majesty's Ship
"The Boreas"
to Frances Herbert Nisbet, Widow

Dominica ꞉ Caribs on the Imperial Road

The Ceiba Tree: St. Lucia

CHAPTER IX

THE WINDWARD ISLANDS

"DOMINICA's pride is in its trees, rivers and mountains," wrote Stephen Haweis in his brochure on what he describes as "the loveliest of all the islands"; and which is, in addition, the largest as well as the most mountainous of the Lesser Antilles. Landfall of Columbus on his second voyage, November 3, 1493, Dominica received its name from the navigator—the day being *domingo,* Sunday. Although Columbus merely cruised about the island, probably owing to the hostility of the Caribs (landing instead at little Marie Galante, which he named for his own gallant ship), so much impressed was he with its beauty that, upon his return to Spain, he crumbled a parchment and tossed it upon a table—the tale waxes monotonous. Had we not heard the same told of Jamaica and Puerto Rico?

It was on a Sunday, the fourteenth of May, that our own gallant ship, the *Lady Drake*, steamed to anchor off Roseau the harborless capital of Dominica, an island not unknown to the distinguished husband of our vessel's namesake, nor yet to Hawkins who also, on occasion, sought shelter here to rest from his labors. Captain Clarke had smoothed our path by despatching a cabin boy with coffee, toast, and eggs to our stateroom at dawn. By seven we blessed the Commander for sending us ashore and speeding us on our way to Sylvania, the estate of John Knowlton.

Henry Francis, dusky driver of Car H5—an impeccable Ford owned, so Francis told us, by a Syrian—was in waiting. The murky Roseau, a drab gray settlement when unenhanced by its famous double rainbow, was left behind without reluctance. It was with relief that we discovered that Henry Francis conversed in the English tongue rather than in what Ober has wittily described as "niggard French"—a patois not understood by Frenchmen. Dominica, lying between Guadeloupe and Martinique, was, by a treaty of European powers in 1748, declared to be Carib territory. Despite this agreement, French colonization continued until the French Revolution, when the British established their claim.

Canefield, the estate of Andrew Green of Chicago, was passed. Money has been lavished upon this model plantation where rum is fabricated and citrus fruits flourish. From a higher level we looked back upon the blue of Woodbridge Bay. It was farther up the coast, at Batalie, that Dr. John Imbray had dwelt generations ago—he who, after the total devastation of the coffee crop by blight, had been inspired to plant limes. Observing that some venerable lime trees grew on his plantation of Batalie, and that the fruit was not garnered, and remembering the prosperity of Sicily because of the citric acid contained in its lemons, the doctor made a voyage of investigation to Italy. The result was a pioneer industry for the British West Indies, including the fresh fruit, "green, and pickled limes, lime juice, essential oil, and otto of limes," an industry continued by Dr. Nicholls under the guidance of the Imperial Department of Agriculture, and introduced to Montserrat, in the early days, by Mr. Burke from Dominica.

A few wattle houses, fashioned as though by beavers from stick and clay and topped by thatch, showed that man has encroached thus far upon the forest. "Trash houses," the English call these dwellings, whether because of the material used in their building or, perhaps as a term of opprobrium toward the nature of the inhabitants (whose skins would deny their inclusion as "poor white trash"), we did not know.

Below us as we mounted, rivers roared in cañons. Bamboo, reaching to astounding heights, edged precipitous curves. Tree-ferns formed fantastic labyrinths. Bottle-blue humming-birds flashed from flower to flower. Every tree had its blossom, forest giants for whom we had no names. Acajous we could indeed recognize: the profusion of their florescence was phenomenal. At a sudden curve, a landslide blocked the way. Henry Francis was equal to the emergency. Boulders were laboriously shifted, and, by a feat of circumnavigation, the chief obstacle was skirted. Lianas festooned the denizens of the forest... lesser vines with heart-shaped leaves clung to trunks, daintily, reminding us of gold and silver heart-shaped earrings seen at Antigua.

The Imperial Road, over which we traveled, was constructed in 1899 at a cost to the government of £15,000. Although it has opened to cultivation the fertile plateaus known as Layou Flats, it comes to a dead end at Bassinville, in lieu of the desired continuation to the Windward coast. As yet the towns of Dominica—the most sparsely peopled of the major islands—are connected only by boat. The Valley of Desolation must be traversed to obtain a view of the geyser known as Boiling Lake.

The air had grown fresher as our car climbed. Springfield estate was passed, gay with hibiscus. Its owner, of the Rockefeller connection, comes rarely and expensively by plane, landing at Guadeloupe or Martinique. Abrupt turns in the road

The Boiling Lake of Dominica ✦

disclosed, ahead, glimpses of a distant peak. It
was not, however, until we stood upon the terrace
of Sylvania, at an altitude of 1,700 feet, that we
beheld the Trois Piétons, clad with virgin forest
unchanged since the days of Columbus, and
Diablotin, highest summit in the Lesser Antilles.
A downpour welcomed us to the estate; and the
following sunshine, during our stay, was punctuated by sprays of rain. Showers are the order
of the day on an island where rainfall varies from
eighty inches a year, on the coast, to three hun-

dred in high valleys. The luxuriance of vegetation could not otherwise be attained. Dominicans take pride in numbering their rivers, tempestuous torrents rushing to the sea, at three hundred and sixty-five—one for every day of the year.

Sylvania citrus estate is a monument to the industry and good judgment of John Knowlton, its owner, who has made an outstanding success of orange growing at an altitude where the former proprietor had failed. We found Mr. Knowlton not yet departed for Massachusetts, where he and his family spend the hurricane season. Sunday breakfast on the vine-sheltered veranda at Sylvania with the Knowltons and Mr. Stephen Haweis, their neighbor from the estate of Mount Joy, is a cherished memory. Sunlight and cloud played upon the mountains, water trickled from a fountain, orchids swung from hanging-baskets. Upon the house wall Mr. Haweis—an English artist, who has discovered "joy" in the tropics— had depicted a map of our host's three hundred and more acres. He had lately returned from Nassau where, for the third time, he had painted a rich man's loggia, periodically destroyed by weather.

"Yes, *Music and Morals* was written by my father," he admitted, in answer to my inquiry about the Victorian classic. "I shall never live it down." He reminisced of artist friends in common. In Florence he had known Howard Pyle.

Mr. Knowlton told of a visit, some years before,

to Martinique with "Jimmie" Roosevelt. The American consul at Fort-de-France had informed the young men there were no birds and no snakes on the island.

"But," said our host, with an infectious grin, "I heard the birds!"

The talk turned to the alluring bird, now probably extinct, from which Mont Diablotin—a former haunt—has derived its name. It seems the creature was web-footed, with hawk bill and eyes of an owl, and that runaway slaves, in the old days, trapped these soot-black petrels to salt and send in quantities to Martinique, bartering them for muskets and ammunition.

Our exquisite hostess, a type more French than English, was wistful because of lack of information on the point as to whether her infant, Hetty, must go to school in the United States consecutively from thirteen to eighteen, in order to obtain citizenship. If she did not, would she become a citizen without the right to vote or would she become a British subject?

Farewells were reluctant. Our eyes dwelt lingeringly upon the hills and, more especially, upon the little party outlined against the low house upon the ridge, with roof of beetling thatch and sheltering clumps of drenched bamboo, connecting it, in our minds' eye, with remembered prints of Old Japan.

The Botanical Garden, noted for its collection

of palms, under the supervision of the Imperial Department of Agriculture, covers forty acres of the Bath estate at Roseau. It was established in 1891. Here we were shown some of the tree wonders of the tropics: we were to renew our acquaintance at St. Vincent and at Trinidad. The sausage-tree amazed us, and the *Butea frondosa* from India, rivaling with its beaked vermilion blossoms the flamboyant; but none could, for sheer fantasy, equal a native of British Guiana, the cannon-ball tree. Huge heavily-scented blossoms, of lotus pink, with centers resembling passion flowers, hung upon rootlike stems—mistaken at first glance for a powerful vine, and, simultaneously, after the fashion of the tropics, hung with "cannon-balls," large and brown as coconuts. Our guide pronounced, with earnestness, that this was the Garden-of-Eden fruit!

Immediately above Roseau rises precipitous Morne Bruce. In times gone by the hill was fortified, but now its reputation depends upon the beauty of the view to be had from its plateau. We encountered upon this eminence a leather-skinned man of Carib descent. His features were, indeed, akin to the American Indian, as was his hair, but the chocolate color of his countenance betrayed a mixture of races.

The word "cannibal" is said to have its origin in the misreading of the written word, "Caribales"—the Spanish name for the warlike tribe accused of having killed and eaten their enemies, the peace-loving men of the Arawaks. There seems to have been no William Penn among the European settlers of the West Indies, nor were the Caribs friendly Delawares. In the year 1640, long-boats, manned at Dominica with as many as a hundred painted Indians, descended upon Antigua; their savage occupants burning, pillaging, and, as has been stated, carrying off the governor's wife. As late as 1748 "by treaty agreement between the European states with interests in the Caribbean, Dominica, St. Vincent, St. Lucia, and Tobago were declared Carib territory." Eventually, as the white man pushed his way into these mountainous strongholds, the Caribs were granted two reservations—one at St. Vincent, destroyed by the eruption of Soufrière, the other at Dominica, which has become the last stand of a disappearing race.

Drake, who described the Caribs of Dominica as "very personable and handsome strong men," would hardly recognize the fishermen and tillers of the soil who dwell in what is known as the "Carib country"—extending three miles along the windward coast, between Mahoe and Crayfish rivers, and as far inland as the inhabitants care to cultivate. Salibia is the nearest approach to a village. Although the headman is known as the King of the Caribs, gone are days when men and women alike dyed their bodies yellow, encircling their eyes, formidably, with bands of black and white. No longer is one tongue spoken by the men, another by the women. Nowadays, after the way of Indians, they are noted chiefly for their basketry. The fame of the Carib panniers—waterproof baskets woven of layers of mahoe with interlining of wild plantain—has traveled far.

As with unwilling feet my Illustrator and I boarded the launch of the *Lady Drake*, we registered a vow to return to Dominica, and when the shore receded, perhaps as an omen of the ultimate (and, as it happened, swift) fulfilment of our intention, an unanticipated radiance arched the heavens. Thus Dominica bade august farewell, brandishing as though in our unique honor what, in the Carib tongue, signifies "the plume of God."

St. Lucia possesses one asset that might well be the envy of its sister islands—a harbor, at Castries, its capital, where vessels may dock. Dominica, some say, could utilize Portsmouth, but owing to oft-recurring malaria among the inhabitants of that town, Roseau is preferred as a port of call. Castries itself is a black-man's city, the site being unsuited to the white man who dwells on the slopes of dominating Morne Fortune. In the eighteenth century wars and yellow fever raged in St. Lucia. It has been stated that at least twelve thousand Englishmen were buried in the West Indies in one year alone, 1794—the year in which the Duke of Kent (father of Victoria) raised the

flag on Fortune. To-day, despite the evil reputation of its swamps and lagoons, St. Lucia, paradoxically, has one of the most popular hotels in
the Lesser Antilles, the Saint Antoine—an unpretentious dwelling to be found in a bower of verdure, at no great distance below Government
House, on the terraced flank of Fortune.

"The island of strife," Sir Frederick Treves
has called St. Lucia. Discovered by Columbus in
1502, on Saint Lucy's Day, the island has, between
the years of its first settlement, 1650, and the year
1814—since which time it has been a part of the
British Empire—been shuttled, with appalling
loss of life, fifteen times between the rival powers
of France and England. It was from Gros Islet
Bay that Rodney's fleet (as the French left Martinique) issued forth to maintain supremacy of
the seas for the English nation, and, incidentally,
personal renown and a peerage for its admiral as
hero of the Battle of the Saints.

History tells that "whoever holds Morne Fortune holds the island." The classic view from the
summit has not been overestimated. A reviving
breeze greets the traveler on arrival at the wireless station which crowns the mount. From this
point of vantage the eye beholds the harbor, the
historic hill of Vigie, Pigeon Island from which
Rodney observed the manœuvers of the French.
Still more distant is Diamond Rock, once manned
by Hood with the crew of a British gunboat to

harass the French—a job they performed with consummate success over a period of seventeen months. Martinique itself may sometimes be discerned. It was into Castries that the S. S. *Roddam*, weighted with tons of volcanic ash, crawled for succor on May 8, 1902, the only vessel from the harbor of St. Pierre to escape, but not unscathed, during the eruption of Pelée. After admiration of the windblown ceiba, the traveler turns his eyes inland to the distant peaks—*pitons* in the vernacular—known as Gros Pitons and Petit Pitons but dubbed by sailors the Donkey's Ears.

As though war and pestilence were not enough drawbacks to discourage the white man's settlement of St. Lucia, floods and the deadly rat-tailed viper or fer-de-lance have been thrown in to tip the balance against the island's chief asset—unusual fertility of soil. Apropos of the Pitons, a story has been echoed by West Indian raconteurs since it was recorded as a "local legend" by the historian Froude. Four British seamen, so the story goes, attempted to scale the Gros Pitons—a peak slightly under three thousand feet but hitherto unscaled. With field-glasses, messmates watched the progress of the climbers. Half-way up one was seen to fall by the way, then, later in the ascent, another, and still another. The fourth had almost reached the summit when he, too, disappeared. The surmise is that all were struck down by the fer-de-lance. "Death of the Woods" is an-

other name for this nocturnal serpent, long as a
man is tall, which, when curled during the day,
will strike without provocation. It is said that the
French introduced the snake (unknown in the
other islands of the British West Indies) from
Martinique with the intention of driving out the
Caribs. In the year 1869, the Legislative Council
offered half a crown for every five heads of the
reptile. The first year fifty thousand were collected. In 1872 the bounties amounted to £465.
Later the situation was controlled by the introduction of the Indian mongoose.

The town of Castries was named by the French,
in 1785, for the Maréchal de Castries. Although
the English were nominally in possession after
the taking of Morne Fortune in 1794, the Brigands' War did not terminate until the surrender
of French and Negro terrorists in 1797.

On a memorable afternoon my Illustrator
and I set out, via the Cul-de-Sac Valley, to the
pass known as Bar de l'Isle. The divide was a
high and lonely region in which to find ourselves
as shadows lengthened. Impenetrable jungle lay
about us ... lavish growths of the tropics among
which we were beginning to recognize familiar
tree-ferns, the immense leaves and scarlet blossoms of the wild banana, forest giants half-stran-
gled by encircling parasites, sturdy rope-vines
hanging free of trunks. Parrots passed us by,
raucous voiced, red, blue, and green of plumage.

We watched their flickering flight over the tree-tops down valley toward the distant sunset-transfigured hills.

Our chauffeur divulged that he had driven James Bond when that authority was gathering material for his book *Birds of the West Indies*. The topic on which the man expatiated, however, until his listeners had difficulty in concealing inappropriate amusement, was that of "the disaster" of the previous November. Landslides had occurred in three places; a hundred road-workers had been killed, and numberless cottagers. Scars on the bare cliffs were insistently pointed out, whence, during torrential rains, the avalanche of mud and stones had descended. Sugar-fields had been inundated by the river, and bridges swept away. Questions on other topics would not distract our narrator but merely inspired continued gestures toward more and more graves and the telling of more and more gruesome tales of corpses. Had his not been one of the first Fords to enter the valley? Had he not trailed his own hand in the water, sitting in his driver's seat? Had he not talked to the woman who, having gone alone to the outer kitchen, returned to find husband and children missing?

Country folk were straggling home from picnics, guitars still twanging. The smell of cooking mounted from open-air fires. Frog-choruses echoed in the lowlands, the hoarse voice of the

"crac-crac" rose from the forest, while mammoth
fireflies swung their lanterns far and wide. Steep
curves brought us again to the slopes of Morne
Fortune. Narrowly avoiding pedestrians, horn
blowing, lights blaring, we descended upon the
twinkling town, intermittently revealed by a flashing ray from the lighthouse.

Like Dominica, St. Lucia, and Grenada, St. Vincent has its Soufrière or Sulphur Mountain. Unlike the others, however, the Soufrière of St.
Vincent is a notorious volcano. The eruption of
1912 destroyed the eastern end of the island. Volcanic dust spread over an area of a hundred miles
... reaching, to windward, to the island of
Barbados.

On May 6, 1902, preceded by several years of
premonitory warnings, "an enormous cloud of
steam rose from the crater, and later the whole
mountain was illuminated by flame, followed by
jets of steam, mingled with fire, and frequent detonations." Next day, according to an eye-witness,
a "vast column of smoke and mud ... arose." The
people along the leeward coast fled before the
rain of stones, ashes, and dust, but those in the
Carib country were apathetic. Two thousand of
them lost their lives and thousands more became
homeless refugees. "Earthquakes," says Stod-
dard, "accompanied the eruption, and the coast
at Wallibou and Morne Ronde sank into the sea."
The eruption at St. Vincent occurred the day be-

fore the still more appalling catastrophe at Martinique.

The natives of Kingstown, we learned on arrival at St. Vincent's capital, insist upon the pronunciation of every letter in the name: "King's town."

"Das so!" "Das so!" came the soft voices of the boatmen surrounding our steamer. "Cartwheel" blue was the lining of the rowboats, and poles at sterns were surmounted by bunched bougainvillea. On the tender that bore us to the shore an inter-island passenger, in whom a touch of the tar brush could be detected, spoke of the grandeur of the "awful column of smoke at the time of the eruption." In her mind's eye she could never think of St. Vincent otherwise.

Fort Charlotte, overlooking the bay, is second in historic interest only to Brimstone on St. Kitts. Every chauffeur, so ours told us, before obtaining a driver's license for the island, must make the ascent at night—the drive is no child's play even by day. Having ascended to the fort we found the view panoramic. Years of peace have had a mellowing effect even upon the instruments of war. Our attention was called, by a wide-eyed pickaninny, to a bird nesting in a cannon's mouth.

"Top-knot bird," said he

"Bird with crown?" said I.

"Yes, das it, das it," he beamed.

St. Vincent is divided into five "parishes," St.

George, Charlotte, St. Andrew, St. David, St. Patrick. Like St. Lucia, the island suffered severely during the Brigands' War, when French and Indians killed and plundered. To establish order the English deported five thousand Caribs to Ruatan, an island off the coast of Honduras. The story is told of the wreck at St. Vincent, in 1675, of a slave ship from Guinea. The white survivors were put to death by the Caribs, but the black were welcomed. As a result, the Indians of St. Vincent became, eventually, divided into two tribes, the yellow or pure Caribs, and the Black Caribs. The latter, as generations passed, observing that the black men were the white settlers' slaves, flattened the foreheads of their own children to make them easily distinguishable.

Although the climate of St. Vincent is in its favor, and there are no marshes among its jagged hills, yet, since the eruption of Soufrière, the island has fallen into disfavor with the white man. Few descendants of the early Scottish settlers remain, their successors being chiefly Portuguese and Hindus. A Scotch reminder is the Free Library donated by Andrew Carnegie. The books are augmented by a collection of Carib weapons and tools.

It was to obtain seeds and plants for the Botanical Garden, established in 1763 for the "acclimatization of tropical exotics," that Captain Bligh set out on the ill-destined *Bounty*. The story of the mutiny, the Captain's voyage for four thousand miles in an open boat, the settling of Pitcairn by the mutineers, has become popular history. Nothing daunted, Bligh set forth on a second voyage—this time aboard the *Providence*—and brought back for the feeding of the slaves, along with hundreds of other treasures to benefit the Indies, the tree, now naturalized on the island, that won for him the appellation of "Bread-fruit Bligh."

The Botanical Garden, the oldest in the New World, has been called the "Cradle of tropical agriculture." Here cloves were introduced from Martinique in 1787 and nutmegs from Cayenne in 1809—flourishing here to-day as in neighboring Grenada. The staple of St. Vincent, however, is arrowroot (the *ararautu* of the Caribs). The roots, resembling salsify, are seen at the local markets and, along the streams, at primitive arrowroot mills. St. Vincent's Sea Island cotton is considered the best in the world. This material is used in the fabrication of parachutes. The entire crop of the West Indies was purchased during the World War.

Grenada, the debonair "Isle of Spice"... the mouth waters at the name. No less does the eye delight in the picture presented, while the mind rejoices in the thought that Grenada is the isle of thrifty small-farm owners: there are fourteen thousand with holdings of less than five acres.

S t. Vincent ‡ The Botanical Garden.

The inner harbor or Carenage, where lesser boats may dock, is a center for white-winged sloops whose sails flutter in the trade winds like pinions of sea-going birds. These are the boats that ply to the Grenadines, that enticing chain of isles stretching almost to St. Vincent. Jungle green presses from hills to the water's edge. A mountain spur juts into the sea, dividing the Carenage from the more populous hillside section of the capital, St. George's. A tunnel links the two portions of the town.

Our Lady Liner was a scene of especial animation on arrival at Grenada, owing to the presence aboard of the Catholic bishop of the Windward Islands, returning to the seat of his bishopric. The prelate, a Celtic type, and his satellites, sun-helmeted and robed for the tropics, were greeted by an ecclesiastical flag flying from the high-perched Cathedral. Anglican and Presbyterian towers and spires, substantial red-tiled houses, angular steep streets give St. George's the appearance of an old-world provincial town. On a nearby bluff stands up-to-date Santa Maria Hotel.

Columbus, after leaving Trinidad in August, 1498, sighted, on August 15th, what is now Grenada and called it Conception—its neighbor, now Tobago, Assumption. For a century or more after this discovery the Caribs held undisputed sway. In 1609 the English attempted settlement; in 1629 the French claimed the territory for the

Company of Islands of America, founded, at that time, by Richelieu. The following year the island was granted by Charles I to the Earl of Carlisle. It was the French, however, who were long to hold Grenada, only to cede it, in 1762, to Great Britain —since called upon on more than one occasion to defend it with bloodshed.

Escaping from the turmoil of the dock, where basket venders and turbaned mammies with bunches of heavily-scented khus-khus besieged us, my Illustrator and I threaded our way to the river, beside which huts cluster beneath straggling cocopalms, after which our car began to mount the seventeen hundred feet to the crater lake of Grand Etang. Grenada is a lush and hilly island. Because of the fertility of its soil it has been compared to Java. As we passed the famous nutmeg orchards—not dissimilar to orange groves —boys tossed us branches from the laden trees. Inside yellow hulls, bursting already, the dark nutmegs were revealed laced vividly with scarlet threads—to become, piquantly, the mace of commerce. In a year one tree may yield as many as five thousand nuts.

The jungle, as we mounted, recalled the riotous vegetation of Dominica. Wild bananas bore flaming torches as though to light the scene, while, spasmodically, we were brought back to earth by charred patches caused by the carelessness or malice of man.

Grenada

The lake, located in an ancient crater, proved a melancholy climax to a drive in itself its own reward. The bush had encroached to the water's edge. A brooding loneliness assailed the heart as we lingered—the shadows lengthening—at this solitary tarn. The "Home of the Mother of Rains," the natives call the Grand Etang, in their caressing tongue. Thoughts of tales told at Grenada press upon the memory—of Le Morne des Sauteurs, still shown on the north coast, where, rather than submit to foreign rule, the last Caribs flung themselves into the sea. The hour was late. Our descent to the capital was, perforce, rapid.

"Dominica, Grenada; Grenada, Dominica," the rhythmic oar-beats murmured in my ears as two coal-black boatmen rowed us, past blue-sailed pleasure boats discernible in fading light, to the ever-looming Lady Liner.

"All visitors ashore, please, all visitors ashore!" came thrice-repeated the warning in the golden voice of the wireless operator. The Chinese gong resounded, notice of immediate sailing from the twinkling lights which were St. George's.

Guadeloupe: The village of Bananier

The bridge at Basse-Terre

CHAPTER X

RUSTICATION IN GUADELOUPE

"GUADELOUPE is ferociously French!"—the words the youthful Breton governor had spoken to us—sum up one phase of the island's characteristics. Abandoned, after discovery, by the Spaniard in his search for gold; settled, in 1635, by the French, before whom the Caribs fled to neighboring Dominica—a base from which, it is true, they made furtive attempts to regain their Elysium; occupied for several brief periods by the English, the island of Guadeloupe has been, since the year 1816, indisputably French territory.

As Sorin, not without pride in his capacity as Governor of the island and its dependencies, re-stated its position in his Armistice Day address: "La Guadeloupe, province de la France d' Outre Mer." A colony, yes, but a colony considered an integral part of the homeland, with a senator and two representatives in the Chamber of Deputies in Paris. For a time the words *Patrie, Travail, Famille,* supplanted—in public speeches but not, one would say, in the hearts of the island's patriotic citizens—the more exalted *Liberté, Egalité, Fraternité.* (Since 1946 Guadeloupe and Martinique have ceased to be colonies but have become legally Departments of France. Prefects have replaced governors. As social security benefits have not been given, labor unrest remains acute.)

With its sister island of Martinique (from which it is separated by the English Dominica), Guadeloupe and its satellites—Marie-Galante, la Désirade, les Saintes, St. Barts, and a portion of St. Martin—form all that remains of the pretentiously planned and once far-flung Amérique française. The creoles of Martinique are renowned for their elegance—"*ces messieurs de* Martinique," while those of Guadeloupe are familiarly called "*ces bons gens de* Guadeloupe"... nowadays a no less honorable title. Although Guadeloupe can lay no claim to being the birthplace of an empress, nor to such sophisticated elegance as is to be found at Fort-de-France, yet, after her own unworldly fashion, she is no less—if not indeed even more—endearing than her only rival in the Indies that combines uncontaminated French atmosphere with abandon of tropical verdure. To those who seek release from urban ways, the lure of Guadeloupe is potent.

There are, I must hasten to add, two islands, united by a newly-constructed bridge, and together known to map-makers as Guadeloupe. Facetious writers have stated that though one of those isles is named Basse-Terre and the other Grande-Terre, the former is the higher and the latter is the smaller. The second idiosyncrasy is true, but Basse-Terre (guide-books to the contrary notwithstanding) is the name of a town, the capital in fact, and not of the island upon which this center of government stands. Indeed, this territory possesses a far lovelier nomenclature, none other than Guadeloupe *proprement dite* or, to our intents and purposes, without qualification, Guadeloupe. That the smaller, flatter, less picturesque isle of Grande-Terre (on which Pointe-à-Pitre, the commercial center is situated) should lay claim to the title at all is a mere convenience of geographers and politicians, Columbus having named the mountainous island for the Sierra de Guadalupe. The names of the islands, however, very slightly concern the sojourner in search of tropical rustication. He will tie more especially to the place names, depending on his choice of base, of Dolé-les-Bains, Matouba, or St. Claude.

Dolé-les-Bains, what fond memories the words evoke! Dolé set in verdure that gives to Guadeloupe, as well as to Ireland, the privilege of calling itself the Emerald Isle—in this case the Ile d'Emeraude. Dolé, from the French windows of whose incomparable inn may be seen the glittering sapphire of the Caribbean, the visionary Saintes (revealed to Columbus on All Saints' Day), the heaven-aspiring Dominica or — to landward — spurs of the *massif* of Soufrière. Dolé, set in an aura of rainbows—uplifting to the spirit as the aurora of northern lands; Dolé fanned by the trade wind, resplendent in the light of the moon: Dolé, even in our day, warrants the title that Columbus bestowed upon another island, the title of a terrestrial Paradise.

Swooping from the skies, the Pan-American plane flashed earthward to deposit us at the floating dock in the harbor of Pointe-à-Pitre, and to refuel and make a swift departure. Deserted, dazed, we stepped from the company's launch almost into the arms of Monsieur Party—eighteen years out of France—on whom the success or failure of our stay was almost wholly to depend. The incredible had come to pass. For at least a week all connection with the outer world was severed.

"Why Guadeloupe?" In the British islands the query was not unusual. "Why, may I ask, Guadeloupe?"

The answer, until then mere intuition, was evident the moment we set foot upon the land and lifted our eyes to the range dominated by la Soufrière. From the time we crossed the bridge and entered Guadeloupe proper it became so obvious as to be entirely dismissed.

The road—not surpassed by any in the Indies north of Trinidad—opened vistas of hill and dale, of cascade and rivers known to Columbus; the port where he watered his ships; steep plantations and palm-sheltered coves, emphatically green Bananier. Skirting the shore the strand of the highway which circles the island wound, now worming between palms, now threading its way through villages.

"The interior has no settlements," the host of Dolé-les-Bains, at the wheel of his Renault, informed us. "Not even roads, you can see by the map...nothing but mountains.

"Our warm springs at Dolé come from la Soufrière. Have no fear. There's not been an eruption since 1799. The craters form our safety-valves. The volcano breathes.

"Dolé is thirty-four miles from Pointe-à-Pitre and only six from Basse-Terre—but what a change of air! You notice the difference already in the hills? In winter we used to have American tourists, in summer we still get Guadeloupéens, escaping from the towns."

The Station Thermale of Dolé-les-Bains has, in all probability, a future. The present establishment was founded by Dr. Pichon in 1917. In the salle-à-manger of the hotel an impressive certificate may be seen:

Exposition Coloniale International
Paris 1931
Le Jury International
des recompenses décerne
un Diplôme de Medaille d'or
à la Source Dolé

As an aside to his hotel and market garden, Monsieur Party is, in normal times, in the habit of making frequent trips to France where he purchases articles perhaps a trifle out-of-date—anything from a brass bed to a refrigerator—and sets a style in Guadeloupe. I was reminded of the classic tale of the 42,000 warming-pans introduced into the West Indies by a progressive salesman. In his autobiography one Timothy Dexter (later Sir Timothy) of Newburyport relates how Martinique received 10,000—owners using them for cooking and displaying them to the envy of the neighbors. It is obvious that the white man is not, as a rule, in the tropics for altruistic motives.

The predicament of Dolé to-day lies in the fact that it is beyond reason to expect that more than a minority of visitors will be of European race. White may be the irascible bearded chaplain at the table next our own, demanding more than a fair share of the services of an ever-willing bonne; but African is his table companion. Chocolate is this companion as the suit he wears, and flashy as the watch chains and finger rings, the display of which gives him such evident satisfaction.

The incomparable inn, I find I have written. My mind runs over the reasons for the adjective: the view from our windows—seen down-valley, with foreground of highway and spindling palms, of les Saintes, Dominica; the lilting trade wind— out of bounds at night, drowning the voice of mul- titudinous tree toads, banging furiously the tall shutters, threatening to carry off mosquito cano- pies; the lavish fruits of the soil—the Hôtel- Restaurant is set among palms, bougainvillea, and roses; among radiating plots, edged by crotons, of pineapples, beans, tomatoes, and cabbages. (Be sure to sample the maron-like mammee conserve in syrup of brown sugar, flavored with *gousses* of vanilla!) And against all this, on the other side of the ledger are found the following: the ques- tionable modernity of so-called modern plumbing; the hilarity of sporadic Negro visitors to whom billiards, radio, and records constitute a lure; the emphatic gutturals of Syrian merchants depart- ing with the dawn; the scarcity of paint and im- ported delicacies; the all-inquisitive, though harmless, ants—whose presence on checkered cloth or linen sheet is sheer impertinence.

Keeping a nice hold upon the situation is the indispensable Marcel Party—French of the French—his wife, a reticent Haitian hostess, pearl-earringed, coated à la Chinoise. Perhaps the scales would merely balance were it not for the startling revelation—kept like wine at the Mar-

Dolé-les-Bains ‡ The mirror of the pool

riage of Canaan—of the old stony-surfaced road
to the spa, a road bordered by mighty Mammea
Americana and flaming *immortelles,* with its
dénouement of the pool.

French artistry has created the pool—or connecting pools, the shallower for the ladies. Nature
has supplied the climax of the setting. Unobtru-

sive bath-houses cluster against the forested hillside, the path leading between Valhalla boulders.
The refreshing (though singularly unbuoyant!)
mineral waters, at a temperature of 95°, from the
molten heart of la Soufrière, rush from various
channels and even bubble irrepressibly beneath the
surface of the pool. Clumps of bamboo lead the
eye across the dappled mirror of the basin to a
pair of veteran figs (of the banyan tribe) whose
slim youth is long forgotten; ample of form,
spreading of limb, mothering a motley host of
adopted offspring ... wild pines, clinging jungle
vines, and dangling tentacles. As though this were
not enough delight, between the matriarchs is a
vista of valley and not-too-distant Caribbean isles.
Birds flit among ponderous branches, the stillness
is broken only by a gurgle of waters descending in
exuberant cascades.

Let those to whom creature comfort is of primary importance hesitate; let the painter and the
horticulturalist hasten to the Hôtel-Restaurant at
Dolé-les-Bains. As a base, to my mind, Dolé has no
rival in the hotter, low-lying Basse-Terre or fever
ridden Pointe-à-Pitre.

Basse-Terre, seen from the Caribbean, delights
the eye with its dominating background of la
Soufrière. Tropical cataclysms have spared its
cathedral and much substantial masonry. The approach by bridge—between the Champ d'Arbaud
and Jardin Pichon—is as dramatic as that to a

Guadeloupéenne

Pyrenean hill-town. The French flavor is emphasized by the almost medieval Fort Richepance—
erected on the foundations of that built by Governor Houël in 1647—guarding the capital from land
and sea. Here are tombs still revered, that of
General Richepance, a victim of fever at the age
of thirty-two, and of Governor Gourbeyre who
rode the forty-five miles.to Pointe-à-Pitre on horseback to give succor after its destruction by earthquake and fire, in 1843, and for whom the district
in which Dolé stands is called.

Conscripts have recently returned to Guadeloupe from overseas—of twelve thousand mobi-
lized in 1914, fourteen hundred lost their lives. A
bevy of recruits, on week-end furlough, distinguishable as embryonic soldiers only by their
khaki caps, emerged from the fortress as we
passed. Where Frenchmen, including our linen-
clad host, indulged in the casque or sun-helmet,
and even certain black-skinned functionaries, it
amazed us to note that ardent francophiles of
African descent often wore the minute woolen
béret Basque.

The market-place—situated not far from the
dock and the Cours-Nolivos, the town's most popular promenade—was a favorite haunt of my Illustrator. Here fishermen in the coolie hat made and
worn at the Iles des Saintes may be seen beach-
ing their boats, displaying their still breathing
catch of tuna and lesser fry. Here—with insatiable

curiosity and the unending patience of the artist, sketchbook in hand, kodak whipped from pocket —T. O. would linger, in broiling sunshine or tantalizing shower, to be on hand when the wearer of a creole costume emerged from the melée. As at Martinique, the traditional woman's garment is voluminous, long-skirted, and looped in front, disclosing a lacy starched petticoat. The bandana or madras, as it is known locally, is worn *en éventail*, the fan in front replacing the "ears" of that worn at Martinique. Not less vivid in color were the venders with their burdens of tropical fruits, their more carelessly bound turbans, their gaudy cotton frocks—beneath which, incongruously, horny feet emerged.

Poverty, abject poverty may be seen, but begging, in the French islands, is practically unknown. Taking refuge from the sun (not as sometimes in the Indies from beggars) I stepped into a pharmacy adjacent to the market and noted jars marked as follows: Fleurs de Coquelicot, Queues de Cérises, Bois de Panama... titles that whet the curiosity.

In contrast to the crowded dwellings of the city beside the sea, more airy and actually modernistic structures have been erected on the terraced hillside, a hotel—of none too appealing character nor any too well placed—the Court of Appeal, and, at higher altitude, overlooking the Caribbean, the really superlative Governor's Palace and Legislative Council. Here we had the privilege of an interview with the vivid Sorin—his name is coupled in my mind with sea-worn Brittany, dear to my heart—who, as governor, wished us to bear the message to our countrymen of Guadeloupe's intention to remain an integral part of France, while pursuing the policy of "the good neighbor." As to the color question, it does not exist in Guadeloupe, we were told. People are considered merely as human beings. ("Worth," Thionville was to say, "not color decides eligibility to the Mountaineers' Club.")

We had already made acquaintance with the name of Victor Schœlcher to whom a bust was erected on the Cours-Nolivos in honor of the centenary of his birth, an anniversary which occurred on July 4, 1904. Under-Secretary of the Navy and of the Colonies in 1848, Schœlcher used his influence toward the freeing of slaves in the French islands—a freedom granted on April 27th of the aforesaid year. His picture hangs beside the governor's desk. Descending the stair of honor after our interview, we were shown a monumental head of the Liberator that divided our interest with striking murals of Guadeloupe and Colonial scenes from the life of Père Labat—the "Bellicose White Father" whose labors during twelve years spent in the Antilles have been compared to the labors of Hercules.

On an excursion to the north of Basse-Terre to

Guadeloupe : The forested

slopes of la Soufrière

316 BEHOLD THE WEST INDIES

desolate Vieux-Habitants we were to remark, in
passing Baillif, beside the sea, the ruined tower of
Père Labat—the Dominican "priest, soldier, doctor, engineer, historian, and savant" who played
such a part in the colonization of Guadeloupe. He
it was who, in 1702, directed the building of the
historic Fort St. Charles, the predecessor of Fort
Richepance.

Less sinister than Pelée, la Soufrière (superior
in altitude) is equally cloud-topped. If seen between Baillif and Rivière des Pères only the middle forested slopes are apt to be revealed. Strewn
is the base with lugubrious-looking rocks, charred
reminders of volcanic output, recalling to my Illustrator the petrified Hans and Schwartz in *The
King of the Golden River*. Lingering in the partial shade of palms for further revelation of the
peak we were to speculate on the mystery of life.

Does not man himself, emulating his Creator,
"move in a mysterious way his wonders to perform"? Were the peaks of this world as obvious
to all men at all times as earth's level places . . .
if genius were a constantly open book . . .

"Look," I cried, cutting short my soliloquy, as
before our watchful eyes the thinning mists dissi-
pated, revealing a tentative pinnacle, and then,
wholly, generously, if only momentarily, against
a pearl-white cloud bank, the cratered cone of
tender green . . . a modern miracle in this our own
especial Eden.

As we turned carward my Illustrator murmured, " 'Why, may I ask, Guadeloupe?' "

Even the memory of la Soufrière is enough to
quicken the heart-beat of its amateurs. Among the
most ardent of these is Camille Thionville, distinguished gentleman, aged, blind, yet vitally concerned in the fate of the paths, the forests ... in
all the doings of the Club des Montagnards of
which he is both President and Founder. Having
hung on the words of Monsieur Thionville's timely
La Guadeloupe Touristique, we were to search out
its author and find him at his Villa Jeannette at
St. Claude—perched on the very slope by which
Soufrière is approached by climbers who, after
traversing the "high woods," must cut their way
with machetes through fern and shrub. After an
active life, spent partly in Senegal where his children were born and where his wife died of yellow
fever, this son of French sires is content to spend
his declining days at Guadeloupe—land of his
birth. He dwells within sound of the torrent, but
a stone's throw from his son's dwelling. His exuberant Louisiana daughter-in-law—the only
American who lives permanently in Guadeloupe
—in presenting her children to us said she hoped
they were Americans, as all three were born in
the United States. We could not help recalling the
words (told us, laughingly, by Sigrid Undset) of
a Norwegian abbot, uttered under similar circumstances:

318 BEHOLD THE WEST INDIES

"If the cat had kittens in the oven would they be biscuits?"

In the cool purlieus of St. Claude are found the governor's residence, the Military Hospital, and Camp Jacob. It was at St. Claude that, in the year 1802, the colored Colonel Delgrès—cornered by the troops of Richepance—having vowed to "live free or die," dynamited himself and three hundred men ... a hard thought to intrude upon dwellers in the most modern villas of Guadeloupe. Still more tranquil is neighboring Matouba, where may be seen long-haired East Indian agriculturalists, growers of chives on a property bequeathed to them by a former master of the name, for which the locality is called, Papaye.

St. Claude, being at an altitude of over two thousand feet, is famous for its coffee estates: the manor of the Propriété Dain is reached through an inviting allée of cocopalms. Coffee and cacao—mainstays of cultivators before the cyclone of '28—are, in this region above Basse-Terre, variants on the ubiquitous theme of the banana, as, too, at Dolé, in the district of Gourbeyre, connected with St. Claude by the scenic Route de Choisy.

The culture of vanilla at Guadeloupe dates from the year 1860. Tons are shipped yearly overseas. Both the *vanillon* and the so-called Vanilla of Mexico (*Vanilla popona*) have their advocates. The wax-like vines of *Vanilla planifolia,* twined

around the slim trunks of *immortelles,* are a rav-
ishing sight at blossom time. As the preparation
of the *gousses* or beans is a cottage industry, it
was a delight to the nostrils to pass through Gourbeyre in the month of February, when the subtle
fragrance of sun-drying vanilla mingled with
agreeable whiffs from the establishment for the
preparation of chocolate.

Like St. Claude, dominated by the giant Soufrière, the heights of Grand Fond Dolé (from
which one may look down on Dolé's hotel) are
reached in first gear, between banks starred with
tangled thunbergias. Here sheltered coffee plantations vie—in interest though not in color—with
the wind-tattered broadsides of bananas ... key-
note in the color scale of this tropical Erin.

In quite another direction, at indeed the extreme southernmost tip of Guadeloupe, where the
Pointe du Vieux-Fort juts into the Caribbean, the
best coffee is said to be produced, as well as the
most daring fishermen. Beyond Trois-Rivières we
jolted one day over a rarely-frequented stretch
of the old-time Colonial highway to the village of
Vieux-Fort, called the "cradle of French colonization." In 1638, ten years after Esnambuc settled
St. Kitts, two of his lieutenants, Charles de l'Olive
and Duplessis, with five hundred men recruited in
France, took possession of Guadeloupe. The in-
intrepid de l'Olive erected a bastion against the
Indians, driven to Dominica but returning bel-

ligerently in war canoes. Not alone for the fragmentary ruins of Vieux-Fort but for the scenic
wonder of the coast I could recommend the drive,
were the road but wider than a car. I shall not
forget the brink of a cliff overhanging the sea,
our car perched perilously upon the bitter edge;
our chauffeur—tinkering amidst dismembered automobile parts, a fractured exhaust—blowing into
a feed pipe, eyes and nostrils doused with gushing
gasoline; myself, by the roadside, somewhat pride-
ful of my power over sensitive plants, of a sudden
deflated by a noxious douche. My Illustrator remembers more vividly the aftermath of near-as-
phyxiation, a drive in indescribable heat, ourselves
bathed in unrestrained blue fumes from the exhaust, our efforts to keep the door held open, our
turtle heads thrust out for air.

Having seen the fort from which the French
defended themselves against the aborigines, on
our next excursion, we turned our resuscitated
automobile seaward from Trois-Rivières, almost
to the fishing-village of Bord de Mer, to view the
Roches Gravés Précolombiennes, or Carib Stones.

The learned Monsieur Blanche in his brochure
The Caribs: were they Monsters? has proved the
contrary. Columbus, he says, believed to his dying
day that he had discovered a new route to India,
Japan, and China. He was confirmed in this belief by the fact that the Antilles lie in the same
latitude as the Gulf of Bengal. A firm believer in

the tales of Marco Polo, he carried with him letters to the Grand Khan. At Hispaniola he had
been told of the ''monsters,'' eaters of human
flesh, to be found on other islands. This tallied
with the description of those encountered by
Marco Polo.

Warlike and cruel the Caribs undoubtedly were,
says Monsieur Blanche, armed with bows and arrows while their Arawak enemies possessed only
spears, and with the further advantage of means
of transport. Their long canoes were built to carry
eighty braves. It was not unusual, says this
scholar, among South American tribes to eat the
flesh of warrior captives, sacrificed, in consecrated
places, to tribal divinities. It may be safely stated,
however, that the Caribs did not live on human
flesh and that the name of cannibals—by which
they were first called by Columbus—was unjusti-
fied. That the misrepresentation hastened their
near extermination can not be denied. A report by
Juan Ponce de León, confirming (without due evidence) the cannibal tendencies of the tribe, was
the cause of permission granted to Castilians to
enslave the Caribs. This the Spaniards were un-
able to enforce, and the French could only expel
these Indians—known to them as Karukéra—
from Guadeloupe. By the year 1660 a mere six
hundred remained, segregated on the islands of
St. Vincent and Dominica. To term all others bar-
barians, says Monsieur Blanche, makes slavery

plausible ... the treating of men as beasts of burden. The same idea may be found, he goes on to say, as the origin of all wars.

Primitive as were their attempts at stone engraving, the Caribs' choice of a site for their grotto gives proof of artistic perception. Beside running water, in the deep forest, though near the sea, they found boulders inviting their crude tools. Not in musty museums should pre-Columbian relics be seen. In the open, in their natural setting, they become transformed.

The guardian, an aged man, might well have been a Carib descendant. Down a well-shaded path he led us, crossing the uproarious brook by stepping-stones, to the idyllic valley chosen by the Caribs.

"The Cacique," the old man explained, pointing to a rock from which a round face stared inscrutably, "the chief, you see he wears three feathers in his hair." Foremost is the burial grotto—bearing a variety of impish countenances and unintelligible hieroglyphics.

Scrambling to a height, beneath a sheltering bread-fruit tree, the guardian dashed water on the images to bring them into broader relief. We praised the well-swept path—knowing the propensity of the bush to engulf man's traces—to be informed that Cuban visitors were expected. We had then to break the unwelcome news that the coming of the long-anticipated vessel to the Exposition at Pointe-à-Pitre had been postponed, owing to a minor Cuban revolution.

The mangrove swamps of Panama are no more forbidding than their replicas that have discouraged frequent ingress from Guadeloupe proper to the island of Grande-Terre. In the old days the crossing of the Rivière Salée, a salt Strait, was made by a lighter known as the *Gabare*, notorious for its propensity for capsizing in midstream. On October 27, 1940, however, the indefatigable Sorin had the honor of opening the new span by which the National highway crosses the river, uniting the two islands of Guadeloupe. He referred to the bridge as a symbol of the indissoluble union which unites Guadeloupe to France.

Since the dredging of the harbor at Pointe-à-Pitre, the capital, Basse-Terre, with an open roadstead, has lost the greater part of Guadeloupe's commercial trade. Pointe-à-Pitre has been destroyed by fire, earthquakes, hurricanes, little of any worth having survived the hurricane of 1928 —one of the three worst of the thirty-two recorded since 1653.

A local guide-book (with translation for the English-speaking) describes Guadeloupe's chief cities as follows: "Basse-Terre, the capital, silent under its grey antiquity... filled with sightseeings." "The glamourous and cosmopolitan city of Pointe-à-Pitre all crawling and swarming with 35,000 peoples."

Glamourous! Cosmopolitan! Pointe-à-Pitre was not, as we saw it, but crawling and swarming, indeed, as a Chinese town. ("Hongkong," my Illustrator comments.) Especially is this true of its Main Street, Rue Frébault with its metal-shuttered shops and tiers of iron-roofed balconied apartments. In full sunlight its open-air market, where humanity jostles within narrow bounds, is essentially Oriental. European notes were posters announcing Cigarettes Job, Pneus Miche, Galeries Parisiennes, and Bon Marché; while streets bore such metropolitan French names as Rue Raspail, Lamartine, Alsace-Lorraine, Gambetta, Victor Hugo.

With our host, Monsieur Party, we had come from Dolé, on a day's excursion in the invaluable battered Renault, to visit the Exposition de la Mer et de la Fôret, held in a building adjoining the Custom House upon the dock of Pointe-à-Pitre. It was an opportunity to see the town en fête. Guadeloupéennes—wide-eyed *doudous* (sweethearts) rivaling the daughters of Martinique—attired in madras and elegance of amplified Empire costume, crowded about the cages where wild doves, ibis, and long-legged *crabiers* were on view, lizards, green or brown iguanas, raccoons. Within doors were displayed butterflies blue as those of Brazil, moths the size of bats. Here was to be seen modernistic furniture fashioned of native woods. In the section of the Sea were nets and boat models, dried fishes and conchs ingeniously utilized as lighting fixtures, tortoise-shell objets d'art.

The Place de la Victoire—named for a defeat of the English in 1794—was, we thought, the only other location for which to linger in Pointe-à-Pitre. It offers benches beneath the shelter of sandbox trees, centenarians with distorted trunks. Here, during the Terror, stood the guillotine. Twenty-seven Royalists were executed on October 6, 1794, and here an expiatory fountain plays. Although noteworthy ancient buildings are conspicuously absent, and no outstanding modern ones have been erected, there may be seen giving upon this Place the Chamber of Commerce, a cinema, a market, a Club Nautique on Perrinon Quay, with pleasure sloops at anchor, and near-by the cluttered masts of schooners that ply between French islands.

In the Place de la Victoire stands, too, the Monument aux Morts. We were shown photographs of black-skinned throngs, a sprinkling of whites, sun-helmeted, at the ceremonies held here on the occasion of the Tricentenaire of Guadeloupe and Martinique, 1635-1935. Here also, on Armistice Day, the Governor had addressed the veterans of two wars, 1914-1918 and 1939-1940, in the presence of the Mayor and of Admiral Rouyer, Commandant of the training-ship then in port, the cruiser *Jeanne d'Arc.*

Guadeloupe, no less than Jamaica, is noted for

her export of sugar and excellent rum. (The word *rhum* to the creole of African descent to whom the letter "r" is anathema, becomes a less palatable "wo'm.") Of the numerous sugar factories of Guadeloupe the largest is on the island of Grande-Terre. Indeed, the Usine d'Arboussier is one of the most important in the Indies. To it the peasant proprietors, from the small holdings for which Grande-Terre is famous, bring the cane in their own two-wheeled charettes. To my Illustrator our arrival at this usine was a highlight of our stay. Traffic jams, in the region, are caused by a congestion of ox-carts. When we found ourselves at a standstill, there was time to count seventy of these creaking vehicles—each drawn by a pair of humped cattle and guided by a vociferous black owner, cruelly free with long-lashed whip where, in other lands, the touch of a pole would have sufficed.

One unforgettable view we had from Grande-Terre, that from the only perfect lunch-room on that island, the Pergola du Gosier. It is high set above the sandy, shaded beach at the town of Le Gosier, known by its island lighthouse conspicuous on the approach to Pointe-à-Pitre by sea. From a breeze-fanned terrace the mountains of Guadeloupe may be beheld across the blue of Petit Cul-de-Sac bay. A Parisian luncheon, including lobster, was served to us, *pourboire compris,* for the equivalent of fifty cents. Our only criticism in parting from this echo of the Riviera—where a blossoming century plant and an ingratiating Siamese cat detained us—was to regret the lack of bedrooms.

The farewell proved to be the forerunner of a final departure by Pan-American Flying Clipper. On that occasion all our attention centered on the rapidly shrinking white-clad and helmeted figure of Monsieur Party. Ominous black clouds had obliterated the Soufrière and no less ominous dark-skinned masses were to blot out all vision of that stalwart symbolic Frenchman.

les Caraïbes

All days are market days
in Fort·de·France

Pelée

CHAPTER XI

SHADOW ON MARTINIQUE

"ITALIA! O ITALIA!" sang the poet, "thou who hast the fatal gift of beauty." Substitute the word Martinique, in lieu of Italia, and the lines are equally applicable. Like Italy radiant as girl budding into womanhood, producing daughters of contours in loveliness rivaling her own, Martinique is a land to stir the heart's depths. From the tropical abundance of fruit, flower, and verdure, of soft-voiced languorous *filles de couleur,* the imagination leaps, unwittingly, to austere Pelée, its barren slopes seared with ash and lava, its treacherous crater bearing aloft a plume all-too reminiscent of Vesuvius.

The fascination of volcanic sites—apt to lie in lands of deep enchantment—is nowhere better exemplified. Browning wore the word "Italy" grav'd on his heart, Queen Mary her lost

Stark Pelée rises

"Calais"; for how many another nostalgic being
—who knows if not for the Empress Josephine on
her deathbed at Malmaison, if not indeed for him
who called the island Le Pays des Revenants,
Lafcadio Hearn, who shared the same profound
emotion (at least until the time when he embraced
Buddhism)—would the word inscribed be "Martinique."

Flying from Guadeloupe we had skirted Dominica with its razor-back mountains, its cloud-hung
heights, where roads dwindle to trails, and trails,

bleakly from the sea

in turn, are lost in untracked forests. For the first
time our eyes rested on unwholesome Portsmouth,
while next, with happy recognition, we spied the
familiar road to inimitable Sylvania, chary Diablotin, and, anon, Roseau, nestling below Morne
Bruce. With reason have the Caribs chosen the
wilderness of Dominica as a last refuge from the
world. Modern ways do not intrude nor are they
likely to do so in our day. Open roadsteads and
lack of level land for runways prevent the alight-
ing of planes by land or sea.

Awe was our first sensation on the approach to Martinique—for Martinique greets brusquely the new-comer from the north. The stark Pelée rises bleakly from the sea, its ashen-gray heights accentuated by contrast with the level blue fabric of the Caribbean. A slight *fumerole* was visible, lost soon in Pelée's "ever-present belt of trade-wind cloud." Like a petrified dragon the arrested lava stream of 1929 sprawls downward to the water's edge, but, amphibian monster though it seems to be, it can find no solace seaward. Nearer to what was once the Paris of the Indies is the more broken, boulder-strewn track of the unprecedented calamity—that of 1902—when between thirty and forty thousand lives were snuffed out within less time than is taken to tell of it. A chastened furtive remnant of St. Pierre is visible to-day along the shore; but, for the most part, ruins answer the new-comer's stare with vacant imbecility.

Gayer indeed—an understatement, for no place could well be less gay than St. Pierre—is the capital of Martinique, the laughing, astonishingly Mediterranean town of Fort-de-France.

On this St. Valentine's morning our plane swept downward between clouds—seemingly buoyant enough to bear the weight of Raphael's cherubs—a modern silver-toned cupid hovering over the sun-exposed breast of this all-too-susceptible island Daughter of the South; a cupid (a Trojan-horse

cupid) from which bounded passengers each
armed with his taut bow of resolve and arrows of
thought ready to attempt onslaught upon the unsuspecting Fair One, the richly-dowered possessor
of "the fatal gift."...

As our motor launch scudded over the surface
of the rippling bay, as spray almost obliterated
the view, we caught glimpses of the hoary fortress
of St. Louis, the safely anchored ships, the well-
built plaster houses, red-tiled as Marseilles or
Genoa. Our thoughts leaped to a similar approach,
past El Morro, to the inner harbor of Havana—
that singularly Old-World harbor of the New
World. Adding to the European flavor of our
initial impression of Fort-de-France was the quality of the shipping. Battleships of France, men-
of-war drab as though awaiting decisive engagement, the cruiser *Emile Bertin,* the aircraft carrier *Béarn,* the banana-boat *La Guadeloupe,* arrived that very day from France—all simulated
the port of Marseilles. (Cherished memories un-
blurred by our recent visit!)

The Gallic flavor was hardly less pronounced
upon our stepping ashore, only a stone's throw
from the Monument aux Morts in an allée crowded
with attentive *bonnes* and children with hoops,
French of the French; while, isolated in the vast
Savanna, towered the statue of Josephine, Empress of France, Daughter of Martinique.

The cluttered streets and markets, where dark-skinned throngs milled to and fro—all days are market-days in Fort-de-France—the turbaned bearers of fantastic burdens, lent a semblance of the Orient, as did the mosque-like dome of the Bibliothèque Schœlcher and the soaring palms along our route. French, and very modern, was the convent school for girls upon the heights, French the Fort Desaix—the historic Fort Bourbon, that once, for a season, flew the British colors and was dubbed Fort George, and where a gold hoard of a billion dollars, smuggled out of France aboard the *Emile Bertin*, was said to rest. French was the car in which we rode, the tongue spoken by our chauffeur, the look of the coquettish villas along the Route de Didier, and superlatively French the pension at the Lido—on the Anse Colas —to be our headquarters during our sojourn in Martinique.

My Illustrator's freshly-polished French was of no avail in stopping an African-looking crone from receiving upon her cushioned head his ponderous week-end case. That he told her it weighed all of thirty kilos (containing, as it did, books, sketching kit, and kodak films), merely made her bare her gums in a toothless grin, and balance—for bravado—an added piece of luggage before marching erect, between century plants, up the terrace stair.

"Je suis forte," she assured us, on being relieved of her burden, wiping the sweat from her

Brooms!

brow. Yet we had noted that she could not lift the load with her poor withered arms.

Forgotten by us was the crone, the exposed seams of life obtrusive in West Indian towns, when we stepped upon the bougainvillea-entwined balcony of our cliff-side dwelling. Below our terrace lay a vast expanse of scintillating Caribbean. In the offing we spied two patrolling United States battleships, sent, according to the man in the street, "to keep off the Germans." The sails of fishing-boats caught the light.

With effusive gesticulation our buxom hostess threw casements open to the breeze, chattering in French with a luscious southern accent.

"You are from Provence?" we ventured.

"My family came from Marseille," she answered, "but I was born here. Alas! I've never been to France ... and now ... one must not give up hope."

"Martinique," I told her, gazing out of the window and speaking before the fading of a first impression, "is uncannily French. If we were dropped from the skies (indeed that is the way we came!) we should guess we were on the French Riviera. Look at your pensionnaires ... those unmistakably French families headed for the beach, and this group of debonair officers mounting your steps."

"Even the lobsters," my Illustrator was to remark at déjeuner "are not *homards* but *langous-*

tes"—the small-clawed Mediterranean variety used in bouillabaisse.

As in all Latin countries, Sunday in Martinique is a day to rejoice the heart. The bells of the Cathedral called to us, but before entering the church we lingered on the plaza to watch the congregation assemble in its easy-going way.

"Le Bon Dieu is no prudish Protestant," the attitude of the natives seemed to say, "carrying a stop-watch in his hand!"

As mass followed mass there was an incessant coming and going, shifting and shuttling. A large group of men and boys preferred to stand just within the main doorway. Huge as is the Cathedral the *grand'messe* found almost every seat filled with a seemingly devout participant; yet Hearn's doubt came to mind—whether the rich and prosperous Church in Martinique possessed any preponderant authority in ethics or politics, citing race-hatreds and "a Polynesian laxity of morals among the black and colored population." French nuns, in blue robes partially concealed by black cloaks, marshaled uniformed pupils to the balconies. Dark-skinned choir boys, purple-clad acolytes, a verger resplendent in white-plumed hat and heavy broadcloth, gold-braided as in France, several priests—mostly bearded chaplains from French battleships—groups of French officials with their families, chic creoles of pure French descent—all would have held our attention had it not been for our all-absorbing interest in the *matadores*—those creoles of mixed blood to whom the wearing of a local costume is as natural as, on a fête day, to an Arlèsienne.

Of the hundred-odd wearers of costume there was one, we thought, comparable in beauty, despite her café-au-lait complexion, to the exquisite Angèle—the poet-chosen Queen of Arles. The dignity and elegance of this Martiniquaise would have been remarked in any assembly, irrespective of the garments worn; but that they were enhanced by the style inspired by robes of the French Empire can not be gainsaid. The girl's trailing costume was of écru brocade, the skirt tucked knowingly under her left arm during the service. A salmon-colored fichu, likewise of brocade, led the eye to the head of this distingué individual—a head silhouetted, from where I sat, against a gray column. Her coquettish madras, beneath which her hair was brushed, was of carmine-and-canary plaid, as chic, in its traditional way, as a Parisian confection. From her ears dangled fan-shaped golden earrings—their tiny balls dancing at their wearer's least genuflexion. Other girls might take their places, with head-dresses gay as butterflies, yet none eclipsed or even rivaled the bewildering fascination of my first love. Older women, eschewing black, might choose, for instance, chintz trellised with pink roses, kerchiefs of sky-blue silk foulard, but their

madrases were apt to be plaques of yellow, checkered, as with fishnets, of brown. Gold and coral
heirlooms, necklaces, earrings—the quest of
beauty—distracted my mind from thoughts of devotion.

On the Rue Isambert next day we were to search
for antique jewelry but to find only facsimiles of
brooch and earrings at seven hundred francs the
set. As for the madras (imported from India) we
were told by a couple from Avignon, owners of
the shop whose name, Mireille, had attracted us,
it takes a modiste an hour to fold a madras in a
fashion becoming to the face of its wearer. Perhaps the French mode of turbans fitted to order
had its inception not in a Parisian millinery establishment but in Martinique.

At Mon Rêve on the Route de Didier we admired an Ali Baba jar of vari-colored hibiscus,
posed against the house wall of the dining-porch,
an arrangement which would have won a prize at
any flower show—irrespective of visiting humming-birds, which could hardly have been transported! Our hostess, white-clad even to her pearls,
seated in a toile-de-Jouy-covered armchair, was,
we should have guessed, a gracious Parisian
châtelaine, had she not told us that she was born
in Martinique—although, in happier days, a frequent holiday-seeker in France.

"Shall I ever forget," she said to us, when
speaking of the friend we had in common, "the

La Martiniquaise

dogwood at Valley Forge, lovely as the cherry blossoms in Washington.''

"You accept," I answered, "this hibiscus, this bougainvillea as a matter of course ... the tree-ferns at your door."

Across the way was the modernistic white mansion of Captain Pierre Benech, former French naval attaché in Washington and then Chief of Staff at Admiral Robert's Admiralty Headquarters, the soul of hospitality to friends and friends of friends. To be waited upon at dinner by a girl wearing a madras and by a French seaman in uniform was as much of a novelty to us as to hear that the elaborately French repast had been cooked with charcoal, the baking done in a portable oven.

"Two months ago," Madame Benech told us, "you would have found no bread and, naturally, no cake! You are lucky to have come after the arrival of flour from the United States. We were a week without flour or gasoline."

In some quarters the popularity of the United States had risen sky-high, while in others it was muttered, without a grain of foundation, that the American sailors on the battleships ate all the bread! Bread, as much of a staple here as in France, was still in the limelight. We had noticed an American taking a newsreel of women leaving the bakery with wheel-sized baskets of long loaves baked with American flour. Young Scherman, too, en route to Trinidad—next in the limelight—was photographing for *Life,* all unaware that his own life would so soon be jeopardized aboard the torpedoed steamer *Zamzam.*

Whenever we motored into Fort-de-France we were sure to pause beside the monumental Empress Josephine, work of the sculptor Vital Dubray, erected by the inhabitants of the town in the reign of Josephine's grandson, Napoleon III. On a pedestal of the best classical tradition, surrounded by a circle of royal palms, the exquisitely feminine Empress stands in her robes of State, her left hand resting on a medallion of Napoleon but her eyes seeking her birthplace at Trois Islets across the bay.

"Only the bewitchment of her lives," the author of *Two Years in the French West Indies* wrote of Josephine.

Not finding a suitable boat, we were to make a detour, by way of Lamentin and Ducos, to reach Trois Islets and, afterward, to return by way of Diament with its famous Rock. It was before reaching Lamentin that we were to look down on the red roofs of aviators' barracks and see the marooned American-built planes, two hundred strong, no longer rusting under cover but glittering boldly in the sun.

As well as at the tomb of Josephine's mother the authorities of the village church at Trois Islets have erected a tablet, commemorating the christ-

ening of its parishioner, later Empress of the
French:

ICI LE 27 JUILLET 1763

A ÉTÉ BAPTISÉE

MARIE-ROSE JOSÉPHINE

TASCHER DE LA PAGERIE

COURONNÉE

IMPÉRATRICE DES FRANÇAIS

EN 1804

The baptismal certificate may be seen in the
humble musée, around the corner, possessing massive mahogany antiques "of the period" and one
touching item, the narrow, slender-post, girlhood
bed of Josephine.

Encouraged by the quaint Old Mam'selle in
charge of the Museum (garbed, I verily believe,
in a biretta and soutane discarded by Monsieur le
Curé!) we pushed on a mile or so to a rough rutted
lane, not known before to our chauffeur, leading
to the shut-in valley with ruins of the birthplace.
Few stones of it withstood the hurricane of 1767
that ruined its owner, the planter Lieutenant Joseph Tascher de la Pagerie, but somewhat more
of the *sucrerie* stands, the mill where the family
dwelt after the destruction of the house. The only
sign of life was a grazing pony. A tangle of cacao
and mangoes has usurped the former haunt of human beings, a dank thicket from which, at dusk,
one could well imagine might emerge the sinister
slithering uncoilings of the nocturnal fer-de-lance.

The Empress
JOSEPHINE

For in Martinique not even the inroads of the vicious mongoose have been able to destroy this most dreaded of serpents, this inflictor of the "Death in the Woods."

Although Josephine de la Pagerie was destined

to leave Martinique in her sixteenth year to marry the son of the Marquis de Beauharnais, a former governor of the island, at the age of twenty-five she was to desert her husband and to spend two years in Martinique; after which she returned to Beauharnais to remain at his side until 1794, when he was executed during the Terror. It is recorded that at a time after the Battle of the Accajou at Martinique—when prisoners fraternized with their jailers, and, temporarily, the forts of Bourbon and St. Louis flew the tricolor and bombarded the capital, then known as Fort Royal—that, without time for a last farewell to her mother, Josephine de Beauharnais and her daughter Hortense boarded the *Sensible* bound for France. How little could the young woman have foreseen the blazing light of publicity that would fall upon her, the deepening shadow. At thirty-six she was to become the wife of the thirty-year-old Napoleon. Fascinating, clever, tactful, tender, warm-hearted she has been called; by some, shallow and frivolous ... her influence was ever for peace and moderation. It was Napoleon who said of her: "She has no more sense of resentment than a pigeon."

Most of the "incommodities" found at Martinique in the year 1640 by the Jesuit father Jacques Bouton (whose record was reprinted at the time of the Tricentenaire of Martinique and Guadeloupe in 1935) no longer obtain to-day. It was to be expected that the new settler should

suffer fever four or five times, that he should live
in dread of the manchineel-poisoned arrows of
the Caribs (loath to relinquish the island called
by them Mantinino) and of the menace of foreign
fleets, not to mention the venomous serpents in-
festing the forests. In order to live long in the
colony, Père Bouton advised a formula not inap-
plicable elsewhere: hard work, the avoidance of
sleep by day and above all of melancholy. No
longer is smallpox the dread destroyer described
by Hearn. The major ''incommodity'' of Martinique, an incommodity indeed so great that, at
one time, the suggestion was made that the French
evacuate the island, may be summed up in the one
word ''Pelée.''

''La Montagne,'' itself the climax of a stay in
Martinique, may be reached, overland, by one of
the most nearly flawless roads in the Indies. A
seventeenth-century map of the island in the National Archives gives the dignity of mountain to
it alone, Vauclin as well as Carbet being desig-
nated as *pitons,* while the lesser hills, which form
a backbone between volcanic heights, are known
locally as *mornes.* It is along the highway to
Pelée (a stretch of thirty-eight kilometers) that
passengers, discharged at St. Pierre by such boats
as the *Georgic* and, twice, by the *Normandie,* were
met by taxicabs from the capital and motored,
wide-eyed with wonder, to overtake their ship at
Fort-de-France. What bananas are to the culti-

Sugar

vated hills of Guadeloupe and Jamaica, the battalions of tree-ferns are to the mountainous interior of Martinique. Armies of them invade the
hills and camp upon the verge of the abyss, prod-
igally prolific, fantastic beyond wildest dream.
There is no parallel to them—seen thus across the
ravine, from the cool watershed to which we
mount, with the background of the three Pitons
de Carbet from which torrents tumultuously de-
scend; or again, glorifying the foothills backed
by the formidable Pelée.

From St. Pierre the traveler should return to
Fort-de-France by the Atlantic Coast road, in order to gain an impression of its rugged cliffs and
winsome *anses* or coves: only the port of la Trinité

is dignified with the name of *havrę* or harbor. The towns, in comparison with those of Guadeloupe, are prosperous, elusively French; especially is this true of Marigot, substantially built of buff plaster with conspicuous stone, festooned nets and sails drying on sea-walls . . . above which the town ever-so-picturesquely mounts. There is a look of well-being upon the faces of workers returning from the sugar-fields. It is worthy of remark that the natives of Martinique are friendly to the stranger. They never are beggars nor are they garbed in the tatters remarked in other islands: although the author of *Mon Pays Martinique* would have us believe that "scandalous unmerited fortunes" have been amassed and that there are "abysses of misery, of suffering and servitude." The social conscience, after long slumber, stirs, as in the days before the liberation of slaves; and, in this respect, the voice of Martinique is but a part of a world chorus. Among the better-class creoles each Martiniquais has ambitions to build himself a permanent home, whereas a Guadeloupéen is more apt to spend his hard-won funds in France and return to his island penniless.

Sugar and rum are the prosperous islanders' chief source of revenue as once they were in Jamaica. Lafcadio Hearn tells of the peril of the fer-de-lance at time of the sugar-cutting in Martinique. "The nearer the cutlassers approach the end of their task," he writes, "the greater the danger: for the reptiles, retreating before them to the last clump of cane, become massed there. ... Regularly as the ripening-time, Death gathers his toll of human lives from among the workers.''

Around Lorrain and again at Ste. Marie, on the Atlantic coast drive, trains on the narrow-gage railway (leaving the workers to trudge afoot after the fashion of the Indies), engines puffing like grampuses, lurch by with ludicrously top-heavy loads of sugar-cane.

It is thought that Columbus first saw the island now known as Martinique in 1493, and that, on his fourth voyage, he landed on its shore, June 15, 1502. Carib tradition tells that this landing took place at the *parages* du Carbet and that the white man remained for three days. Not until September 1, 1635, did the adventurous Pierre d'Esnambuc (coming from St. Kitts) disembark his eighty colonists. Under the governorship of his nephew Du Parquet, the island was to become among the most prosperous of the Antilles, a reputation it was to regain when stimulated to new endeavors by that ardent, red-blooded Dominican, Père Labat. The first settlement was at Prêcheur, a little to the north of St. Pierre, beneath the shadow of Mount Pelée.

How much of one's own reaction to the ruined St. Pierre, dominated by its evil genie—the djinn awakened in unfathomable depths of Pelée's being by the rubbing of some subterranean magic lamp—how much is actually due to what is presented to the eye, how much is the result of reading of the heart-rending tales dramatically told by eye-witnesses of the mountain's wrath—Kennan, Heilprin, Perret? Aside from the walk to the Grande Coulée and the lava-flow of 1902, where feet sink shoe-deep in volcanic dust, where pumice-like lumps of stone invite the collector, where carbonized rocks have been thrown or carried upon the lava stream, the most rewarding hour may be spent within the Musée Volcanologique on the Grand' Rue, in what was once the center of the town. On this slight eminence dominating the roadstead, a spreading mango stood, and here Lafcadio Hearn was wont to seek the shade, while engaged in writing his *Two Years in the French West Indies*—a book of as rare quality as the author's better known works on Japan.

Martinique has been variously called the "Pearl of the West Indies," the "Queen of the Caribbees," and, by the creoles the "Pays des Revenants." ... Who, once having seen Martinique, would not return? In my own acquaintance I know of but one exception to this rule. To the imaginative natives it seems that even the souls of the dead return; that Père Labat—in life forbidden to go back to the colony—bearing a flickering lantern, haunts the heights of Morne Rouge.

In order to form some idea of the magnitude of the cataclysm we tried to picture to ourselves, as we poked among the ruins, the St. Pierre of happier days. The Cathedral, not utterly destroyed, has been restored. Of the opera house built to accommodate four thousand not a stone remains; nor of those residences, so debonair as to green jalousies and Parisian dormers, along the shaded boulevard bordering the sea . . . the boulevard that had been the setting of some of the gayest fêtes ever held in the Indies.

Was it, perhaps, because the only other recorded activity of Pelée, in 1851, had subsided harmlessly, that the people, terrified by the smoke and fall of ashes on April 2, 1902, the earth-tremors at the month's end, the eruption of May 2nd and 3rd, could actually have been planning an excursion to the new crater on the Sunday before the fateful May 8th? It has been surmised that the news of the activity of la Soufrière at St. Vincent lulled St. Pierre to a false sense of security. Among seafarers in the harbor only the captain of the Italian barque *Orolina,* familiar with Vesuvius, recognized the symptoms of an eruption and refused to tarry, sailing with only half a cargo and without clearance papers. Of all the varied shipping along the shore only the *Roddam* escaped, crawling to St. Lucia with tons of ash upon her decks, her crew for the most part dead or dying.

Fugitives, it is true, had left the gayest city of the Indies on the eve of the disaster, to find refuge

St.Pierre beneath

the shadow of Pelée

in the capital, Fort-de-France, turning a deaf ear to scathing sarcasm of local journalists apropos of their departure. The Governor and his wife, the British and American consuls with their families remained in the ill-fated metropolis. The Receveur des Poste at Fort-de-France, telephoning to his colleague at St. Pierre, was the first to report an electric shock and the sound of a terrific explosion. The disaster has been described as "a flaming whirlwind," "a red-hot hurricane," directed horizontally toward the heart of the doomed city. In less than three minutes the population of St. Pierre, estimated at over thirty thousand, had perished with the exception of one solitary prisoner, Auguste Ciparis, all-but-forgotten, in the partial shelter of a cell.

On May 14th, George Kennan, an intrepid journalist, sailed from New York to the scene of disaster and interviewed the survivor in Father Mary's lazaret at Morne Rouge. Père Mary himself did not escape the "tornadic blast" which— in the course of one minute on August 30th of the same year—was to destroy by heat and fire his village, taking the lives of 1,200 of his parishioners.

In the words of Professor Angelo Heilprin: "There can be no question that all the havoc that had been wrought on this fatal August 30th was the result of one explosive blast . . . or of a series of such blasts following rapidly upon one another.

It is singular that we, who were passing the evening at the absolute foot of the volcano, much closer to it than some points that had been destroyed, and remarking upon the magnificence of the electric display, absolutely above us, should barely, if at all, have noted the detonations which preceded, accompanied, or followed the explosions.''

Like Professor Heilprin, geologist of the Academy of Natural Sciences of Philadelphia and author of a study on the catastrophies of 1902, the American volcanologist Frank A. Perret has risked life and limb to study Mount Pelée. His book on *The Eruption of Mt. Pelée 1929-1932* deals with the three-year activities which filled the Rivière Blanche Valley with volcanic detritus and formed the ash deltas of the Grande Coulée. Both scientists have waxed poetic in the depiction of what Heilprin describes as ''mushroom clouds,'' while Perret speaks no less lovingly of ''non-luminous ash clouds of cauliflower form'' and of the alternating non-explosive phase where lava is active in dome and spine building: but above all he dwells upon the explosive *nuées ardentes,* ''fiercely active and supremely swift avalanches.''

Writing of the lava discharge of the Peléan type, Professor Perret states that the ''mass of discrete particles separated by vapor films 'flows' down any slope with incredible speed because it is frictionless; the extreme manifestation of power in explosive action.''

In the realm of Science a Perret manifests anew, by his unflinching devotion, that the spell of irresistible Martinique remains unbroken.

Barbados : Isle of Sugar

Barbados

CHAPTER XII

BARBADOS, ISLE OF SUGAR

BARBADOS, "Gem of the Caribbean"; Barbados, "Sanatorium of the West Indies"; Barbados, "the tight little, right little island"; Barbados, "The Happy Island"; Barbados, "Little England"; these are the terms in which its admirers depict the Isle of Sugar and Planter's Punch.

To my mind Barbados is by no means the "Gem of the Caribbean," a title contested, among the British West Indies, by Dominica, but won, in my judgment, by Trinidad.

The forefathers of the planters would have been astonished to hear Barbados claimed to be the "Sanatorium of the West Indies." In their time yellow fever raged and was, according to Aspinall, "attributed to the sickly climate instead of to the stegomyia mosquito and new rum." Nowadays we shall not contest the claim. The sea air freshened by the "trades" of Barbados is of the purest, as is her bountiful supply of water underground; her tropical climate is exemplary. Indeed the island is noted, among West Indians and South Americans, as a health resort.

Perhaps Dibdin would have said Barbados fulfilled the qualifications of "The Snug Little Island" of his song. I know not what a "tight little island" may be, but I could not say that Barbados merits the appellation of a "right little island." The fabulous wealth of the early planters was created by slave labor; the freeing of the slaves was followed by no slackening in pace because, in so thickly settled a colony (over a thousand inhabitants to the square mile), unemployment would have meant starvation to the workers. (It is said to-day that only China is more densely populated than Barbados, where about 96 per cent of the land is under cultivation, but all of it in the possession of plantation owners, in contrast to Grenada, where the natives may acquire plots of ground, or other islands, where workers have the use of Crown lands.) To-day, despite the excessive insularity of Barbadians—both black and white—prosperity fluctuates with the price of sugar . . . the one outstanding crop. When Napoleon introduced the idea of beet sugar for France, he struck a deliberate blow at Britain, the consequences of which were felt at Barbados—the British Colony where cane had been first intro-

duced. Foreign bounties have added to the planters' problem . . . in 1902 the sugar industry on
the island seemed tottering to a fall. "Tight little,
right little". . . one scans the record of the Negro
rebellion of 1861, of the Pope Hennessy riots; one
remembers that, although the island has an elected
House of Assembly, the Colonial Office in London
appoints officials. Save for Newfoundland, Barbados is Great Britain's oldest colony.

"The Happy Island," well, owing to the health
and disposition of its people, the title, paradoxically, does not, for the moment, seem too much
amiss. Moreover, the Mother Country has of late
years shown a disposition (unknown in Froude's
day) to put her hand in her pocket to protect the
welfare of her colonists.

Barbados, "Little England," the designation
most often heard, sounded absurd to me before I
made the place's acquaintance. " 'England,' " I
thought. "Impossible!—a flat tropical island, with
140,000 of the 160,000 inhabitants black men—
absurd, preposterous!" However, in striking
contrast to the other islands, one feels this
"Englishness" almost as soon as one steps
ashore. Although the name, Los Barbados, was
given by the island's unknown Portuguese discoverers, some say the word is derived from the
"bearded" banyans at that time plentiful upon
the shores. Barbados was first claimed by Sir
Oliver Leigh of Kent in 1605, aboard the *Olive*

Blossome headed for the Spanish Main. "Finding no opposition," Kent took possession in the name of King James I. Permanent settlers, arriving twenty years later in the *William and John,* discovered the tree on which their fellow-countrymen had carved "James K of E and of this island."

Barbados is the one Caribbean island wholly English throughout its career. Since the English came into possession it has never been invaded. It was originally divided into six parishes, and colonists were obliged to "conform to the government and discipline of the Church of England." Nowadays the map shows the island partitioned, quaintly, into eleven "parishes," whose sons and daughters are, for the most part, professing Anglicans. The language spoken is not only ostensibly but actually English. Astonishingly, therefore, the title "Little England" is, in consideration of these facts, not far-fetched.

By whatever name we choose to call the colony, we shall, in all probability not agree with Nelson, who, writing from Barbados, but longing to be in Nevis with Fanny Nisbet, headed his love-letters, "Barbarous Island." Lord Nelson has been forgiven this youthful lapse owing to the fact that, when in 1805 the united fleets of France and Spain were reported off St. Lucia—to the terror of all British West Indians, the Admiral, aboard the flagship *Victory* and at the head of the British fleet, came on the morning of June 4th to Barbados, entering Carlisle Bay. By the fearless pursuit of the enemy fleets to Caribbean waters Nelson had, in the eyes of the natives, become the savior of Barbados. News of the chase of the French and Spanish squadrons to Europe, the victory at Trafalgar on October 21st and the death of Nelson reached Barbados simultaneously. The second statue (the first being in Montreal) erected to Nelson stands—it must be admitted without impressiveness, artistry, or even commanding dignity—upon the capital of Bridgetown's Trafalgar Square.

Our debarkation at the capital was by means of launch. The usual native boats thronged about the gangway, their black oarsmen diving for pennies. More powerful in physique than those of other islands, grinning as affably as Chinese coolies, they claimed attention with unprecedented courtesy. The Barbadian Negro is noted for industry and reliability, some assert, because his ancestors came not from the Slave Coast but from Sierra Leone. To Americans, especially to those from south of Mason and Dixon's Line, he seems no stranger.

White-coated and helmeted black police had the hordes upon the docks well in control. By comparison with the capitals of the lesser islands, Bridgetown recalled—not London, indeed—but a provincial town of England. Carlisle Bay, the island's only attempt at a harbor, was alive with shipping. In the ceaseless trade wind steamers fluttered many flags. Lighters were transferring Canadian lumber and codfish ashore or filling Canadian holds with "fancy" molasses to sweeten the fare of Nova Scotians.

White-frocked mammies, whose beaming countenances were offset by snowy turbans, displayed crude pottery jugs upon the docks of the careenage, where schooners mostly flying the British colors rode at anchor within a stone's throw of Nelson's statue.

"Spiders"—hogsheads on two wheels hauled by natives—ambled spider-wise along the quays. Donkey-carts piled with cane or produce added to the general clatter. Not of "sugar and spice and everything nice" are moneyed Barbadians made, but of sugar, molasses, and rum . . . two products and a by-product of the cane. Barbadians will tell you that their rum is the best on the world market.

Barbados is approximately the size of the Isle of Wight. It is always with England that Barbados is compared.

Our first excursion was to Hackleton's Cliff, a dozen miles from Bridgetown, on the Windward Shore. The monotony of the ride was of the very essence of Barbados. Fields on fields of cane, punctuated with mills or planters' estates screened by mahogany groves, formed the pat-

Mills punctuate the Barbados' fields

tern of the island's plan. White dust swirled along the straight coral road ahead of our speeding car, like spume blown shoreward from the ocean of undulating cane.

Cutters were at work in the seemingly unbounded fields. Powerfully built they were, despite their African origin sweating beneath the blazing sun, forcefully wielding cane bills—broader and shorter implements than machetes. This is man's work, as is, also, standing upon a loading wagon and receiving burdens from the women who gather the cut canes. A female "boss" stood aloof, supervising the women workers. Despite its stored sweet juices the ripe crop looked moistureless, save for the topmost tufts. These are useful for feeding cattle and are hauled to their destination by donkey-carts, dwarfed, like their pedestrian drivers, by the height of the cañon walls of uncut cane.

Although long-winged mills of substantial masonry were passed, we noted that Barbadians are transferring allegiance to the central manufacture with power supplied by steam. We lingered at the greatest sugar factory, whose indoor machinery seemed eagerly to be awaiting fodder. Mammoth cranes were already at work to feed the insatiable maw. Six-mule teams rushed, regardless of bystanders, to unload their cargoes. Oxen, of zebu extraction, six to a cart, strained at their yokes. The acrid smell of the sweet juice we found repellent, but not so the savory odor of boiling molasses.

Arrived at Hackleton's Cliff we drew long breaths of dust-free air. From a height, a sheer thousand feet above the plain, we looked down upon the faraway beach and vast tempestuous Atlantic—a striking revelation to eyes long accustomed to the blue waters of the more circumspect Caribbean.

The region is known as "Scotland" from a fancied resemblance of its hills to the only ones worthy of the name at Barbados. On this coast-line nestles the town of Bethsheba, famed, as is Speightstown on the west coast, for its fleet of smacks used in the capture of flying-fish. On these wild beaches Barbadians gather sea-urchins. In this region, too, dwells a colony of "Redlegs"— the forlorn descendants of Royalist Scotchmen sent by Cromwell as slaves to an island whose settlers were themselves Royalists. Scant welcome was afforded the new-comers from the established settlers of the vintage of 1605, at what is to-day Holetown; or yet from those of 1628, founders of Bridgetown, who had emigrated under the protection of the Earl of Carlisle, to whom Charles I had granted twenty-two islands with more generosity than power to bestow clear titles.

Only one of the Redlegs has attained anything like fame—and that in the dubious category of a pirate. The career was not of Redleg's choosing

On wild beaches Barbadians

but was forced upon him after this fashion. Escaping from his harsh masters he took a desperate chance, as a boy, in swimming to what he mistook for a Dutch ship in Carlisle Bay. The vessel proved to be a pirate craft, whose captain Redleg was in due time to become, after seizing command by the traditional methods.

Near Hackleton's Cliff, picturesquely situated on a bluff, stands one of the best known churches in the West Indies—St. John's, in the "parish" of the name. The original building was constructed in 1676, but destroyed by hurricane in 1831. The present edifice, with its square tower and Gothic arches, is essentially similar to those erected in England a hundred years ago. Outstandingly different, however, is the variety of

gather sea-urchins ✳ ✳

woods decorating the interior, as well as the
character of the trees growing within the graveyard. The church's ceiling is of pitch pine, brown
with age, the pews of white cedar. The elaborate
pulpit was carved by a local craftsman a hundred
years ago from native woods—pine, mahogany,
ebony, and locust—while its massive frieze of
grape vines is of the notorious manchineel. An immense sandbox tree guards the entrance to the
church while seaward, with outstretched arms, as
though in protection of the cherished graves,
gnarled veterans cluster; scarlet-clad cordia and
flamboyant; white-plumed ebony, frangi-pani, battered and twisted; casuarina, whistling shrilly. A
worthy bodyguard they form to a scion of emperors interred in one of the ancient tombs:

HERE LYETH YE BODY OF
FERDINANDO PALEOLOGUS
DESCENDED FROM YE IMPERIAL LYNE
OF YE LAST CHRISTIAN
EMPERORS OF GREECE
CHURCHWARDEN OF THIS PARISH
1655 - 1656
VESTRYMAN, TWENTYE YEARS
DIED OCTOBER 3, 1678

"Barbados lies out of the track of hurricanes" is a sweeping statement to be printed even by the most ardent promoters in the face of the destruction of the original St. John's and the historic hurricane of 1898 when eleven thousand habitations were destroyed and many lives were lost. The assertion that Barbados has had no earthquakes and no volcanoes seems to be safer ground.

The most awful episode in the history of the colony was in the year 1812, the famous day on which the sun did not rise. Visitors are at first mystified by references to this phenomenon. The livelong day a leaden-gray ash, more blinding than snow, sifted over land and sea. The natives, fearing doomsday, waxed hysterical until reassured by the normal revelation of the setting sun. This was not to be the last occasion that the eruption of Soufrière, on the island of St. Vincent, ninety-five miles to windward, fertilized Barbados.

Substantial as the Grand St. Bernard, the Grande Chartreuse, or some other Old-World monastery—in imagination transporting the visitor overseas—is the two-hundred-year-old building, an inn for sixty years, known as the Crane Hotel. The name of the promontory, of which the building seems an integral part, is taken from the fact that once a cove sheltered steamers and, so we were told, "a crane was used for hoisting goods." Nowadays there is no creaking crane to distract the traveler's attention from the pounding of the surf upon the wind-blown coral shore, for the hostelry—in contrast to those at Bridgetown, thirteen miles away—stands upon the exposed southeastern coast, with naught to windward save the tumultuous Atlantic. Luncheon specialties are Crane chub and rum omelette; and, if the visitor has no time for a longer stay, he must not be content unless he has explored the ground-floor rooms, with massive four-post bedsteads, overlooking as from a deck the expanse of water; the ancient sunken tubs with showers; the courtyard where potted plants flower beneath luxuriant shade, and where life is lived in the open with an informality less English than Provençal.

In comparison with the glories of Crane's the stuffy quarters of the tawdry Aquatic Club at Bridgetown pale to insignificance, though the management may endeavor to tempt the epicure with menus of eddoe soup (deliciously like artichoke) and flying-fish. The frying of the captivating creatures, in life iridescent as rainbows and

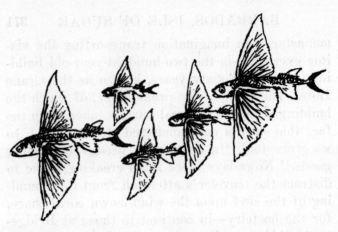

likewise arching the waves, I resented as much as the serving, in Italy, of larks and nightingales.

Opposite the club stands a rather unprepossessing house where the youthful officer George Washington (he was nineteen at the time) resided in 1751 to 1752 with his older brother Major Lawrence, a sufferer from tuberculosis. The pair were the guests of the commandant of Fort James and were lavishly entertained upon arrival until, after a fortnight, George developed smallpox: he bore the marks to his grave. The experience may have given him a distaste for travel. The visit becomes significant from the fact that this was the only occasion on which the Father of his Country ventured beyond the land of his birth.

Barbados has been called the Hongkong of the West Indies because of its being the central port from which goods find their way to England, Canada, and the United States. In proportion to

the importance of its shipping, Bridgetown is a
relatively unimpressive capital, the explanation
being that the plantation owners dwell on their
estates and the transient white population prefers
hotels on the beaches, especially at the fashionable suburb of Hastings. Even Government House
stands somewhat aloof from the town proper, although the public buildings are near the docks.
There is an appalling dissimilarity between the
residences of the wealthy, set in gardens at Belle-
ville, and the shanties of the Negroes.

Barbadian hospitality is proverbial. My Illustrator and I had read of Froude's welcome at Farley Hill in "St. Peter's"; of the Georgian dignity
of the Principal's Lodge at Codrington College
(the Oxford of the Indies) former residence of Sir
Christopher Codrington, its founder; but our own
memorable experience was at Canefield, in the
"parish" of St. Thomas.

Before leaving Bridgetown, on this occasion,
we were to pass innumerable examples of the un-
painted, flimsy quarters of the natives, erected
largely with boards imported from Vancouver.

"Barbados" shutters protected the inmates
from the glare of the setting sun—a purpose
served by the mahogany groves on the estates.
Callender, the driver of our car, enlightened us as
to the significance of certain domiciles that appeared to have been carved in twain, with only
one half remaining.

"Those," said he, "are 'divorce houses.' "

We had already been told of this practical arrangement by which the natives, as a rule "married" but not "parsoned," contrive to settle the difficulty of a broken home. The complainant "walks away" with his half of the hut, while the defendant remains on the premises.

Monotony of scene was characteristic of the drive between sugar plantations, some brown with refuse from stripped canes—no atom wasted, but used for bedding cattle and later returned as fertilizer to the fields. Many estate houses are sheltered by walls enclosing oases of trees, flowers, and vines, amid deserts of dry cane. Canefield has no need of such protection, standing high enough above the plain for views of the sea in two directions, and for a sight, from the guest room, of ships in the distant harbor of Bridgetown.

It is an impressive Georgian house, built over a hundred years ago, with galleries on every side, panels alternating with windows. Upon these panels, wall paper, rich in tone, represents Boston in early days, Niagara, West Point, the Natural Bridge and so on, brought, oddly, from a former Mary Elizabeth Tea Room on Fifth Avenue—for the present owner of Canefield happens to be an American, the mother of the founder of the business, the said Mary Elizabeth. This lady, daughter of a judge in Syracuse, early widowed, at one time in her career penniless, has lived valiantly, undisturbed by her poverty or riches. On Sundays there is open house, for here friends from the island and newly-arrived ships congregate.

Our distinguished hostess—clad in soft gray even to low-heeled suede slippers, with earrings of dangling jade—knowing our interest, showed us her many rooms, dwelling on ancient balustrades, a mahogany sideboard constructed to display pewter, and chairs in the style of Chippendale— fashioned in her own basement by a local mechanic. Rarely had we seen so many hurricane shades, and we remarked the thickness of the walls and the ponderous folding shutters.

"It is the custom to bar the shutters nightly," said our hostess, showing how massive bars slide into grooved walls, "though hurricanes come once in a hundred years!"

Miss Fannie, a daughter of the house, had painted the design of an Aubusson rug on the drawing-room floor, enhancing the elegance of this salon with its studied arrangement of scarlet anthurium upon the grand piano. In this congenial atmosphere we lingered over lime squash and planter's punch.

Especially I remember the dragon-carved chests at Canefield, formerly acquired in China, exhaling an odor of camphor-wood that pervaded the second floor; and the view, framed by a certain window, through the branches of an orchid-laden almond, to the court below where against a salmon wall a white goat stood, checkered in sunlight.

(Canefield, we found on our latest visit, has changed owners. Compared with the Great Houses even the hotels at Hastings—preferred by Americans and English to Bridgetown—suffer. The Marine, one of the most noted hotels in the British West Indies, now shares honors with the Ocean View and the Royal-on-Sea. During our recent stay we were shown, at Holetown where it had been constructed, a replica of the *Santa Maria*. "Christopher Columbus" had recently been filmed. At time of "location shooting," oddly attired "sailors" landing at Bridgetown were asked when and where shipwrecked!)

From Hastings Rocks, an enclosure to which entrance was had on payment of a penny, we watched the sun set beyond the lithesome pines to the decorous accompaniment of miniature breakers. Invigorating salt air blew upon us, a whiff of seaweed. Tanned British children played at our feet, under the surveillance of stiffly-starched and white-capped nurses. "Barbados," we remembered having read, "is a nice island for nice people."

An echo of our Barbados visit came on the eve of our steamer's arrival at Trinidad. I had been seated at table, beside the Captain. A Barbadian occupied the chair to my husband's left. This benign gentleman, whose gold-rimmed spectacles hung from one ear, dangling below his chin as he ate, startled us, on introduction, by remarking that he had given orders to have our plane met on our return to Barbados from Trinidad. This had been planned to give us advice as to a hotel —his own, the Marine, being as we knew temporarily unavailable. So it is in the Indies, every one knows everything; the very walls, as in India, listen to the white man's doings.

It was at dinner aboard that the Captain told this anecdote:

"In the World War," said he, "the story goes that the Barbados government, seeking to reassure the British (and with never a doubt of its own importance) sent the following despatch to the home government: 'Barbados is behind you.' This message, according to Trinidad's version of the tale (you remember the relative sizes of the islands), was intercepted by the Kaiser, who sent the following cable to Barbados, 'Join us and we give you Trinidad as a colony!'"

Bamboo and Zebu

Marine Square: Port of Spain

CHAPTER XIII

TRINIDAD, A TERRESTRIAL PARADISE

On the thirtieth of May, 1498, Columbus, the intrepid, set forth from the mouth of the Guadalquivir to seek again the shorter way to India. Three of the six vessels of his fleet he despatched to Española, while the remaining three were swept by a gale southward as far as the equator. Deserted by the wind, with water running low and vessels leaking, the mariner vowed that if his life and that of his crew were spared, to name the first land sighted for the Holy Trinity. On the thirty-first day of July, through a tropical haze, three peaks rose on the horizon . . . a seeming omen. La Trinidád, Columbus therewith called the isle that later he was to describe as "a terrestrial paradise."

"Land ho!" my Illustrator shouted before the

dawn, as in waning darkness our steamer churned its way toward the far-famed Bocas. It was Columbus, we remembered, who had named the northern and southern channels of the Gulf of Paria, separating Trinidad from Venezuela. He had approached, reversing our direction, through the Serpent's Mouth and departed by the Boca Grande, one of the mouths of the Dragon. In the glow of dawn the brilliant lighthouse on Chacachacare—the lepers' island—warned of danger, a stark finger pointing heavenward as though to symbolize the only hope of the isle's inhabitants. In the east a shadowy moon was borne in the arms of a crescent, its brightness echoed by the morning star.

How little did we realize, as we said farewell to our ship, that, for better or for worse, the lure of this tropical Eden was to take such a hold upon us that in time to come—whether we lived on our farmlands or wandered far afield upon the American continent or in frequent thought to France, our first love, or to England, our ancestral home, to Finland and its Scandinavian sisters, to the Orient, beloved and long unseen—an unconquerable nostalgia would tug at our heartstrings, making eventual return to Trinidad obligatory.

Our first day ashore was not spent at Port of Spain but in motoring sixty or more miles southward to visit the Pitch Lake. This pilgrimage to La Brea—with the glimpses obtained en route of

St. Joseph, Curepe, Pointe à Pitre of oil-well fame, and San Fernando, not to mention the Caroni Plain—is essential to the better understanding of the chief city of Trinidad, Port of Spain.

Nine o'clock found us upon our way. Not since a visit to the Orient had we seen Hindus, happily wearing the garments of their ancestral land, dwelling appropriately beneath banyan, palm, or mango, tending extraordinarily East Indian zebus. It was startling to be told that a third of the population of the island is formed by descendants of those Hindus and Mohammedans transported to Trinidad between the years 1845 and 1917 to provide laborers after the freeing of African slaves. The East Indians, introduced on the indenture system, were permitted, after ten years on the land, to return to the country of their birth or to receive a plot of ground. Coming originally from the caste of agriculturalists, these petty farmers often chose to remain; and even those who returned to the motherland of India were frequently moved to come again to Trinidad. Starvation does not stalk on highways laid with inimitable La Brea pitch.

Passing through St. Joseph, we paused at the tracks at Curepe, noting that the sign "Beware the Moving Gates" was repeated in Hindustani. Houses, superior to those in which, in other villages, the Negroes dwell—built of adobe and heavily thatched with palm, walls scrawled with

Along the North Coast Road ‡ ‡ ‡ Maraval Valley

crude depictions of Siva, Rama, Hanuman—
nestled beneath tropical shade; Hindus, as in India, squatted tirelessly upon their heels, while
mothers, clinking with bangles, as in India, carried bare babies upon the hip. A fakir, begging
bowl in hand, passed, impervious to our glance. We
paused at a glaring white-walled temple decorated
after the manner of India. A veritable Gandhi, in
garments dripping from early morning ablutions,
offered us a spray of allamanda, bidding us enter.
A much-bearded priest was sing-songing de-
votions—the sound of his intonations transporting us in time and space to unforgotten mornings
along the crowded ghats at far Benares where,
from generation to generation, pilgrims bathe in
the holy waters of the Ganges.

San Fernando, against its hill, the second city
of Trinidad, the center for the southern, oil-producing area of the island, swarmed with Hindus.
Chinese restaurants abounded. Natives of all
shades of color jostled along the dusty winding
thoroughfares where the white man was conspicuously less in evidence than at Port of Spain.
Trucks (known locally as lorries) lunged perilously near, terrifying me by their British habit
of bearing to the left. On the open road these
emissaries of the oil companies and Pitch Lake
speed unremittingly.

Our car clattered past a gleaming mosque, past
tawdry shops catching the eye with cheap and

over-advertised wares, past trees where vultures congregated.

"Scavenger birds," commented our black chauffeur, whose quaint monkey-face had been distorted as, on a lonely stretch of road, he had enacted in pantomime how, when night falls over the island, the sinuous bushmasters—Lords of the Jungle—issue from their lairs. The emaciated gesticulating body of the man had become so attenuated as he repeated the words "He comin', he comin'," that our imaginations had raced to a point where we felt ourselves menaced by the incarnation of a serpent.

Hanging-baskets of ferns gave a semblance of privacy to second-story porches of the more decent-looking houses on the outskirts of the town. In these the wash was drying below stairs, open on all sides to catch the breeze, while beneath the humbler shanties hammocks were hung.

We thought of an Englishwoman with little children, a passenger aboard our liner, who dwelt at San Fernando. Was her abode, we wondered, on a cliff overlooking the sea? Remembering her hollow cheeks we trusted so, yet feared a negative reply.

Negroes, better able to withstand toil in the sun, are employed for the arduous labor at Pitch Lake. The glare of the tropical sun, baking the asphalt with its rays, is apt to be devastating. We had been warned, however, to engage a car with a top to protect ourselves against what the Bermudians call "liquid sunshine."

"At Trinidad," we had been told, "you'll find fifty showers a day."

It was this same "liquid sunshine" that lent an eerie, other-worldly quality to our initial view of Pitch Lake. Having been cordially received by Mr. Vandeburgh, the American general manager of the Trinidad Lake Asphalt Operating Company, and by Mr. Mathison, secretary, we accompanied the latter, hastening to arrive before noon through the gates and down to the black "lake." On the horny hide of this asphalt monster the scattered gangs of Negro workmen seemed of no more importance than so many ticks. A fringe of green vegetation—where once was jungle—encircles the immense pool save on the side of the refinery; a few spindling palms rear their exotic heads in the direction of the workers' village.

The taking of asphalt from the seemingly inexhaustible lake is done by a simple and inexpensive process. Dump cars running by gravity (which sometimes bound violently from the tracks, we were warned in the nick of time), are hauled back again by cables. Each gang consists of a digger or pitch-cutter and five "headers," who carry the chunks—weighing up to a hundred pounds—to the narrow-gage railway actually laid on the solidified surface of the lake.

As we approached the central gang we were

struck by the extreme mournfulness of the picture. The absence of color seemed accentuated by the darkening heavens. Wielding heavy picks or bearing upon their heads crushing burdens, the black men swayed to rhythmic chanties. "Bearing the Cross" . . . the refrain of a spiritual came to our ears, poignant as though its inherited cadence revealed the misery of men about to be crucified, of slaves late from the Congo.

The acrid voice of a passer-by was carried to us: "Their heads are as hard as bullets. Though they wear bits of old tires to break the blow if they're struck. Pitch is soft compared to the head of a nigger."

"Once," Mr. Mathison told us, as we traversed the wrinkled surface of the lake to stand beside the "mother" in the center, bubbling beneath a rainwater pool, "once, in 1928, a buried tree, not at all petrified after thousands of years, rose in the lake, then, before the month's end, canted and withdrew. A section was sent to your natural science museum in Philadelphia."

The dark surface upon which we stood and into which our feet had a tendency to sink was lightened by pools, at first reflecting leaden clouds and later blurred by drenching rain that sent us scurrying to the shelter of the refinery. Here water is boiled from the steam-heated pitch, which is pressed through strainers into topless barrels, as pitch has a habit of sealing itself. The plant is capable of an output of 400 tons in twenty-four hours, as compared with 1,500 tons in the crude. The former is known as "dried" asphalt and is preferred for shipment to the crude—run by aerial steel ropeway directly into the holds of ships at Brighton pier—owing to a tendency of the latter to coagulate into a solid mass in the hold, conceivably causing a dangerous list.

As we sat at luncheon at the Brighton Hotel—a "hotel" at which money is not accepted—we noted that the only other occupant of the room was a youth in khaki; sent, our host informed us, from England to superintend defense of the wealthiest island of the Indies. Hitler, it was rumored, had established air-bases in Venezuela.

(How little could we have anticipated, on our first visit, that—under "destroyers-for-bases" agreement between Churchill and Roosevelt—fifty square miles of Trinidad would be leased, from 1941 for 99 years, as United States Army and Naval bases. The Army, in lesser numbers since the war, occupies Waller Field—a north central area east of Arima—the Navy, Chaguaramas on the north west peninsula. The Americans have been accepted with good grace by Trinidadians.)

The level of this far-famed deposit has dropped only twenty feet in half a century, during which time five million tons of asphalt have been mined. The substance is actually an oxidized residue of crude petroleum. First used as pavement in the

Trinidad: mournful is

United States, Trinidad asphalt has attained
world fame.

The legendary origin of the lake is poetic. Iëre,
the Indian name for Trinidad, signifies "The
Land of the Humming-Bird." It is said that the
Chayma Indians, celebrating a victory over war-
ring rivals, ran contrary to an ancient taboo
founded on the belief that humming-birds were
reincarnations of human souls. The Indians not
only slew these "feathered jewels" but ate them
and "bedecked themselves with the plumage."
Thus the wrath of the Great Spirit was aroused,
so runs the tale. The earth is said to have opened

the monster asphalt lake

and swallowed the offenders with all their habitations, burying the entire village with pitch.

Melancholy reflections still haunt the lingerer beside the lake. Not more than a few hundred of the company's 2,000 employees are actually at work there, as cutters, loaders, hoistmen, and dumping gangs, but there are, as well, gatemen, pouring gangs in the refinery, screenmen, wrenchmen, pushers—whose wages are scaled to the increased cost of living—cappers of drums, stockrollers, and shipping rollers . . . to mention but a few. Realizing the seriousness of the consequences of strikes and lockouts, here (and at

Barbados where the white man is so greatly outnumbered) one is encouraged to observe that
nowadays the method of settling differences at
Pitch Lake is not by gunboat but by written wage
agreement—the first signed on May 18, 1939, on
behalf of the Company and on behalf of the Oil-
fields Workers' Trade Union, as result of negotia-
tions carried on with the assistance of an
Industrial Adviser.

No warfare, worthy of the name, mars the history of Trinidad. "The annals of Trinidad," it
has been said, "are almost free from blood
stains." The importance of this fact can not, to
my mind, be overestimated. Nowhere, except in
the United States of America, have we encountered such diversity of racial stock. It is, in all
probability, owing to the fact that Trinidad is still
a "promised land," with much to entice the better
class of immigrant, that enterprise, coöperation,
and loyalty to the traditions of democracy are
nowhere more apparent. Whatever may be said of
the lesser islands of the Antilles, at Trinidad
standards of virile youth, not decadence, prevail.

Sir Walter Raleigh paid two visits to Trinidad,
the first on March 22, 1595, when his vessel came
to anchor at Puerto de los Españoles, known to-
day as Port of Spain. Like his Spanish prede-
cessors his search was for that El Dorado said
to be located between the Orinoco and the Amazon.
Having heard from an Indian cacique of the

alleged murder by the Spaniards of one Captain Whiddon, sent by Raleigh to prepare the way, Sir Walter ordered the arrest of his host, Don Antonio de Berrio, the enlightened Spanish governor, and the destruction by fire of San José, the capital. It was on this first visit that Raleigh made the discovery of what he wrote was "called by the naturals Piché and by the Spaniards Tierra de Brea." He also noted the tiny fish in the pools on the "lake" (they exist to this day) and was probably the first white man to caulk his ships at La Brea.

In 1617 Raleigh paid his second visit to Trinidad, this time coming by the Serpent's Mouth and anchoring at Los Gallos Bay. Sir Lawrence Keymis was sent to the mainland to explore the Orinoco, while Raleigh waited impatiently at Trinidad. The search for gold having proved vain, and crushed by the scathing ire of his patron, Sir Lawrence took his own life. Raleigh sailed away, confirmed in his opinion that El Dorado was a myth, though gold, had he known it, did exist at the mouth of the Orinoco, and resources of more value than pure gold.

Columbus, Raleigh, Nelson are among the names evoked upon entrance to the harbor of Port of Spain, the eastern cross-road of the Caribbean. Astounded were the inhabitants, on June 7, 1805, to see the British fleet, decks cleared for action, sail into the harbor and—without a word of ex-

planation—sail out again. Having failed to overtake the French Fleet at Barbados or Trinidad,
Nelson, aboard the *Victory,* continued the chase
to Grenada and Antigua—a chase begun in May
that was to end on October 21st at Trafalgar.

The startling beauty of Port of Spain, as seen
from the water, outweighs, in the balanced scales
of an artist's judgment, the wealth of products
loading at piers and bunkering by lighters, though
these include the riches of the Indies: crude oil
and asphalt, Angostura Bitters, cacao and coconuts, sugar from the Usine of Ste. Madeleine—
one of the largest in the world. (In the British
Empire only Canada, in the Western Hemisphere,
surpasses Trinidad in trade—a trade now increased
by industrialization.) All this, as I have said,
is naught to the artist, who, standing aloof upon
the deck, first communes with the beauty that is
Trinidad. Not Nelson, whose hurried glance was
only for the French fleet, could have felt it to the
full, nor Raleigh, blinded by his passion for
Midas' touch of gold, but Columbus—to whom
gold was but incidental to the quest—before de-
parting by the Boca Grande must have had the
vision of this shore ... though not, indeed, of this
Aphrodite city, rising hill-crowned from the sea.

To those of us nurtured in youth on Arabian
Nights, Marco Polo, and Kubla Khan, mental
word-pictures of ancient splendors have been
painted that are rarely rivaled in our modern

world. Not in the Americas nor yet in Europe do our dreams take pictorial form nor often even, paradoxically, when in the presence of traditional wonders of the world. Yet there come times to the initiated—in quest of the rare, the exotic—when reality surpasses fantasy as truly as, on occasion, the godhead in man puts unbelief to shame. In a life crowded, beyond deserving, with impressions of mind and matter, wedded to form victorious wholes, I recall precisely three previous manifestations of the spirit of a civilization taking such sensuously perceptible and vivid shape: celebration of a Cantonese New Year, the last under the Empire; an echo of Imperial Russia enacted by Orthodox Monks at Valamo; and, on landing from a P. & O. steamer, first sight, in blazing sunlight, of turbaned throngs at Bombay. A fourth manifestation awaited me at Trinidad. True, I had known tropics—Burma, Penang, and Singapore, islands such as the Hawaiian and Dominica—but not in the Western Hemisphere had I foreseen this meeting-ground of Oriental pageantry and South American jungle. Existing pigments, odors, sounds, can but partially reveal the splendors inherent in the very title of this tropical isle of heart's desire—Trinidad.

"The character of Barbados," says the author of *If Crab No Walk,* "is robust and straightforward, Trinidad, and especially Port of Spain, has a curious subtlety that is baffling." . . . It is in-

Hindus, dwelling beneath banyan, palm and mango

deed those on whom the sameness of "Little England" palls who revel in the infinite variety, the
freedom of Trinidad. Instead of a homogeneous
British population, greatly outnumbered by the
descendants of African slaves, the racial stocks of
Trinidad may, roughly speaking, be classified as
one third East Indian (descendants of Hindus
and Mohammedans), more than a third Negro, the
remainder divided between a sprinkling of Chinese (who were for ten years introduced by in-

denture) and those whose ancestors were among the early Spanish, Portuguese, and French settlers (the patois is, to this day, French), Americans of both continents, and the dominant British. The population has to-day far exceeded half a million, in contrast to the eighteen hundred it had attained after nearly three centuries of Spanish rule. "Trinidadians," so states a history used locally in the schools, "are a mixed people, intelligent, handsome, and lively." Cold of heart, indeed, would be the unprejudiced American who, on wide acquaintance, found them less than irresistible.

Although within ten degrees of the equator, Trinidad has a mean temperature of seventy-six degrees in winter, eighty degrees in summer, with a drop of over ten degrees at night. Avoiding what Ober terms the "miasmatic effluence" of the swamps—distant from Port of Spain—and the direct rays of the sun, the white man, thanks in part to the trade winds, thrives in Trinidad. Moreover, the island is without volcano and out of the path of the hurricane.

Glamour (an abused word of late) is the quality that best describes both setting and things seen from the Taj Mahal Hotel in Bombay, the "Q. P. H." or Queen's Park Hotel in Port of Spain. The ancient caravansary at Trinidad has largely been rebuilt on modern lines—for is it not a stopping-place for those ultra-modern Cosmo-

politans, the passengers of international airways?
Taxis and limousines load and unload (here
it was that Christopher Hasnally, exemplary
chauffeur, was to await us daily), tourists and
business associates brush shoulders in the airy
lobby or crowd around the iron gates of the cocktail bar. Soft-voiced natives seize luggage, while
bath- and chambermaids give a welcome to
"mistress" that at once elevates her to the rank
once held by "memsahib" in India.

The appointments of our room were the last
word in taste and comfort. . . . "It was not ever
so," a knowing one murmurs. Mosquito nets were
lowered—a precaution against an imaginary foe.
On the first morning of our stay, however, I had
an encounter, in the immaculate tiled bathroom,
with a formidable adversary: a tarantula, large,
I could swear, as my outspread hand. I sprang at
it with my slipper, it retreated to a corner of the
wall. Again I missed in my aim and, instantly,
the hairy creature bounded to attack (I had not
known they did!). My third blow was a knock-out.
The thing fell, quivering, to the floor.

"Fancy, in the new wing!" remarked our English friend. "Courageous of you!"

"There wasn't time to get help," I assured him.
"I couldn't risk having the thing at large."

Outside our French windows, giving on a balcony, lay the Savannah or Queen's Park, on which
the hotel faces. At all hours of the day a pageant

was presented. Vehicles, crowds afoot, thronged the highway. Race-horses were exercised by jockeys: course, grandstand, and stables all were outstretched before us, the extent of the Savannah being 199 acres. Here Boy Scouts and Girl Guides indulged in hockey or paraded on Empire Day. Here cricketers, of various shades of color, white- or red-shirted, drew crowds more interested than the few who watched of a morning the "route drill" of sun-catching cavalry or dusky, white-helmeted infantrymen. At intervals the strains of "God Save the King" floated to our ears, not, however, downing the insistent note of friendly kiskedees, yellow-breasted and apparently still French-speaking, reiterating:

"Qu'est-c' qu'il dit? Qu'est-c' qu'il dit?"

Spreading shade trees indicated the location of an ancient cemetery. Above all and dominating all a ridge of mountains presided over the plain, barring somewhat the passage of the trade winds, but lifting the soul by their majesty.

From the convenient base of the Queen's Park Hotel excursions may be made to all parts of the island. Rewarding as are trips into central Port of Spain, they are of secondary importance, especially to those susceptible to heat. Tourists revel in the shops on Frederick Street, many displaying East Indian or English wares: curios—reptile, cacao tree, or native—fashioned of balata rubber. A few find their way to the Royal Victoria Institute to see, with their own eyes, an anchor salvaged from one of Columbus' vessels. Exceptional is the man who omits a visit to the renowned manufactory of Angostura Bitters. Native Calypso singers should, unquestionably, be heard. The Anglican and Roman Catholic Cathedrals are points of interest—the latter between Marine and Columbus Squares—while Woodford Square is ornamented by moss-bearded samans. St. James Village (Coolie Town), now part of Port of Spain, is the Mohammedan quarter, and here annually the lauded festival of Mohurrum is held with such colorful East Indian authenticity as to justify a journey from New York.

The Mohurrum may rightly be reckoned one of the glories of Trinidad, unsurpassed by the celebration of Hindu weddings, the fabulous beauty of the Zebu Herd, the blossoming of the *bois immortel*. Add to these attractions the tropical seas and palm-fringed beaches, the blue or cloud-tipped mountains, the "high woods"—the name by which the almost impenetrable virgin forests are known —and the new-comer begins to realize why this island has been called the "Paradise of the Caribbees."

To name the essential expeditions is no easy task, but none of the following should be overlooked: Pitch Lake, the Royal Botanic Gardens, the Government Stock Farm, Mount St. Benedict, Santa Cruz Valley, Maracas Bay and the Blue

Basin; Morne Bleu, via Arima, if not Blanchis-
seuse, Toco and Balandra, and the Hindu village
of Tunapuna. The garnering of all these gems
will aid in building the mosaic that is Trinidad.

North Coast Road, "symbol of British-American
cooperation," runs for seven miles over the Northern Range then plunges to Maracas Bay. Bronze
tablets tell of the building of the road by the U. S.
Navy, in exchange for inclusion of Tucker Valley
Road in the U. S. Naval Base. Completed in 1944,
the highway was carved out of the mountain. It
abounds in vistas—to seaward or over Maraval
Valley to the Gulf of Paria. Drives to Maracas
Valley (Cadbury cocoa estates, idyllic residences—
one of these a remodeled cocoa house), The
Imperial College of Tropical Agriculture are
"musts," also lunch at Hotel Normandie, dinner
at Tavern on the Green, shopping and advice at
King's Wharf Passenger Centre, Port of Spain.

Trinidad, separated from Venezuela only by a
narrow strait, boasts a continental fauna and
flora, unrivaled elsewhere among Caribbean
islands. The Royal Botanic Gardens, established
in 1818, are comparable in beauty to those at
Penang. R. E. Dean, several years out of London
when the curator, has written an efficient guide in
which he tells how Lockhart, the first botanist in
charge, visited "Venezuela and the countries of
the Orinoco discovering Humboldt's Cow Tree . . .
and the Saman or Zaman. . . . These, with many

The Hindu Temple : Tunapuna

kinds of orchids, he introduced into Trinidad.''

''You should see a Hindu wedding,'' said Mrs.
Pashley (Port of Spain artist, exhibitor at the
San Francisco World's Fair). ''This is the
month.''

It was through the good offices of our friend
Wilson Minshall—gifted with the power of frat-
ernization with rich or poor, white, yellow, or
brown—that the invitation, by word of mouth,
came. Of a Thursday evening at Tunapuna two
sisters were to be brides, and at this double ceremony we should be welcome.

''Not before nine, though,'' had been the warning. ''The drums beat from seven and, if men have
been drinking, there are apt to be street fights.''

A sound of drums was in the air as we approached; a crowd was gathered before the house;
drummers led the men's delegation. Pushing our
way through a group of onlookers, their dusky
faces illuminated by the light of flares, we entered
the palm-dressed pavilion—recently constructed,
for an Orthodox Hindu marriage should take place
in a new building. The illusion of transition to
India was instantaneous. The room was packed
with Hindu women and children, arrayed in colors of the rainbow. All were swathed in silk or
cotton saris, many were bedecked with nose-rings,
nose-studs, and silver bracelets massed janglingly
from wrist to elbow. Our reception by Dorbalshaw,
our host—an agriculturalist, neat in white coat,

Hindu of Trinidad

dhoty cloth, and turban—was cordial. A man-serv-
ant, emaciated as only a Hindu can well be, placed
chairs for us beside the two mounds or "altars"
and opposite the flower-like bevy of the female
relatives.

Wick-lamps swung from the low ceiling, festooned with elaborate cut-paper fringes of scarlet,
white, yellow, blue, and green, as were the two
bowers prepared to receive the couples. The bamboo posts of the crudely erected "temple" were
outlined with upright fronds of palm—a design
worthy of perpetuation in marble. Bunches of
tropical mistletoe added to the air of festivity. On
the earthen floor the low "altars" of manure from

the sacred zebu were molded, sprinkled with water, knowingly patted by the lean hand of the servant who later dusted between his deft fingers a design in rice flour.

An enlightened Hindu wearing European dress, a mechanic in Pan-American Airways, talked to us earnestly, explaining the ceremonies. In India, he said, the ancient Hindus knew of the purifying power of ammonia in cow dung and used the latter in actuality as well as for a symbol. Lotos are not merely of brass but of a mixed metal that purifies the water within. The hours-long beating of the drums, too, stirs the air and, therefore, purifies. The older Buddhist philosophy has degenerated in India and Brahmin rites and gods, too, are taken literally by the ignorant—as are images in Catholic countries. The youth spoke feelingly of Gandhi and expressed an intention to pay a visit to India.

After long delay the first bride entered, muffled in voluminous white, as though in purdah, so that none could recognize. Attended by a matron gorgeous in dangling earrings and other antique jewelry, the girl crouched in front of the "shrine," beneath the canopy of fluttering ribbons; only her brown hands and bony bare feet emerged—the latter to be painted, in the sight of all, in brilliant red design. The process of the preparation of the bride might have seemed to drag interminably to other than enthralled guests. To the chanting of women, attendants—graceful as the milkmaids of Krishna—circled the bride thrice, tossing coins, to be gathered by the servant. Flower-girls arrived with fragrant offerings. The second sister, likewise heavily veiled, was escorted to the other bower. Gifts were presented from the first bridegroom, to be inspected critically by the bride's brother: a tray of stuffs, a golden necklace, earrings and anklets of silver; and they were accepted.

"Are they ever," I queried, "rejected?"

Clouds of incense arose, a pungent odor. Noisy spectators—some Negroes—pushed their way within.

"It is a time to welcome all," said a neighbor. "A quarter of the guests are not invited."

The pundit had arrived, a slim corded Brahmin, immaculate in white. Courteously he came to press our hands and explain that although the ceremony would be in Hindustani there would also be a part translated into English. He introduced his father, fantastically pink-turbaned, who would unite the second couple.

The bridegroom cometh! How biblical, how Oriental the scene—even to virgins with flaming wick-lamps. Resplendent in silken robe, the youth —he was but twenty, the bride fifteen—attired in flaming cerise, wore upon his turban a high openwork marriage-crown of silver and green beads; dangling tassels partly concealed his features.

Sheepish, we thought he looked. Was it mere self-consciousness or did he think this ceremony tedious and unnecessary? Obviously all he cared about was to possess his bride. (Were this an Arya Samaj, instead of Orthodox wedding, remarked a bystander, the groom would wear European dress with turban and no crown.)

The father of the bride made gestures of foot washing for daughter and prospective son-in-law, showing no difference between them, both his children now. Mango leaves, representing freshness, were tasted by both, their garment knotted in a symbolic link. Unhusked rice (how rice and weddings are insolubly linked!) was poured by the bridegroom upon the altar.

The solemnity of the intoning by the pundit was impressive, and especially of interest to us was the portion of the service we could understand. Seven requests the bride makes of her spouse. Five stipulations are made by the bridegroom. One is that should he chastize her she should not return to her parents but consider it a benefit for her own development. She shall, even in his absence, entertain his friends.

The preparations having consumed two hours, the first ceremony was completed by midnight, while the two daughters of the house were not finally wedded to their lords and masters until the early morning hours.

A gesture of good will had been our inclusion

at the nuptials. Hopes for the happiness of the newly-married wives, Phoolmathidevi and Jasv-dradevi—whose features were, seductively, not to be unveiled in our presence—occupied our thoughts on what was, alas, the final evening of our first stay in Trinidad.

Trinidad, Caribbean magnet, revisited! As our thoughts turn thither we seem to stand again upon the flight deck of H. M. C. S. *Magnificent* and hear the band—as the Canadian aircraft carrier's host, the Commander, welcomed His Excellency the Governor. Or thoughts dwell on the night when, canopied by the starry heavens, we sat in the Royal Botanic Gardens watching unfold, against backdrop of rustling bamboo and soughing palm, the fantasy of *A Midsummer Night's Dream,* with added loveliness of luscious English intonation, of music, of an impish Puck. There was moreover the evening when Beryl McBurnie—exotic as a tropical flower, waxed eloquent in telling of native talent, traditional ceremony, minimizing her own phenomenal success as a dancer, assuring us that she was at heart a teacher—an upholder of the torch of beauty. Haunting in the moonlight was the Calypso music of the steel bands—each prosaic oil-drum tempered to respond as by magic, only to its dark-skinned player who, in concert with fellows, poured forth his innermost being by means of hypnotizing rhythm.

Mohurrum

Tobago: Seaward-leaning palms

CHAPTER XIV

TOBAGO

Tobago! embodiment of a poet's fancy, isolated from the hurly-burly of world affairs, land of high hills and deep valleys, of rushing streams and tropical vegetation; hail to you with your profound Atlantic harbors, your scintillating Caribbean coves. Tobago! forgotten by white men save for dreamers and an occasional planter, paradise of the black man, and no less of songbirds and waterfowl; land of cacao and of coconut... in the darkness of the world to-day I close my eyes and am enraptured by a vision of your green-and-silver palms, your sun-checkered coral sands bordered by your limitless encirclement of blue. My wish was father to my deed. I have lived my childhood's imaginings. I have, like Man Friday, printed my foot upon the sands of an island envisaged by Defoe. Starry-eyed I have shared wonder known hitherto only through the pages of Robinson Crusoe.

Trinidad is not Trinidad alone. One of its glories lies in the fact that, politically, it has a ward and is in actuality—so it is written in legal black and white—the colony of Trinidad and Tobago. To the initiate Trinidadian, to whom his islands bulks large as a continent and quite as full of affairs, there is always a way of escape: the door (in this case none other than the cabin door of a coastwise steamer or the enticing entrance to a plane) lies open for a Tobagonian holiday.

Petulant from pouring over the pages of musty history books, I have revolted against telling the truths recounted. What of it that England, Holland, France, and Spain made a veritable bone of contention of this idyllic retreat: enough to know that the island has changed owners more often than any other in the Antilles. What if a naval battle raged off Bloody Bay staining its limpid waters, what if men thought of a harbor forty fathoms deep and of soaring bird-life in terms of men-o'-war, what if sugar-barons grew fat on the toil of slave-labor till "wealthy as a Tobago planter" became a by-word in England: what is all this to us to-day? Truth under these circumstances is not of half as much value to the venturer into new tropical fields as fiction. Let us clap to the stained pages, smelling of midnight

oil, and spread open to the light of the sun the
following:

"I descended a little on the side of that delicious vale, surveying it with a secret kind of
pleasure, though mixed with my other afflicting
thoughts to think that this was all my own; that
I was king and lord of all this country indefea-
sibly and had a right of possession; and, if I could
convey it, I might have it in inheritance as completely as any lord of a manor in England."

Hardly less did my Illustrator and I, swimming in forsaken coves, exploring solitary slopes,
feel, each in his own right, "king and lord," or,
collectively and more realistically, king and queen.

Black men have taken over the tiny capital,
Scarborough, upon the Caribbean shore, black
men nowadays as much a part of the theatrical
setting as Carib Indians would be (Man Friday
was of their number) and less disturbing to the
mere hundred white men who stalk across the
island stage. At Scarborough even so small a boat
as the *Tobago* must land its passengers in rowboats—I was about to say canoes. Ruined barracks of Fort King George still stand upon the
dominant hills. Sights to be seen in the capital
are refreshingly nil. There is, it is true, a tempting market held in the open beneath shadow-
casting tamarinds and Friday's Gift Shop, but
the days on which shops in Scarborough open are
rare. Plymouth, on the north coast, offers, if it be

Scarborough : A tempting market
is held in the open.

possible, still fewer attractions, still more ruins, a lesser number of inhabitants.

It is on leaving the settlement of Scarborough that spirits rise—even if it be to go no farther afield than to the Tobago Botanical Garden. I recall the soul-satisfying red of Royal Poincianas, flaunting starred blossoms upon banners of bloom to skies of white and blue; an *Oreodoxa oleracea*

(how tall a palm!) rhythmically weighted with
pendant nests of yellowtails, swaying in "the
trades," and, sole human being to be seen, a
youth plucking the strings of a guitar.

A mile from Scarborough, on Rockly Bay, is
one of the island's most tempting hotels, the well-
known Robinson Crusoe. We were to turn, however, a like distance on the Windward Main Road
to come upon our idea of a tropical headquarters,
Bacolet Guest House, with its bungalows, private
beaches, its river, hills and flats, its twelve-hun-
dred-acre coconut estate—an inheritance of its
Americanized Portuguese owner, Walter Mendes.
Here we were to partake, with other native delicacies, of the dish which, of a Sunday, is the
Tobagonians' idea of a chicken in the pot, calaloo
—a delectable concoction of crab-meat and leaves
culled from the dasheen. Ten days, our American
hostess told us, must land crabs be kept in their
"crawl," subsisting on greens, to prevent the
possibility of their feeding upon the poisonous
manchineel. Here, ensconced in Sea Gull Cottage,
no less than had we been in its neighbor on the
cliff, Pelican Cottage (named by a writer for
Punch), could we watch specimens of the latter
self-engrossed bird plunge from heights into the
Caribbean. Here, of a morning, we trod the downward trail to the beach and waters we shared
with seaward-leaning palms, with conchs and Portuguese men-of-war, and not, by the grace of God,

with barracuda. Here, after sunset, to the chorus of vibrating frogs, we were reminded of our approach to equatorial latitude by an all-but horizontal new moon, while, at a later hour, the impression was emphasized by the luminous quality of that heavenly symbol, the Southern Cross.

"Why don't you clean off the trees? Why so many weeds?" was the typically English reaction of a father, visiting for the first time his son's estate at Tobago. "Wild bananas? If they are of no use why keep them?"

To which the son replied, "It costs to clear weeds that grow overnight like beanstalks." "Clean off" his trees!—the artist soul of the resident shrank at such a threat to his cherished growth of wild orchids and other epiphytes.

At Terry Hill—its owner Gervaise Casson was to be found at Trinidad—the author of the novel *Hecla Sandwith* was installed, awaiting his friend Casson's return, a matter of perhaps a year or years, quien sabe? This born raconteur, trained otherwise at Haverford College ("I could not live in Philadelphia," he told us, "where people demand, 'Who was her grandmother?'") in his youth had sailed the seas to Cocos Island—the record to be found in A. W. Roberts' *Rough and Tumble*—later living in Japan, where he had rented a house with two servants flat on their backs with beri-beri and two others who could not cook ... but the law of the land forbade dis-

missal. The gentleman was immaculate in shirt
and sky-blue shorts. His lean face was still flushed
from the exertion of endeavoring to save the garden from an onslaught of "cockles"—beetles
whose backs are spotted with two uncanny
"eyes." On our arrival, his gaunt form had been
bent double, bagging cabbages against the pest.

" 'Are you employed?' is the question asked
me," he said. One English lady had exclaimed:
"Do get my husband out of the hammock!"

Employed, yes, but our host was employed on
writing a book of his own psychic experiences, yet
thirsty withal for news from outside, especially
of the world of modern art.

At Trinidad we had felt India near—happy the
accident that named these isles West Indies. At
Terry Hill, beneath a saman commanding valley,
bush, and Caribbean, it would take the concen-
tration of Buddha not to be diverted from other
purpose by the distractions of this rival to a bo-
tree. The tree, similar in scope to the mighty plane
in which Anthony Adverse passed many boyhood
hours, was encrusted along trunk and branch with
a wealth of living green, feathered with tiny
ferns, host to cactus vivid with crimson blossoms
—spiny leaves erect or trailing like some slithering green snake to hang inquisitively along a
bough ... there was, indeed, a lazy serpent, basking in the sun. Beneath the spread umbrella of
the crown, the great saman was aflutter with

wings—whirring wings of humming-birds; wings
of russet-headed woodpeckers, flitting from limb
to limb; wings superlative in bright turquoise
beauty, tanagers—with Chinese kingfishers—
bluest of blue birds. A tree of dreams, a tree in
itself a world apart, a tree where watchers of the
life therein find an hour passes swift as a stolen
minute. All hail to Casson who, seated within the
shade of this thought-absorbing "bo-tree," has
strength to attain the mystic's peace of the abyss.

Beyond Terry Hill the coast road, a legacy
from the French (the English did not possess
Tobago until 1814), leads to Speyside, a distance
of twenty-five miles from Scarborough. Having
left the southern flatter portion of the island,
where roads abound, this old military route clings
at times to the cliff—a rock-hewn cornice bordering the ocean. As yet the encircling of the
island by highway is incomplete. The gap on the
mountainous north coast from Man-o'-War Bay
to Castara is traversed only by bridle path.

Pembroke, a typical village, was passed on our
drive to Speyside. Its setting is in the local tradition, with coconut groves encroaching to the
water's edge. Pickers of coconuts, agile as monkeys, average anywhere from two to five thousand
a day, Henry, our chauffeur, in his caressing
singsong, told us. The gathering from the ground
and splitting open is done by women, and shells
feed the furnaces used in the preparation of the

Tobago: Pembroke Village

copra. Natives wielded gallettes, the instruments by which cacao pods are shorn from branch and trunk without injury to the "cushions." After "sweating," the beans are literally "danced" upon after the time-honored method of treading grapes for wine. We wondered if more modern means were employed at the much advertised Co-operative Cocoa Fermentaries.

From the cliff above Speyside we had one of the island's famous vistas. Across the green of tropical hillsides, across the emerald waters of a bay ruffled by current around Goat Island, we had a glimpse of Little Tobago, which is to Tobago as Tobago is to Trinidad, an isle of sheer romance. At Bird of Paradise we were to lunch copiously—jack-fish broth was, I remember, a feature—and to learn more of these two islands. The first, composed of jagged rocks, is the abode of a lone woman writer. The second, densely wooded, a mile in length, stocked some years ago by the late Sir William Ingram with birds of paradise imported from Dutch New Guinea, was presented by his sons, in 1929, to the Government of Trinidad and Tobago on condition that the birds be protected. Therefore, at intervals, the water bottles of these gorgeous creatures are refilled and the paths to their nesting grounds "kept tidy."

"Take a guide along," we were warned, "if you visit Little Tobago. Don't be like the American from your hotel who went alone. His boat

capsized in the swift current at the moment he
was counting shark fins!''

Jean Batten, the New Zealand aviatrix, said our
host, had been spending weeks at Speyside-on-
Sea, reveling in the walks and swims, escaping
crowds. She would have liked the Bluehaven.

It was at Speyside that we were to see a copy
of *Crusoe's Island,* the effusion of a youthful
pair written after six months' residence in Tobago. The copy, brought to the hotel by a Yale
professor, had, judging from its appearance,
passed through the hands of every white islander
although, be assured, Tobagonians resent publicity and would on no account purchase the volume.

Man-o'-War Bay, with its nestling village of
Charlotteville, exceeded our expectations—although we had indeed read that in its waters
a "fleet of windjammers could manoeuver." No
windjammers hove in sight, phantom or otherwise, but man-o'-war birds—those frigates of the
air—did, in lieu of army planes, give a demonstration of technic, defying imitation. Fishermen,
in loin cloths, busy with nets, showed interest in
the unwonted arrival of a car. A statuesque man
of iron mustered courage to inquire where we had
come from and where going to, what our life calling ... in embryo a born reporter.

"If crab no walk he no see notting" is a Negro
proverb. The author of the volume *If Crab No
Walk* believes that the name Tobago is derived

from the Indian name for tobacco, which was grown there at the time of the discovery of the island ... a name already adopted by the Spaniards elsewhere. Others think the appellation can be traced to a fancied resemblance in the island's contour to an aboriginal tobacco pipe. The crop is no longer profitable but has given place to cacao and the all but ubiquitous coconut. Sugar likewise has been largely abandoned since the failure, toward the end of the last century, of a firm owning two-thirds of the estates.

Having a mean temperature of eighty degrees, with almost constant sea breeze from December to June; being outside the hurricane zone, with cyclones exceptional; being freer than Trinidad from poisonous reptiles and disease-breeding swamps, Tobago has much to offer the white settler. On the reverse side of the ledger is the lack of congenial companionship. Relations between the races are harmonious, as the Negro (of whom there are some 27,000) is not—as at Barbados, for example—dependent upon outside employment, but will, if the spirit move him, devote whole- instead of half-time to the tilling of his own garden. This unescapable fact tends toward his receiving just treatment by planters.

"Drive care-foo-lee," black youths in shorts called to the gentle Henry as our car approached Scarborough. Still in his early twenties but with years of experience in driving, Henry is em-

ployed, he told us, by a "dark lady," a seam-
stress who pays him monthly. He ranks, among
a score of chauffeurs, as the island's premier.
"Ask for Henry," "Ask for Henry"—the words
graced both sides of our windshield.

Leaving the galvanized roofs of Scarborough
behind us we drove past the airy Government
School at Mason Hall, due north to the bamboo
clumps, bananas, and cacaos of Moriah—where
four thousand Negro Moravians dwell. As bird-
lovers—many make pilgrimages to the island
noted for its birds of plumage—we had long anticipated visiting the wild reaches of the region between Moriah and the hills known as Les Coteaux.
No disappointment was in store. The cocrico (a
pheasant peculiar to Tobago) crossed our roadway, while a large proportion of the hundred and
fifty varieties listed by Ober—blue creeper,
crested cacique, tropical kingfisher—were sighted.
Excitedly we recognized the two we had most
wished to see, those bank-nesting birds, the motmot and the jacamar. The latter, a woodland sym-
phony in copper, chestnut, and green, is the
smaller white-throated bird, while its frequent
companion has somewhat the same color scale,
substituting for white a predominant blue. The
motmot—easy to recognize because of the bare-
ness of its feather-tipped tail—has for its style
been titled the King of the Woods. Gray-headed
kiskedees perched by the roadside; while black-

birds—the "boat-tailed" Barbardos variety, corn-birds, or yellowtails—and "old witches" or Roman-nosed "tick-birds" were seen in companies.

Plymouth, with its fine harbor, need not delay the sight-seer, nor palm-edged Mt. Irvine Bay, nor yet Store Bay with its rocky cliffs and firm sands. He may tarry in surprised admiration of certain coco-groves in the district where thrift is well applied. The best grafted stock is used, and, in contrast to all other plantations on the island—many untidy even measured by the standards of the superlatively untidy tropics—these are cleared of trash. Mahogany trees edge the immense property, traversed by well-kept roads. Henry informed us that here fallen coconuts are used as fertilizer, and that the profits, instead of being paid for taxes, are spent on the estate—its owner's delight.

Reminders that we were on Crusoe's island were constant. Defoe, we remembered, had in all probability based the setting for his masterpiece, published in 1719, upon data obtained from the account of an eyewitness, Captain John Poyntz, printed in 1683, *The Present Prospect of the Famous and Fertile Island of Tobago;* although Alexander Selkirk (the Scotchman—marooned in 1704, on Juan Fernandez off the coast of Chile—by William Dampier, following a quarrel, and rescued by Woodes Rogers with Dampier as

I was king and lord of all this country

pilot), known to Defoe, was the prototype of Crusoe.

Pigeon Point to the north of Store Bay has its Aquatic Club called the "Lido" of Tobago...a Lido where close-serried palms crowd to the water's edge. Our final expedition, in search of the cave of Crusoe, led us to the south of this point: indeed, to the extreme southwestern tip of the island known as Crown Point. Store Bay Road—most roads in Tobago are known as "streets"—meandered rurally across government land, dwindling finally to a vanishing lane. Beyond Crown Point was moorland deserted save for roaming fowls and startled doves—pink-tailed in flight, perhaps the "pigeons" of Pigeon Cove.

Our quest for the cave of Crusoe was, seemingly, unprecedented. The cavern's hidden location, to be reached pathlessly afoot, was unknown to Henry, omniscient as to roads. Our resourceful driver, finding the owner of the roaming fowls, was directed to a clump of gru-gru palms, where an urchin who would serve as guide searched for edible grubs. Past the "trash" house where hens nested, our oddly-assorted quartet filed, past calabashes where chickens already roosted, over a ragged field rough with coral formation, across slippery fallen palm leaves. For stealing a coconut, Henry drawled, the fine is six months in jail, or maybe a month for first offenders.

Sounds of breakers reached our ears as we

neared our destination. To have come so far, my
thoughts registered, and to be thus daunted! We
stood upon the margin of a cliff. Below lay a
rocky chaos where ocean dashed and roared.
I looked at my tropical footgear and longed for
the staff or rope of a mountaineer. But Henry,
the mild and gentle-faced Henry, leaped, literally,
into the breach.

"Come," said he, standing perilously upon a
slippery rock below, "I take Madame on my
back"! To be lifted on to the lower grade was
the thought in my mind; but this was not the idea
of Henry, who, like a patient Christopher, trotted
off with a grateful, clinging passenger. Oncoming
tide threatened the cavern's mouth: hastily Madame, deposited on earth, was pushed into the
cave.

Alone, so I supposed, with not even the "shining eyes" of a dying goat to confound me—as
they had Crusoe—with thoughts of the Evil One.
I staggered on into the dark, barking my shins on
jagged rocks, brushing the low arch overhead. A
dank odor engulfed me.... Do creatures come
here habitually to die? I wondered, as something
stirred at my approach. A stench, a sudden rush
of air (what bird of prey would strike me to the
heart?) Perforce, I stood my ground against an
onrush of invisible Things. No time to call for
Jack Robinson, or the shade of his tribesman
Crusoe.

"Thornton! Henry!" I shouted, my voice drowned by the waves.

"Bats!" came the distant unruffled tones of Henry.

"Vampires!" I called, trembling from the suddenness of the onslaught, thankful as Crusoe "upon discovery of the monstrous, frightful old he-goat," having, like him, feared "some creature whether Devil or man."

Friday

Curaçao ‡ Primitive and arid

Curaçao.

CHAPTER XV

DUTCH WEST INDIES

ALTHOUGH Saba lacks the importance of Curaçao, although we were never to land upon the island, my impression of it is, none the less, vivid. Our plane, winging its way from Martinique to Puerto Rico, flew low as a plane dares. Before our astounded eyes was unfurled the unexpected scroll of Saba. Donkeys, discernible dots, could be seen upon the steep path cut from the hillside. Freed from the necessity to land by boat on the few yards of rock-threatened beach and thence to mount abruptly the nine hundred feet to Bottom, we were, nevertheless, able to look down, although with tantalizing briefness, into a crater-mouth, and see upon its bottom the red roofs of the oddly titled capital. Had we come by boat there would have been no alternative to the route we had seen, save the still more perilous approach known as the Ladder.

Romance hangs like a halo of cloud over the

isle. No more in extent than a single extinct volcano, Saba captivates the imagination not only by its history—its crater was the last ditch of the buccaneers—but because of the temerity of Dutchmen in converting such an inhospitable place into a base for sailors and boat builders. Used as they were to flat lands below the level of the dykes, these Hollanders (who in their homeland have utilized the sea) have at Saba, with no less ingenuity and courage, fitted to their use this partly hollowed mountain. The island has been Dutch since 1632, no other nation coveting its possession. Dutch is still taught in the schools, and English likewise is spoken. Owing to its salubrious climate—the smaller villages, Windward Side and St. John's, stand at altitudes of 1,200 and 1,900 feet—potatoes and strawberries, impossible to raise at low levels in the tropics, are grown and exported to St. Thomas. Perhaps because of this climatic advantage and also because of its isolation from the black hordes of the larger islands, the native Dutchmen, some 2,000 of them, have kept their blue eyes and rosy cheeks. The few Negroes employed here remain a race apart.

The porters of Saba were outspoken in protesting the introduction of donkeys: how archaic it sounds in a machine age! Man power is still used, however, for hauling lumber up the steep Ladder and carrying down the sea-worthy boats (not schooners, as has been said, but surf-boats from fifteen to twenty feet in length) to launching. While their men are thus employed, in boat-building or as seamen on the high seas or as em-ployees in Curaçao's oil refineries, the women of Saba, artists of the needle, busy themselves with intricate drawnwork.

Those who, like Ripley, would venture to this island—dubbed long ago by a sailor, Bonaparte's Cocked Hat (the tip of the "hat" rises to almost 3,000 feet)—may do so on the fortnightly boat from St. Kitts.

The Dutch portion of St. Martin—the island divides allegiance between France and Holland—St. Eustatius, better known as Statia, form, with Saba, the trio of Dutch possessions, dependencies of Curaçao, off the Leeward Islands. Statia, almost twice the size of Saba, is formed of two volcanic cones and, as a picture, composes well from sea or air. This was Rodney's Golden Rock and was once the scene of the world's most sensa-tional auction. The Dutch, having made Statia a free port, enjoyed the patronage before the Ameri-can Revolution of trade with England and her Colonies and of France. The place was known, too, as a rendezvous of smugglers. It was, at one period, the chief mart of the West Indies, with sometimes seven hundred vessels off the roadstead of Port Orange: harbor there is none. In 1780 the popula-tion numbered 2,500, and the wealth stored in the great warehouses—whose ruins gape to-day—

made it a prize worthy of Rodney's mettle when he took the Dutchmen unawares on February 3, 1781, and also, by the strategy of keeping the Dutch flag flying, captured additional laden vessels. Merchandise from ships' holds and vast storehouses was disgorged and put up at an unrestricted sale, netting the conquerors £4,000,000 sterling.

Lying close to the Spanish Main, Curaçao and its lesser neighbors Aruba and Bonaire—known, conveniently, as the ABC islands—complete the roll-call of the Netherlands West Indies.

Aruba, at the mouth of the Gulf of Venezuela, is ideally situated for the transfer of oil—brought by shallow draft vessels across the bars at the entrance to Lake Maracaibo—to sea-going tankers. Subsidiaries of the Royal Dutch-Shell and of the Standard Oil Company dominate the activities of this flat and unprepossessing place, where some 2,000 Americans dwell. Oil refineries belch soot-black smoke. The reek of petroleum offends the new-comer.

Curaçao has, no less than Aruba, been revived from lethargy by the "open sesame" of oil. It has been said that the true ruler here is not Queen Wilhelmina but King Petroleum. However this may be, we were given to understand that the Queen is the chief stockholder in Dutch-Shell. The Curaçaosche Petroleum Maatschappij—a subsidiary of the Royal Dutch-Shell—is not only

Aruba.

one of the largest but also one of the most up-to-
date in the world. Oil from Maracaibo (most prolific source of oil in South America and one of
the main oil-producing areas of the world) is delivered by a never-ending stream of tankers, to
set forth again, after refining, on other journeys
in the form of gasoline, kerosene, fuel oil....

Approaching Willemstad aboard the S.S. *Colombia,* my Illustrator and I were greeted by the
"Three Brothers"—the hills that dominate the
harbor. An old fort tops the central eminence;
silvery oil tanks to the left bore the name
S H E L L in letters that all might decipher, while
to the right, as our boat made slowly for the
narrow channel, on the curved side of another
mighty container was revealed the startling
H E L L.

Few visitors, even though they come fresh from
Holland, can be otherwise than astounded at the
mirrored resemblance of Willemstad to towns
along the Zuyder Zee. Substantial house-walls,

gabled roofs topped with red tile, chimney-pots, tiny windows with their full quota of panes make the overnight voyager feel that he has awakened in an Old World port.

Centuries ago, we thought, as our steamer went through the ceremony of taking aboard a pilot, Curaçao probably looked much as it does to-day. Peter Stuyvesant, governor of the island in 1643, would no doubt still feel at home here, although he would miss the slave-market of the Indies, instituted by him and bringing such prosperity to his island that Stuyvesant was promoted to become governor of New Amsterdam.

The entrance by which steamers gain the inner port is so narrow that it is ordinarily spanned by a pontoon bridge (the clever invention of an American consul), designed to swing aside on a vessel's approach. Obsolete forts, Riff and Amsterdam, guard the passage theatrically, in keeping with the Dutch stage-set of the city.

"How can it be real?" I queried. "How do they keep it so Dutch?"

The answer was that Shell employees come from Holland—usually for four years. Likewise the traffic police come, absurdly garbed in green, with metal helmets (and this the tropics!) and startling bayonets; soldiers, too. There were fifty new-comers aboard our steamer—Protestant Deaconesses and Catholic Sisters, and doctors in the hospitals (Dr. Aars, of St. Elizabeth's, in the

Medical Service of the Dutch East Indian Army, was going next to Java and Sumatra). From the Low Country, too, come the business potentates, lesser officials, as well as the governor of the Netherlands West Indies, who should, we thought, when we saw his eighteenth-century palace, wear a costume in keeping with its early tradition.

Although the Hotel Americano (in Otrabanda, Punta lies across the bridge) looks best from a distance, it is a convenient base in Willemstad from which to watch the ebb and flow of traffic. The pontoon bridge connecting the two sections of the town, when opened to admit a steamer, flies a black flag—reminding us that it was in the safe inner harbor of the Shottegat that pirates used to conceal their ships, to sally forth, on signal from the watch tower, upon the approach of galleons from the Main. We were amused by the never-ending formality of tankers from Maracaibo exchanging salutes with the port flag. Their scarlet pennants bore their company's emblem, a shell flaunted upon a ground of white. We became familiar with the sloop that bore the mail from Bonaire. There were, too, as ever in Holland, stalwart Dutch schooners. Cobbled were the quays: only the wooden shoes were missing!

Shopping at Curaçao is one of the favorite indulgences of cruise passengers. Being, to all intents and purposes, a free port, Curaçao displays articles from Europe and the Far East to be acquired at reasonable figures. The Oriental goods, however, are disappointing to globe-trotters who know the East, the coats of strident color and gold-encrusted kimonas, for example, having obviously been concocted to tickle the taste of vulgar Occidentals. The famed liqueur known as Curaçao is on sale but—we were disillusioned to hear—is made in Hamburg and Amsterdam. An important ingredient, however, the skin of a bitter orange, is, indeed, shipped from the island. (We were to see a grove of these oranges at the Governor's week-end house at Hato.) Huisvlijt (Women's Home Industry Exchange) has for sale the drawn-work of Saba, home-woven hats, and irresistible balata from Dutch Guiana.

Costumes of native women lend local color to the shopping thoroughfare. Worn with the full skirts of Holland is a black shawl undoubtedly derived from the Spanish mantilla and suggestive of the black fringed shawls of Venice. Dutchmen, tourists, Negroes, Indians, and Venezuelans—the latter living aboard the sloops in which bananas are brought from the mainland—add to the confusion of tongues. Although most street signs are in Dutch, Curaçaons have a nondescript tongue of their own, borrowing a little from English, Spanish, French, and Dutch: Papiamento, a written as well as a spoken language.

Maduro's Bank is one activity of a noted family; other Maduros are agents for Standard Oil,

Willemstad ‡ Venezuelan banana boats

making frequent trips to and from the United States. Some of the Maduro mansions are among the handsomest and most original in the town— situated in the Jewish quarter, for the family is Hebraic, of Portuguese descent, having been four hundred years on the island. Old Elias S. L. Maduro is buried in front of his palatial abode. Salmon or sage-green plaster, with white trimmings, are these engaging gabled dwellings.

In a public park, the Damesclub "Entre Nous" (founded by Rebecca Cohen Henriques) has erected an effective statue of Wilhelmina Konigin der Nederlanden, commemorating a period of fifty years' reign, 1880 to 1930. How little could the ladies have foreseen the vicissitudes to which their estimable queen was to be subjected! In the office of the Chamber of Commerce we remarked a photograph of H.K.H. Prinses Juliana and Z.K.H. Bernhard, in robes of State, and another of the *Niew Amsterdam*, flagship of the Holland America Line. It was in the office of the Compagnie Générale Transatlantique that we did business with the very French descendant of a royalist from Bordeaux. The ancestor had fled from his homeland, following the execution of Louis XVI.

"My family has lived at Willemstad, in the same house, ever since," our courtly interlocutor explained, "and it was never necessary for us to change our views, as all are royalists here."

The American consul—eager some day to record his own impressions of the land, ever scribbling—told us his duties might be divided into two chief sections: one is oil, the other the recording of the birth of Americans...in the Netherlands West Indies they average about one a day.

"Take your choice," said he, "as to their relative importance!"

Fortunate indeed were we that our week at Curaçao was spent at the Piscadera Bay Club. That we were received was through the good

offices of a friend in Trinidad. Permission for a
stay may sometimes be arranged through officials
of steamship or airplane. The club is primarily
intended as a vacation center for Dutch families
—workers in Shell. Here these Dutchmen send
their women and children in the hot weather, here
they come from Maracaibo and Aruba to spend
their "short leaves"—leave worthy of the name
was, before war-time occupation of the Netherlands, the opportunity given every three years
for a sojourn in Holland.

Our arrival at the Piscadera Bay Club—about
three kilometers from Willemstad—was on a Whit-
monday. Crowds had come to lunch and dine in
the open-air restaurant, to swim in the deep-sea
"pool"—heavily netted against sharks—to dance
in a pavilion where trees in tubs were as gaily
lighted of an evening as evergreens in an American suburb at Christmas. Almost continuous,
during our stay, was a stiff breeze from the
ocean; only occasionally, with a land-breeze, came
the all too familiar whiff from the oil refineries.
We were, of course, to visit the model village for
employees—a garden city with commodious bungalows, known as Emmastad, where, like mush-
rooms, oil tanks sprout. Oil, though malodorous,
is not the stench to the sensitive that were former
notorious causes of prosperity: piratical attack
and the nefarious slave-mart.

Curaçao, according to Ober, was discovered by

Where cactus and oil tanks sprout

none other than Amerigo Vespucci, although one authority credits the honor to Vespucci's comrade, Ojeda. Indian giants are said to have been the original inhabitants. The name Curaçao is attributed to them. Nowadays the population, some 35,000 in all, are mostly of African descent. Asylum has often been given to Venezuelan revolutionists, and emigrés such as members of the Gómez family. Indeed, it has been because of the

instability of Venezuelan governments and con-
stricting red tape tied by officialdom that American interests prefer to bring Venezuelan oil from
Maracaibo to Aruba to be refined under the laws
of the trustworthy Dutch.

Rain falls in Curaçao only ten days in the year.
If there were no ocean breeze the place would,
we thought, be uninhabitable. At Willemstad a
salt water distillery has been established; also,
much drinking-water is imported. The arid characteristics were especially apparent as we set
forth on a tour of the island.

An experimental ostrich-farm was given up,
said our chauffeur, because Curaçao is too dry
for ostriches! Green parrots, with daffodil-yellow
heads, flitted in hedges, while trupials, orange
below, blue-black and white above, frequented the
wild calabashes. Next to the tree-cacti—the natives actually eat one variety mixed with corn-
meal—and the aloes, the outstanding feature of
the trip was the distorted forms of divi-divi trees,
all violently wind-blown from the northeast. Their
pods, used in tanning, rank high as an export.
The country, barren in appearance, was sparsely
settled. A few plastered huts showed thatched
roofs above cactus hedges. One estate was noticeable because of walls of sea stone, built by slave
labor at a time when slaves were brought from
Haiti.

At Savonet were twisted manchineels and, more

A
Divi-Divi Tree

prepossessing, an old farmhouse still owned by the white descendant of the Dutchman who had built it four centuries ago. Its buff walls, red-tiled roof, and arid setting suggested to our minds a Provençal *mas*. At greener West Point, family huts were to be had for one or two gulders a day, while husbands were employed in oil or government work. Each village had its Catholic church and school. At St. Christoffel were many of what our chauffeur called "the people's bicycles"—donkeys—as well as cactus "fences" on which newly-washed garments were drying among thorns.

"Notice how the women chew wood," said our driver. "Only a few old girls smoke cigarettes, from Santo Domingo, known here as 'fire in mouth.'"

The climax of our ride—indeed of our Curaçaon stay—came at the sea cavern at Boca Tabla. After long miles of travel through semi-desert dust, after the weary monotony of cactus and aloe, aloe and cactus, how liberating to come at last upon wild surf! In winter, waves dash to the rocks beside which we parked our car, and gales completely fill the cavern. After a rough-and-tumble climb over sand and coral we scrambled into the mouth of a Crusoe cave, the main approach to the grotto: and what a grotto! Remote from man or signs of men, as we had been at Tobago, we gave ourselves up to appreciation of sponge and shell and Portuguese man-of-war and, more especially, to the extraordinary wonder of the deep blue strip of Caribbean, where breakers burst to foam, framed by the cavernous overhang of our cool refuge fringed with spray, as though with icicles.

Caracas Country Club

Puerto Cabello

CHAPTER XVI

VENEZUELA, BIRTHPLACE OF BOLÍVAR

ABOVE the port of La Guayra rise the cloud-capped Andes. Cold and unemotional indeed would be the man unstirred by the vision. The town is strung along a mile of coast, clinging for bare foothold to the base of the range. A high-perched fort has been immortalized by Kingsley. Proudly the mountains lift their heads abruptly from the shore to a height of eight thousand feet.

The Spanish Main! what a turmoil of conflicting emotions, what events the words evoke ... its discovery by Columbus, its exploration by Ojeda, accompanied by that "Italian pickle-dealer of Seville, Amerigo Vespucci," the exploitation of its fabulous resources by the Spaniard—brutal

445

alike to Indian and to imported African slave—
its battles to the death of treasure-laden galleons
with high-pooped vessels of the buccaneers, the
conflict in the philosophies of Elizabeth's England and Philip's Spain.... The list might be in-
definitely prolonged.

Venezuela, Scruggs states in his history of
the Republic, "comprises an area of territory
greater than that of either France or Germany
[obviously written before Hitler!], and greater
than that of Italy and Spain combined." He
speaks of the fact that because of a "fancied
resemblance to Venice," Ojeda, having observed
an Indian village on piles on the bay of Maracaibo (a type still in use; it was one of these, the
oil town of Lagunillas, that was destroyed by fire
in 1939 with appalling loss of life), called the
region Little Venice—a name later applied to the
whole country. Thus it was that a vast and mountainous land was destined to become known by
the absurdly inappropriate, although musical, title
of Venezuela. The population of this immense
and largely undeveloped country—which has been
compared in size to the entire Middle West of
the United States—is only about that of New
York and New Jersey combined.

Since the completion of the breakwater in
1891, passengers debarking at La Guayra need
no longer dread damage to life or limb. Our first
impression, on a Saturday evening, was of a for-

mal Spanish tiled park, of a walk along a boulevard by the sea-wall where thoughts of olden days
and sound of surging waves were drowned by
the horrid roar of amplified jazz blaring from
loud-speakers. Shops were closed; loafers and
strollers, players of dominoes upon the quays,
seemed impervious to the tumult, accepting if not
applauding it with Latin-American grace.

Lying at anchor were the *Virgilio* from Genoa
and the freighter *Sesostris* flying the stark
swastika—her seamen little foreseeing that April
first morning of 1941 when, on orders of their
superiors, they would, in company with the crews
of three Italian tankers, sabotage their vessel in
the harbor of Puerto Cabello and leap overboard
to escape the flames.

The ascent from La Guayra to Caracas is a distance of seven miles as the sea-bird flies, but
twenty-three miles by sensational rail, where cars
hang, breath-takingly to passengers, upon the
margin of the abyss—threading tunnel and deep
cutting to attain a height of over three thousand
feet in little more than an hour. It was to be on
our descent by automobile, above grandiose
gorges where rivers had gone dry and via panoramic curves studded with aloes and cacti—merit-
ing more respect than to be plastered, as they
are, with billboards of medicinal pills and American tires—that we were to come again upon La
Guayra, its Leper Hospital, housing five hundred

Above the port of La Guayra
𐌙 𐌙 𐌙   rise the cloud-capped Andes

(there are another six hundred lepers at Maracaibo), and the site of the landslide that had recently carried away a hundred houses and twenty-four human souls. It was on this occasion that we visited Mercuto with its Hotel Miramar; Mercuto, where the pigeons, accustomed to Gómez's Sunday visits, are still fed; Mercuto, with its green-berried sea-grapes beside the shore; a once popular resort, never, we trust, to see again the orgies held there during the period when the dictator Castro, predecessor to Gómez, was supposedly resting to restore his health.

At dusk, as might fly mariners' souls to the sea, the swallows of La Guayra, twittering on the wing, return from the mountain to their habitual roosts along the docks. The lifeless air is fanned by their whirling, darting, and swirling.

Puerto Cabello at the head of its bay, protected by hillside forts, is one of the most ample and gracious harbors on the Caribbean—why thus limit its praise?

"A vessel is safe here," said the Spanish navigators of old, "if anchored by a *cabello*—a single hair."

Man-o'-war birds swooped low to the eagle of dull gold on the towering shaft of a dock-side monument, as our steamer slipped into port. Wisps of cloud hung over the hills, touched the mauve blossoms on gigantic podded trees. Twice had we come to Puerto Cabello—this time we should say farewell to our vessel—and still a third time we were to return, and yet my memory is only a picture of a drive by clustering red-tiled Spanish houses, gay with brightly painted grilles, less ancient than those of La Guayra; and of a certain Tobago bread-fruit tree, magnificent in blossom, turning my thoughts to the isle of my dreams. There is, too, the vivid remembrance of Venezuelan flags enlivening the harbor traffic.

The colors were first displayed by General Francisco de Miranda in 1806. Venezuela declared her independence from Spain in 1811. The

Venezuelan flag was adopted by a special Commission with this explanation: "The yellow will stand for the golden coast of Venezuela separated by the blue of the ocean from the red which symbolizes Spain." The stripes to-day are all of the same width; whereas Colombia, to which Venezuela and Ecuador were at one time united by Bolívar, uses the same colors, the yellow band being half again as wide as its prototype; while the ensign of Ecuador, save for its coat-of-arms, is similar to that of Colombia, as both use the old Venezuelan flag.

It was, too, in 1811 that the monument to General Miranda, comrade-in-arms of Washington, known as El Precursor—The Forerunner of Bolívar, the Liberator—was erected on the plaza at Puerto Cabello. Although his rebellion against Spanish domination was unsuccessful—Miranda died in chains in Cadiz, and his American followers from the North were shot on the beach at Puerto Cabello—Venezuela has never underestimated this assistance. The shield of the United States—there were at the time but fifteen stars—displayed on this memorial, beside that of Venezuela, affords a surprising welcome to North Americans.

In the days of Gómez, Caracas was not in reality the seat of government, for the dictator dwelt at loyal Maracay. Beneath the peaceful waters of Puerto Cabello lie the fetters of political prisoners, fourteen tons of leg-irons, thrown there when jails were emptied upon the death of the despot.

To Maracay we were to turn our steps, or rather the wheels of our car, to Maracay by way of the former Spanish capital Valencia. Dramatic is the ascent from Puerto Cabello. Huts of Indians by the roadside were distinguished by crosses, hung outside, after the fashion in the Basque country— which, by no undue stretch of the imagination, these hills do resemble. It being a Sunday, the Cathedral on the square at Valencia was crowded. Men predominated, although there were many women of Spanish descent wearing black or white lace *mantas*. Golden were the oranges, fragrant the groves on the approach to Valencia. Not alone for the beauty of its daughters is the ancient capital noted. When Saint Valentine's Day is passed, how many Americans have hesitated between the relative merits of a King of Siam orange and a sun-ripened Valencia? While from April to August no "color added" labels need mar the beauty of Lue Gim Gongs—a cross between the Valencia and Mediterranean Sweet.

Gómez possessed the Midas touch—Venezuela is to this day on a gold standard—yet the wealth that flowed into his private coffers as well as into the treasury was chiefly derived from the tax on "black gold"—oil. Venezuela asserts that, next to the United States, it is the largest petroleum producing country in the world. Economically Venezuela may be said, like the Allies in the World War, according to an English statesman, to have "floated to victory on a sea of oil." Gómez, the illiterate mountaineer, was clever enough to outwit the "tricks of the foreign legal minds," writes Thomas Rourke in his dynamic *Gómez, Tyrant of the Andes.* "On all oil produced, a royalty of from ten to fifteen per cent was collected ... a law that assured his nation a proper percentage of the profits, that would still not discourage the foreign exploitation which was so much to be desired." When the oil companies entered Venezuela, in 1918, no accurate maps existed. This work alone of the engineers has been of inestimable service to Venezuelans.

The Hotel Jardín in Maracay, with palatial inner court and fountain suggestive of the Alhambra, tells louder than words of the prosperity of this pseudo-capital in the days of Gómez. From the windows of our suite we overlooked the public square with rows of flamboyants leading the eye to the cloud-topped mountains beyond the barracks which were Gómez's pride, while at a little distance stood the Hospital and Opera House ... farther afield was the bull-ring. Roads were Gómez's delight. (He brought the railroad from Puerto Cabello to Valencia.) Conscript labor was employed upon the highways to Caracas. Of an evening—about the hour when Anglo-Saxons drop to sleep—the fox-trot in our hotel began, compet-

Maracay ‡ Hotel Jardin

ing with the military band upon the plaza. Roller-
skaters usurped the sidewalks so that the owners
of shuffling feet were of necessity honked from
the highway by passing motor-cyclists and drivers
of local buses. Trucks thundered, venders with
bells announced their wares, while sibilant voices
on balconies vied with the shrill note of whistling
frogs.

"How does any one ever sleep at the Jardín?"
I haggardly inquired next morning of Charley, our
chauffeur, who replied:

"When the Grace Line people are here the police stop the honking."

There are, it seems, disadvantages to independent travel. We had discovered that even a stay of a week or two in Venezuela involved the signing of a paper that we had no intention of fomenting revolution, that we must be newly vaccinated, and that carry each of us must the required doctor's certificate. Mine, bearing the signature of my own physician and the official stamp of the consul in Philadelphia of the Estados Unidos de Venezuela, read as follows:

"To whom it may concern.

"This is to certify that, after careful examination, I find Mrs. Thornton Oakley of Villa Nova, Pa., U. S. A., is not suffering from Leprosy, Trachoma, Insanity, Epilepsy, in the acute or grand mal form, or from any other disease that may endanger Public Health."

How much I had always taken for granted, in lieu of being devoutly thankful! Street notices relevant to the treatment of Yellow Fever proved to us that the disease is not entirely unknown.

Having digressed from Gómez let us return to the subject long enough to visit the late dictator's town house, the Casa de Gómez, Plaza Girardot, where at the council table business of state was transacted, and the *hacienda*, Las Delicias, in the valley of Lake Valencia. The man was fifty-three when he usurped the power of Castro. Among his sixty-five bastards (some have put the figure at ninety-seven), Juan Vincente Gómez legally recognized only the children of Dionisia Bello, but, in his later years, Dolores Amelia Nuñez de Cáceres was his official hostess and her three sons and five daughters shared the affection bestowed by their father upon the older brood.

The guide who showed us through the establishment at Maracay, to-day a monument to the late President, assured us that even during the lifetime of the General there were the same two thousand portraits of Gómez on view. Among decorations received from various countries we noted a certificate, dated 1931, of Honorary Life Membership in the American Museum of Natural History, New York. The voluptuous scent of clustered white azahar de la India rendered the lifeless air of the patio oppressive. In the plain bedroom, as he had left it, were photographs of Dolores Amelia and of his favorite children, as well as Catholic images.

No inkling does the foreigner gain, from viewing the collection, of the means by which the Tyrant of the Andes ruled. Men lived in mortal terror, not alone of hanging but of poison, prison irons, castration, and ingenious torture. So plentiful were Gómez's enemies that, toward the end of his twenty-seven-year régime, an armed guard allowed the people to approach no nearer than a kilometer during the President's visits to hostile Caracas.

Juan Vicente Gómez
Despot of Venezuela

Animals, this strange creature was said to have remarked, he liked; they would not kill him. At Las Delicias he founded what has become the National Zoölogical Garden and a model dairy. The Department of Agriculture now owns these Gómez properties and blooded herds. A bronze bull, valued gift from Mussolini, stands at the entrance to the zoo, while within the enclosure white egrets —so plentiful in the land—turpials (*Yecturis yecturis*) of Venezuela—gorgeous in black, white, and orange—magnificent macaws, looked happier in the open than did a nostalgic polar bear.

Gómez erected a family vault at Maracay—a dome of brick remotely suggestive of the Kutab Minar in Delhi. After Gómez's death, in 1935, the people hardly dared to believe that they were not tricked, that the Old Man was indeed no longer among the living. Hats were not removed as the cortège passed.

In the environs of Maracay is a saman of immense girth in whose still living branches Bolívar found refuge during a period of two weeks. It is surrounded by a fence of bayonets. Over the gate we read:

UNION

PATRIA   TRABAJO

Groves of lesser samans in the neighborhood afforded shelter to the polished-jade leafed coffee, of which there were frequent plantations. There are planters in Venezuela and Colombia who get a return of as high as eighty per cent annual income on their investment one year, but another year they may lose everything because of local political upheavals.

A Visit to Colombia in the Years 1822 and 1823 is the title of a volume by a distinguished Philadelphian, one Colonel William Duane, who, with his daughter Elizabeth and stepson Lieutenant R. Bache, great-grandson of Benjamin Franklin, traveled twelve hundred miles on mule-back from Caracas to Bogotá. The record is one of hospitality, of guarding against bandits, of Andean scenery, of cactus, agave or American aloe. "The traveler," the gentleman writes, "in these countries, if he passes but a day's journey from the capital towns or cities, should not move without his hammock." The same might apply to-day in a region, save for an occasional highway, singularly unchanged by the lapse of a century. The valleys of the Orinoco and its tributaries—four hundred and thirty-six, all told—are rarely visited by foreigners other than prospecting geologists and engineers. Still less known, even to Venezuelans, is the vast hardwood area to the southward, the Amazonas territory, where Indians range along the Orinoco and across the untracked jungle to Brazil.

On the day of our departure from Maracay to drive over the highway to Caracas, we were, with tooting horn, to plough our way through herds of

On the Maracay-Caracas Highway ✦

cows and calves... stretching beyond visibility, and rounded up by hallooing cowboys.

Panorama follows panorama on the route from Maracay to Caracas, but none compares with the vision of the capital on its plateau three thousand feet above the sea, encircled by rusty hills of which one, La Silla—The Saddle, dominates by its near nine thousand feet. A rewarding view may be obtained from the heights of El Calvario, where the statue of Columbus overlooks the town.

The range of temperature at Caracas is from forty-eight to eighty-two degrees according to hour and season. Venders with samovars of hot coffee are no unusual sight in the chill of morning. The turmoil in the narrow thoroughfares, congested with costly automobiles, is startling to an arrival from the hills. Caraqueños are lively by nature—there are some two hundred and fifty thousand inhabitants—given wholeheartedly to oratory and revolution. (There were fifty-eight uprisings between the time of Bolívar and the time of Gómez). Our first glimpse of Bolívar Square with its tiles and tropical verdure, its four fountains, its central equestrian statue of the Liberator, is impressed on my memory. Within a stone's throw of the Cathedral, and not far distant from the Capitol, a mob was gathered about the Courthouse. Soldiers had the seething masses in hand, but curiosity ran high as to the reasons of the search for concealed fire-arms taking place as men emerged from the main exit. Weapons and their owners were soon parted.

Another sight, odd to North American eyes, was the transfer of sums of gold and silver coin (the silver bolívar is the unit) done with, to us, unwonted publicity. The sight of bags of specie, apparently unguarded, by the street-side seemed not in the least to disturb or even interest the ragged peons in battered straw hats or the more sophisticated wearers of felt. In the days of the dictator, we were told, beggars abounded, thrusting their dirty hands into automobiles halted in traffic, or, if friends stopped to chat on the street, one of their brotherhood inevitably appeared: these, for the most part, were Gómez's spies.

Fascinating was the flower, fruit, and bird market of Caracas, less pictorial, perhaps, than that at Port-au-Prince, but vastly more tempting to the foreign purchaser. Such a bewildering array of fruits artistically displayed had never before greeted this amateur of markets. Luscious pineapples, ripe mangoes, citrus- and jack-fruit, bananas, were stacked beside bunched grapes, Montana apples, dangling one to a string at a price equivalent to thirty-five American cents, California cherries, unrecognized varieties. Pasta de Membrillo—quince preserve—in plunket form stamped with dove or rabbit, rivaled in sales the ever-popular guava jelly. Cones, resembling bayberry candles, puzzling when first seen in trucks, proved to be of sugar. *Papelón* is the local name for this brown product of the coastal plains, molasses-like ingredient of the popular drink *guarapo*.

Upon the plaza was a chatter of caged birds, parrots, trupials, love-birds; but my attention was riveted upon the flowers. Two nuns, black-skinned and black-veiled, carried between them a clothes-basket filled with lilies—both Easter and calla—from the cordillera. Roses, daisies, carnations ... but what were those: orchids! From the branches

El Calvario: The statue of

of trees overshadowing the flower stalls they
tempted, their blooms within reach of prospective
buyers. At Trinidad, in the month of May, we had
seen the collections of the Royal Botanic Gardens,
that of Sir George Huggins, and those specimens
already preened for the annual show by the President of the Orchid Society. We had, as never be-

Columbus overlooks Caracas

fore, luxuriated in orchids. A gift, in quality to be likened to that made by the Queen of Sheba to Solomon, had been pressed into my hands on our departure. Now, in Venezuela, Oncidiums, Cyprepediums, Cymbidiums, Vandas, even the Cattleya mossiæ or "Easter orchid" are not enough of a novelty to appeal, as gift flowers, to Caraqueñas.

No more absorbing playlet have I heard by radio than that given by Andrew Benson (the veteran gatherer) on acquiring the "Flower of Death" orchid on the upper reaches of the Magdalena near Bogotá...garnered against an accompaniment of hostile Indian war drums. Who would not reread H. G. Wells' absorbing tale "The Flowering of the Strange Orchid"? And now comes *The Orchid Hunters,* the saga of two intrepid Americans daring the manifold dangers of the Colombian and Venezuelan jungle, in a spirit of high adventure, to meet the demand of American ladies for exotic corsages of "lavender flame" at Easter.

Fascinating, the word applied to the market, is not applicable to the Palace Hotel at which we resided, nor, was it, to any hostelry in Caracas. The windowless bedrooms, in Spanish style, give upon a grimy tiled patio—sole source of ventilation— from which a glimpse of the mountains may be had. In the colorful dining-room we partook of such delicacies as *meilado* (honey pancake), and *sancocho,* a succulent vegetable soup, made with chicken stock, with which a second chicken is served; dessert of cheese, guava paste, and a demitasse of the powerful black coffee of the region. A simple luncheon in Caracas may cost from two to three dollars, for prices are probably the highest in the world. It is a matter of supreme indifference to this South American Republic, with balanced budget and no external debt, whether travelers come or stay away. Not one tourist in ten thousand, I read, spends more than a day in Caracas! The Avila or Nacional may hold them!

The suburb of El Paraiso reminded us of the newer quarters of Lisbon. Here are the United States and other legations, and, amid African tulip trees, here a Basque châlet, there a Swede's residence, Dalecarlia; the largest restaurant and dance hall in South America; the Museums of Sciences and of Arts, where works are shown by that distinguished Venezuelan painter Armado Lira; and here, moreover, is the Avenue of the Mahoganies.

In the Florida section stands the Country Club. Of Spanish Mission style, this building has been erected on the site of an estate house of a coffee *hacienda*. Between royal palms, across formal English borders and golf-links, rises a distant range, while the Club is backed by a stark peak. To dine on the terrace, to linger beside the tiled fountain in the patio, in congenial company, caps a stay in Caracas.

EL GOBIERNO Y EL PUEBLO DE VENEZUELA

A

JORGE WASHINGTON

FUNDATOR DE LA REPUBLICA DEL NORTE

ERIGIDO EN EL CENTENARIO DEL

LIBERATADOR SIMÓN BOLÍVAR

1883

We paused at the Washington monument to read the above on our drive, in this newest of new residential districts, to the house of our friend, the Managing Director of the Telefonos de Venezuela. On arrival we lingered to admire sentinel trees at the entrance, and the wife of our host admitted having killed a coral snake in her own garden. Venezuela, said the couple, is reborn since the passing of Gómez. In the old days political offenders were thrown into prison never to be released and men were strung up in public places to die. Our hostess, to show how illiterate the dictator was, recalled a time, in the days of silent films, when her seat at a cinema was beneath the Gómez box and she was almost deafened by the clamor of the reading of captions to the despot. The natives used to fear to go out at night. After the death of the Old Andino the revolution was against Gómez's friends and relatives. A ferocious-looking crew of natives, armed with machetes, came to our friends' at-that-time lonely country place, announcing that it was protecting the houses of foreigners against looters, and protect them, with good humor, it did. The people love to joke—in the old days they never smiled. Theirs is a lovable, though often immature, nature. During the dictator's life every householder was obliged to display a picture of Gómez. All consuls and newspaper men were forced to praise him. Eighty per cent of the population is still unlet-

tered but, with the constantly increasing education
of all classes, Venezuela will rapidly be transformed.

The Colonial mansion where Bolívar was born
on July 24, 1783, is now a museum and national
shrine. The massive mahogany four-post bed-
stead, even to crimson brocade hangings, stands
as on that momentous day when the Liberator of
Colombia, Venezuela, Ecuador, Panama, and Peru,
and the founder of Bolivia, first saw the light. At
sixteen the boy was sent to be educated in Madrid;
in 1809 he returned to his own country after visiting the United States. Aristocratic, idealistic,
Bolívar was forced by fate to become a miltary
leader as well as a statesman and, above all, a
patriot. The episodes of his life are graphically
depicted at the birthplace by murals, the work of
the Venezuelan painter Tito Salas, as is the noted
portrait of the Liberator, in uniform, mounted on
his white charger, with a background of Chim-
borazo—the mountain of Ecuador the ascent of
which inspired him to write a now-famous pane-
gyric. This picture hangs in the Miraflores Palace,
residence of the President of the Republic.

After such brilliant accomplishment Bolívar
was to die at the age of forty-seven at Santa Marta
in Colombia. (His remains have since been transferred to the Pantheon at Caracas.) As death drew
near Bolívar had written (it was a time of reaction):

"I see no salvation for the country. I believe everything is lost ... all who have served the Revolution have ploughed the sea."

Little could Bolívar have foreseen the day when a monument would be erected to him in Central Park, New York, and the anniversary of his birth, July 24th, would be a day for celebrations by the Pan-American Society in this country as well as one to which South American liberals would rally.

Eleazar López Contreras, although the head of the army under Gómez, is conceded to be an honest and enlightened man. As President of the Republic, following Gómez, he did not feather his own nest but instigated a three-year plan (admitting sotto voce that perhaps thirty years would be required) for the regeneration of Venezuela. The vast government commissions from the oil fields—an Anglo-Netherland-American monopoly—estimated at $40,000,000 a year, have been spent for the public welfare. Realizing that only 150,000 voters were qualified by literacy test, Contreras launched a comprehensive educational project. Housing and hopitalization have been undertaken on a vast scale: the Sanotoria Anti-Tuberculoso Bolívar on the outskirts of Caracas was completed in 1940. (No longer can it be said that, in Venezuela, surgeons never operate in the third quarter of the moon!) Knowing that his term would expire in 1941, Contreras paved the way for the continuation of his public-spirited policies.

SIMON BOLIVAR
Liberator of Venezuela
New Granada
Ecuador and Peru
and Founder of Bolivia

The new President, General Isaias Medina Angarita, was Minister of War and Navy in the Cabinet of President López Contreras. General Medina has pledged that his administration will be a "second stage of the Bolivarian régime that has been developing since 1936." For the first time the United States and Venezuela have exchanged ambassadors. A paternal dictatorship followed.

By a vagary of fate the Nobel Peace Prizes were created by the inventor of dynamite. Hardly less bizarre is the fact that the founder of the monopolistic Standard Oil Company should also have chartered, in 1913, "the Rockefeller Foundation ... aimed at coöperation with the nations in the control of such diseases as malaria and yellow fever." Now comes this welcome news: "Four committees composed of 33 educators and other prominent persons were appointed by President Roosevelt to-day [July 30, 1941] to advise the government on planning and executing the program to improve cultural relations with Latin American nations. The committees will work with the State Department's Division of Cultural Relations, headed by Nelson Rockefeller." The names of the chairmen, Robert G. Caldwell, Knowles A. Ryerson, Stephen P. Duggan, and Edgar J. Fisher, carry weight.

Coester in his *The Literary History of Spanish America* says the power of eloquent speech is nowhere greater than among Spanish Americans.

"The rhythmic flow of their vocalic language," he goes on, "excites in them an æsthetic emotion incomprehensible to people of other races. To this psychological peculiarity has been ascribed the frequency of revolutions in some countries, especially Colombia. Would the facts of the following anecdote be possible in England or the United States? It is related of Cecilio Acosta (1831-81) that one day after he had delivered a speech in praise of the fine arts before the Académia de las Bellas Artes in Caracas, he was accompanied home by a crowd composed not only of enthusiastic students and ordinary persons but also of members of the society, the clergy and government officials." One of the latter congratulated Acosta's mother because her son had "just uttered the most eloquent discourse that I have ever heard."

North Americans may well echo the words of President Taft when he said: "I know the attractiveness of the Spanish American; I know his highborn courtesy; I know his love of art, his poet nature, his response to generous treatment, and I know how easily he misunderstands the thoughtless bluntness of an Anglo-Saxon diplomacy, and the too frequent lack of regard for the feelings of others that we have inherited."

We of the Republic of the North should not need a Darió to remind us that the Condor exists with the Eagle on the heights.

The fort of San Felipe
dominates the city of Cartagena.

Along the Magdalena

CHAPTER XVII

PORTS OF COLOMBIA

BARRANQUILLA and Cartagena, the modern and the ancient Caribbean ports, are all that the American traveler aboard a Grace Liner or other cruise ship is likely to see of the Republic of Colombia, our nearest neighbor on the South American continent, a country more vast than Venezuela and with a population of over six million inhabitants; a republic, like our own, with outlet to both Atlantic and Pacific; a territory fabulously rich in natural resources—gold, silver, emeralds, indigo, oil, and, next to Brazil, the most famous coffee mart of the Western Hemisphere; a land so mountainous that, according to Baron Humboldt, a traveler needs only a thermometer and a mule to find any desired climate within the compass of a few miles.

Our leisurely journey to Colombia having included the entire sweep of the British West Indies,

Curaçao, and Venezuela, we were astounded, upon arrival at Barranquilla, to be told: "You know our city is only six hours by Pan-American Clipper from Miami."

Perhaps no other remark had ever so forcefully brought home to us the vanishing frontiers of the modern world.

Three ranges of the Andes run in a northerly direction through Colombia, making the opening of the country by roads other than trails a challenge to the engineer. News has traveled at mule's pace. The capital, Bogotá, all but inaccessible from the Pacific, situated at an altitude of a mile and a half above the sea, is reached in from six to fourteen days by river steamer, and a final stage by train, from Barranquilla near the mouth of the Magdalena.

"People that can afford it," said our informant, "fly to Bogotá in less than three hours. The air line was founded by the Germans in 1919, but now is Colombian owned. In this country we travel by boat, burro, or plane."

A few years ago passengers from cruise ships landed at Puerto Colombia, a place of embarkation with naught but its pier to recommend it, and proceeded thence the seventeen miles to Barranquilla; but of late years, since 1935, owing to dredging and a "submarine landslide," Barranquilla has become the preferred port of call for modern liners.

My memories of Barranquilla are two-fold, of uninteresting modern and squalid ancient.... Yet Barranquilla, having developed so far in our century (before that time it was hardly habitable for the foreigner of nice tastes) has in all probability a bright future. In population it has already attained, in round numbers, 150,000.

The modern note is stressed in such an admirable American establishment as the Hotel del Prado with its impeccable cuisine, its up-to-date swimming-pool with fountain, its airy bungalows. Eighty per cent of the guests are English-speaking. Judging from conversations overheard we came to the conclusion that the common tongue is used chiefly in discussion of bridge and golf. Ennui might conceivably encourage inordinate bridge-playing, but how Anglo-Saxons could enjoy golf in such a climate was to us incomprehensible. In the aristocratic district of El Prado we were to meet the Staplekamps (Mynheer was in Dutch-Shell) who assured us that the climate was preferable to many they had known. One of the minor drawbacks of life seemed to be the necessity of locking mahogany doors; windows were protected in Spanish fashion by iron grilles, as even door-mats, if unpadlocked, would be stolen. This it was easy to believe on seeing a cross-section of the population: mestizos or half-breeds, Indians, Negroes, Syrian merchants—the latter a prosperous group in the republic, a minority (said to be

In the heart of Colombia

ten per cent in the entire country) of white descendants of the early Spaniards.

The modern buildings on the streets of Barranquilla are interspersed with adobe huts, heavily
thatch-topped. The imported automobile rubs
wheels with the native ox-cart. The airplane zooms
over dug-outs and stern-wheelers. In the main
thoroughfare stands the inevitable statue of Columbus, discoverer of the Spanish Main, in tribute
to whom Colombia owes its name.

The village of Soledad, seemingly God-forsaken
despite its large Catholic church, sordid but to a
certain degree picturesque because of thatch-roofs,
is inhabited by Indian half-breeds. A few Spanish

dwell the Motilone Indians

houses tell of former prosperity, as does a curious graveyard where cement sarcophagi stand in serried ranks above ground. The unique note, however, at Soledad, is the labor of natives hollowing dug-outs after the fashion of their Indian forebears. The shallow canal beside which they excavate the tree-trunks is, for lack of a road inland, used as a thoroughfare. Men, on donkeys kneedeep in muddy water, bring milk cans from a distance. Boarlike pigs wallow among water hyacinths, a tropical substitute for clover.

Thoughts leaped to the Motilone Indians of the cordillera, in the border region between Lake Maracaibo and the Rio Magdalena, notoriously ferocious, against whose manchineel-poisoned arrows pioneer oil prospectors, sent a quarter of a century ago by the Mellons to Maracaibo, wore bullet-proof jackets—so one of them, a fellow-traveler aboard the *Lady Drake,* had told me. On muleback he had crossed the Andes nineteen times. Snakes, this man, toughened by life in the bush, could deal with—boas, he said, were easy to shoot —but the Motilones, lurking in ambush, cannibalistic, were dangerous as dysentery and the rum taken as a preventive but too often forming a vicious circle with the disease it was imbibed to cure. The, at times, flushed face and heavily-lidded eyes of this engineer—on other days so original and brilliant—haunt me still.

"I've been in hospital," he used to say, "I'm not dead yet. I'll live"; and, again, "Oil, I want to forget oil."

Barranquilla prides itself on its modern waterworks, transforming the turbid contents of the river, at the rate of a million gallons in twenty-four hours, into water fit for man. It was a remarkable sight to see the nauseous scum removed, the intricate successions of machines and vats and sprays, the miraculous result of clear cool liquid issuing temptingly from bubbler fountains.

Traffic on the Magdalena River includes dugouts. One we noted with anti-clockwise swastika upon its sail—not the type chosen by Hitler, inviting ill luck. Boats, for the most part, are stern-

Barranquilla ‡ The coffee port

wheelers, ploughing their way through hyacinths to La Dorada six hundred miles upstream, whence passengers and merchandise are conveyed by rail to Bogotá. Downstream come loads of bulging coffee-bags, bunches of bananas, both piled to fan-tastic heights beside the muddy stream at the delta port of Barranquilla to await trans-shipment. My Illustrator, son of Pittsburgh, one-time traveler by river-boat to New Orleans, was entranced to hear that these paddle-wheelers are fabricated in the United States and assembled beside the Magdalena.

Cartagena de la Indias, the city named for Cartagena in Spain was called—to distinguish it from the mother community that had taken its title from Carthage. Founded in 1533 by Pedro de Heredia, the Cartagena on the Spanish Main was subject to frequent attack by buccaneers, who were attracted by the treasure of the New World gathered here for shipment by galleon to Cadiz. It was in the reign of Philip II that the city's walls were erected at a cost so fabulous as to make the monarch exclaim that they should be visible from Spain.

In 1585, Sir Francis Drake, having received letters of marque from his sovereign, Queen Elizabeth, took Cartagena and exacted a tribute of 110,000 ducats.

Britain having issued a proclamation of war against Spain in 1740 "to open the ports of Spanish-America to mercantile enterprise," Admiral Vernon, the capturer of Porto Bello, attempted, and failed miserably, to raid Cartagena. Forty-five hundred North American recruits accompanied the British Admiral, among them five hundred Virginians whose leader was Lawrence Washington. This elder half-brother of George Washington was the owner of a plantation known as Hunting Creek, to be renamed, because of admiration for the admiral ("Old Grog" to some), Mount Vernon. Tobias Smollett, surgeon's mate aboard the flagship, was to write of this disastrous campaign in which twenty thousand men were lost in the attack: "Good brandy and good rum mixed with hot water, composing a most unpalatable drench, was the cause of failure."

In 1811 Cartagena was the first city in the territory then known as New Granada to declare its independence from the Mother Country, but the besieged town was forced to surrender after four months, in 1815, to troops from Spain. Its valiant resistance won for it the name of the "Heroic City."

Under the leadership of Bolívar the country was to join, in 1819, with Venezuela and Ecuador to form the Republic of Colombia: the others were later to secede. As has already been mentioned, the Liberator was to end his days at a Colombian port, Santa Marta, in the year 1830. The Hacienda where he died has become a place of patriotic pilgrimage. The description of Santa Marta's landlocked bay is already familiar to readers of *Westward Ho!* who will remember the incident of the bishop's kidnapping by Amyas and his henchmen.

El Pastillo

History comes to life at Cartagena, we thought, as our liner slipped between the sun-blistered fortifications of San José and the disintegrating San Fernando and nosed her way along a mangrove-infested shore to her wharf on Drake's Spit. This channel, the Boca Chica, is the only approach nowadays to what was once the most formidable stronghold of the conquistadores in the New World —the Boca Grande having been blocked after the attack by Vernon: the outer forts and El Pastillo had been taken by the admiral. Spindling palms, suggestive of the Nile, arrest the eye on the edge of the harbor, still as a lagoon. Venice has been in the minds of many on first sight of the virtually intact, iridescent walled town seen across the water. For the very flatness of its waterside situation, the sunbaked appearance of its turreted ramparts, it brought to our thoughts the picture of Aigues-Mortes in Provence—"ethereal," as I have written, "as will-o'-the-wisp or glamorous mirage."

Before crossing the Paseo de Los Martires, with its centenary shaft to Bolívar, to enter the inner city of Cartagena, we drove to the Fort of San Felipe and visited La Popa, conspicuous on its poop-shaped hill. The church of an abandoned Augustinian monastery, on the summit of the mount, houses the image of Nuestra Señora de la Popa, the "Candlemas" Virgin brought centuries ago from Spain. As nuns never lived on this exposed height they could hardly (as has been said) have thrown themselves, upon approach of invading corsairs, into the sea. Here, at Candlemas, thousands of pilgrims come by day, by night, on donkey-back or even barefoot. A cross is lighted nightly and will be during the lifetime of its donor, as a thank-offering to the Virgin for the restoration of the health of a beloved daughter.

In the scorching heat of noonday we staggered, half-blinded by the sun, into the shelter of the La Popa Club where we were fortified (the word seems to be inevitable at Cartagena) with food, while Indian crooners enlivened the hour with rhythms garnered from tribes in the jungle of the interior.

Aside from the Cathedral, sadly modernized but still possessing a magnificent reredos, the walled city with its Moorish balconies, its grilles and patios, is essentially still a Spanish town. It takes little imagination to picture it as it rose newly from the designs of royal Spanish architects—the chief attractions are the San Pedro Claver Convent and the House of the Inquisition, facing a square upon which the Green Cross of the fanatics was planted at time of auto-da-fé for Cartagena, no less than Mexico and Lima, was headquarters of this arch cruelty in the New World. We rejoiced that stones had no power to cry aloud.

What thought the saintly Pedro Claver of the Inquisition, we wondered. Pedro was a member of the Society of Jesus. Had he not signed thus his vow—while still a youth in Spain: "Pedro Claver, slave of slaves until death." It is recorded that during his well-nigh forty years of service at Cartagena he brought baptism to 300,000 unfortunates, fresh from Africa, hanging medals around their ebony necks. Fearlessly he won their allegiance by bearing gifts—for which he had begged—to the filthy holds of the ships that brought these fellow-creatures into port, with his own hands tending the sick and dressing pestilential wounds.

Standing within the little room at the head of the convent stair—the very cell in which the padre

Cartagena ‡ The Patio of San Pedro Claver

had lived within easy call of his flock, with view of the water where slave-ships were wont to enter— I glanced upon the stone recording that the venerable padre had died in this narrow chamber on the eighth day of September, 1654.

As we lingered in the silent patio, surrounded by galleried convent and revered church, it was scarcely an effort to people the place with Peter Claver and his down-trodden multitudes of newly-christened parishioners. Canonization of the deserving priest was accorded by Pope Leo XIII.

Rimsky-Korsakov's "Song of India" brings to my mind not Hindustan alone, but, oddly, a memory of Colombia. How often have we heard of late of the Crown of the Andes: the gem-encrusted diadem from the Cathedral at Popayán, in a region ceded in years long gone to the Republic of Colombia. Spared when an epidemic of fever swept the plains, the Spaniards of this ancient Andean settlement were determined to create a thank-offering worthy of the Madonna to whom they attributed their miraculous salvation. Carved from a block of Inca gold (twenty-four smiths labored for six years), studded with four hundred and fifty-three emeralds (the most famous emeralds of the world, more precious than diamonds, are to be obtained in the Colombian Andes), the Crown was ready for the coronation of the statue of Our Lady of the Andes, said to have taken place on December 8, 1599. The Atahuallpa Emerald, weighing over forty-five carats, as its name implies, is reputed to have been worn by the last Inca of Peru. Captured by pirates; held by rival armies; restored to the Cathedral; coveted by Nicholas II, Czar of Russia, whose fate overtook him before the consummation of the purchase—the Crown of the Andes has been sold, by special dispensation of the Vatican, to Americans in order that the poor of Popayán (farther south than Bogotá, high-perched in the Central Cordillera) might be healed and fed. How symbolic of the days to come! Not in Colombia alone, but in the mining of the world's as yet unfathomed resources, may the few not profit but the people be fed.

Panama City ‡ The Cathedral

King's Bridge. Old Panama

CHAPTER XVIII

INTEROCEANIC PANAMA

On his fourth and last voyage to the New World Columbus skirted the Isthmus of Panama, seeking a westward passage. His vessels are said to have entered Limón Bay, where to-day stand the settlements that bear his name, Cristobal and Colón. Despondent, despairing of success, the Admiral returned to Jamaica and, according to Walt Whitman, was vouchsafed a vision:

> Shadowy, vast shapes, smile through the air and sky,
> And on the distant waves sail countless ships,
> And anthems in new tongues I hear saluting me...

a prophetic revelation of modern Panama.

The conquerors of the Panamanian jungle fall into three categories: the Spanish discoverers, covetous of gold; the pillaging buccaneers, no less cruel, still more obsessed by lust for material

489

possessions; and, within the last hundred years, the pioneers of the New Day.

Vasco Nuñez Balboa, having received a commission from the king's treasurer at Santo Domingo as acting governor of Darien—the name by which the Isthmus of Panama was in those days known—and hearing from the Indians of an ocean to southward, pressed to "a peak in Darien" from which he was to behold the Pacific ... the first white man so to do. On September 29, 1513, he strode into the waves, claiming the waters and the lands they bounded for the Sovereign of Castile. With superhuman effort, on his return to the Caribbean, this Soldier of the King undertook, with a band of Spaniards and Indian porters, to transport two dismembered ships across the untracked jungle of the isthmus, to assemble and launch the craft upon the Pacific, the adventurer having heard from the Indians of a wealthy land to southward. (It is said that Balboa's bloodhound, Leoncillo, who drew the pay of a man-at-arms, could distinguish between hostile and friendly Indians.)

Pedro Arias de Avila, having meanwhile been sent from Spain to govern Darien, was filled with the same ambition. In accordance with the new governor's orders, Balboa was arrested on a charge of "contemplated revolt" and straightway beheaded. Pizarro, a former lieutenant of the dead man, was to realize Balboa's dreams of the conquest of Peru. (For Bolívar, exiled at the time of his death from the land of his birth, Venezuelans have named the unit of their currency; similarly in the Republic of Panama the equivalent of a dollar bears the name of the slain Balboa.)

Pedrarias (for so was Pedro Arias known) set about the building of a base on the Pacific. Thus, in the year 1516, was the city called Panama—the Indian word signifies abundance—founded. The site is known to-day as Old Panama—the first town on the American continent. It was eventually to become, next to Cartagena, the most strongly fortified outpost of Spain in the Western Hemisphere. Here was brought in lavish quantities the wealth wrested from the Incas of Peru, and from this base the gold-trains carried the treasure over the Cruces Trail to the Caribbean settlements of Nombre de Dios ("the Sepulcher of Spaniards") and later to Porto Bello...wrought gold and newly-mined silver, pearls and dye woods, emeralds from the Andes.

Little wonder that the tales that got abroad whetted the appetite of Elizabeth's greedy Protestant subjects, intolerant of the fact that so much wealth should be confined to their traditional Popish foes. Francis Drake was knighted by the Queen when he returned in the *Golden Hind* to England after raiding a gold-train near Nombre de Dios and waylaying a hundred Spanish galleons. With craving unsatiated by success, Drake returned to the region (about fifteen miles beyond where to-day Colón stands) for an attack on Porto Bello. On the eve of this venture dysentery overcame the privateer and he was given sea-burial off the harbor. The destruction of the town was later accomplished by perhaps the most relentless of all the buccaneers, who also—daredevil that he was—braved afoot the long trek through the jungle with his desperadoes to vanquish the Spaniards in their established community of Panama.

"On the 24th of February of the year 1671 Captain Morgan"—wrote Esquemeling, a Dutch apothecary who accompanied the raider, and later author of *The American Sea Rovers*—"departed from the City of Panama, or rather the place where the said City of Panama did stand. Of the spoils whereof he carried with him one hundred and seventy-five beasts of carriage, laden with silver, gold and other precious things, beside six hundred prisoners more or less, between men, women, children and slaves."

The city was shortly to be rebuilt by the Spaniards farther along the coast—a few miles west of the ruins. After the destruction of the Spanish Armada and the looting of Panama by buccaneers came an era of comparative inaction.

The Treaty of New Granada between Colombia and the United States in 1846 virtually gave the latter the rôle of protector of the Isthmus of

Panama. During the second half of the century preceding our own a score of revolutions were suppressed by means of this authority. The Colombians, or rather their politicians in Bogotá, who had continually exploited the district of Panama and who had demanded exorbitant tribute from the French Canal Company, finally rejected the terms of an agreement drawn up between them and the United States—and ratified by the latter—for the creation of a canal by the Americans. It is said, in certain quarters, that Colombia has never forgiven the United States for recognizing the independence of the province of Panama—November 7, 1903—four days after its secession; or for the fact that the coveted $10,-000,000, with promised annuity of $250,000, which would otherwise have gone to the gold-greedy government of Bogotá, was paid into the coffers of the new Republic. The Colombian Congress, in rejecting the treaty, had merely been playing for time until the expiration of the French concession, hoping thereby to obtain the sum that would otherwise be given to the French company by the United States in settlement of its claim. That the United States, its patience at the breaking point, bought off the Frenchmen and prevented the landing of Colombian troops at Colón and Acapulco to suppress the revolution, long rankled.

Gold, the magnet that had drawn Balboa, Pizarro, Drake, Raleigh, and Morgan across the Atlantic to the tropical jungles of Panama, was to be the motive for a revival of interest in the isthmus: this time not wrought gold to be wrested from the Incas of Peru but the as yet unmined nuggets of California. At the time of the Gold Rush of '49, the isthmian route, despite its drawbacks—and they were great—was considered a short and desirable cut for American prospectors from the East. (It was at this time that Colón—to this day preserving characteristics of a mining town—came into being.) The method was to sail from New York to Chagres, transferring to native boat for Gorgona or Cruces, thence by mule along the King's Highway to Panama City. In the dry season thousands were known to pass on this route in a single week. Inevitably the Panama Railroad followed, an enterprise that made fortunes for its American promoters. On July 27, 1855, the first engine crossed the isthmus from sea to sea.

The Spaniards had dallied with the thought of the creation of a waterway. This suggestion of "altering God's plan" was considered impious. At the instigation of the Inquisition, Philip II forbade all such discussion. Nelson wanted a survey made for England. The French government, from 1735, had had the project in mind, and in 1877 a Frenchman, Lieutenant Wyse, was granted a concession from Colombia—the concession actually used in the building of the canal.

Ferdinand de Lesseps, engineer of the Suez Canal, completed in 1869, had been created a count and had become the idol of the French. Following an international scientific congress, held in Paris in 1879, de Lesseps was made head of the Compagnie Universelle du Canal Interocéanique de Panama. The old man, probably a dupe of speculators, visited Panama. Work was started in 1881. The sum of $260,000,000 was raised by the sale of stocks and bonds to the thrifty French people and eked out by lottery. In 1889 the company, owing to inefficiency and the lack of knowledge to cope with tropical disease, went into liquidation. In 1892 its promoters, including de Lesseps, father and son, also Eiffel, of tower fame, were arrested—charged with fraud. Two years later de Lesseps, who was not imprisoned, broken in body and with wandering mind, gave up the ghost.

Such was the legacy of failure braved by the Americans on purchase of the French concession for a round sum of $40,000,000, including all implements and other properties in the field and the Panama Railway.

The Isthmian Canal Zone consists of a strip of territory ten miles in width, extending five miles on each side of the center of the canal. It runs from the Caribbean Sea, ''3 marine miles from low-water mark,'' across the Isthmus of Panama into the Pacific ocean ''to a distance of 3 marine miles from mean low-water mark." Colón and Panama City with their harbors are excluded. The United States is granted the use, occupation, and control of this zone, ceded in perpetuity by the Republic of Panama, by treaty ratified in the United States Senate February 23, 1904. Several islands outside these limits, in the Bay of Panama, are included within the zone.

The Canal is a lasting monument to Theodore Roosevelt, whose foresight accomplished the deal which has been of inestimable worth to Panamanians as well as to Americans and other citizens of the world, and under whose administration work began on May 14, 1904; to John F. Stevens, the railroad man whose genius for transportation solved the problem of soil disposal, and to his successor Colonel George Washington Goethals, Chairman of the Commission and Chief Engineer; and, not least, to Colonel William Crawford Gorgas, fresh from triumphs in Havana, as Chief Sanitary Officer. Despite the exaggerated criticism of its "taking"—Panama had more than once before aspired to independence— the bickerings, failures, and resignations of the first few years, the Canal itself and the transformation of the zone from one of the most pestilential areas of the earth's surface to probably the cleanest region in the tropics, singularly free from insects and epidemics, should fill the breasts of Americans with legitimate pride.

Dysentery, malaria, typhus, yellow fever, bubonic plague had decimated the ranks of the Frenchmen and their imported Chinese coolies. Yellow fever likewise thinned the ranks under the Americans—at one time there were sixty-three cases. Accordingly two base hopitals, of 2,500 beds each, were erected at Colón and at Ancon. Increased authority was granted to Gorgas. Rats were exterminated, flies disappeared with the removal of filth, an amazing system of mosquito control was set up, making the introduction of the ubiquitous wire screens almost superfluous. Gorgas had this advantage over the Frenchmen, that the notorious relation of the mosquito to malaria and also to yellow fever had been proved. Of the forty varieties of the insect known to Panama, the culprits were *Anopheles gambiae* (malaria) and *Aedes aegypti* (Yellow Jack). As late as 1940 the Rockefeller Foundation has discovered two other species in Brazil transmitting yellow fever. The Foundation urges the control of the *aegypti,* as in Brazil, to "avoid the threat which in these days of rapid transit might so easily develop into a cataclysm ... should the virus of yellow fever break through the barriers of quarantine, vaccine and medical vigilance."

Now that the waterway is filled it is perhaps less easy to understand how the undertaking absorbed a half-billion dollars than if the visit had been made at the time strikingly depicted by

Panama Canal

W. B. Van Ingen on the walls of the Administration Building at Balboa Heights, or in 1912 when the indefatigable Joe Pennell was working on the spot, immortalizing the saga of the Canal's crea-

℣ The Gaillard Cut

tion by a historic series of lithographs. Of this
period, too, is a fluid water color by my Illustrator,
for Scribner's History of the United States, showing Theodore Roosevelt, in tropical linens, gazing

at the work of excavation, in a steaming Isthmian atmosphere.

"They couldn't pull the wool over Teddy's eyes," said our friend Mr. Mathison, speaking of this visit. "From his private car he noticed in passing a whitewashed workmen's train. He gave orders to stop, jumped off, looked at the far side and asked if the whitewash had given out. The hospital was ready for his inspection. T. R. said he wanted to rest, not visit it. Then shortly after, he stole away unnoticed and arrived just as the old sheets had been put again on hospital beds. 'What would he see?' 'Well, Bachelors' Quarters No. 111.' Some one had given him the tip—this was the one, at all costs, they didn't want to show. Teddy was a canny one!"

On August 15, 1914—ten years and three months from the day of the American occupation—the S.S. *Ancon* of the Panama Railroad Line made the first transit, from Atlantic to Pacific, formally opening the Canal...to be followed, in the course of twenty-five years (the anniversary was celebrated in 1939 when, as the last voyage of her career, the *Ancon* brought up the rear of the participants), by 105,122 ships of every nation of the globe, carrying cargoes totaling over 500,000,000 tons.

Next to disease, landslides have been the worst obstacles to success that the intrepid commission has had to cope with. Soon after the initial opening of the waterway, Cucaracha Slide closed the canal with masses of rock that delayed reopening for more than a year.

The French had planned a sea-level canal, but, owing to a tide of some twelve feet on the Pacific though not on the Atlantic, serious difficulties might have arisen. The monumental locks are, next to the Gaillard Cut, the outstanding features of the entire trip. A "flight" of three pairs accommodates the Chagres River at Gatun, near Colón, another pair marks Pedro Miguel, while Miraflores Locks form two steps down to the Pacific. Suez, one hundred and three miles to Panama's fifty, had neither locks nor landslides to send the cost of its construction skyrocketing.

In Panama the Inter-American Highway ends, and, to southward, the Pan-American Highway begins. Miles of fairly good road lie within the limits of Panama but a section is yet to be pushed through the jungle. The possibility of the construction of such a road has been increased since 1940 when a North Carolinian, R. A. Tewkesbury, against all advice, braving starvation, fevers, boaconstrictors, crocodiles, the hostility of Indians, fought his way through three hundred miles of Panamanian jungle to the Colombian border—the first white man so to do.

Feminine, exquisite as the "Lady boats" of the Canadian National Line, are the sisterships *Santa Rosa, Santa Paula,* (some choose the cargo *Santas*) of the Grace Line, built for Caribbean and South

American cruises, tastefully furnished in American Colonial style, with domed dining-saloons open to the stars. Our farewells to the *Santa Paula,* that had brought us to Panama, would have been the less reluctant had it not been for an odor in our stateroom, inexplicable by our Chinese steward, but finally discovered to be, by some whim of faulty ventilation, an odor emanating from the hold—not fertilizer but the sickening and henceforward unmistakable stench of a cargo of green coffee.

Panama in June! Lost were the trade winds; the rainy season was upon us—that change of season that brings in its wake prickly heat almost unbearable. Breathless sultriness marked the days, rainbows arched the harbor, alternating with tropical downpours and sunsets that burnished the dazzling waters to ruddy gold. Refuge we found within the spacious quarters of the United States Government-owned Hotel Washington, where amiable Barbadian Negroes, round-headed, anxious to please, offered such grandiloquent replies to an order for a serving of cobina, if the fish were not on the menu, or for a variation in the iced drinks as:

"My lady, I shall endeavor to accomplish it for you."

As day followed day our delight was never lessened in the view from our windows of ships of divergent nationality and tonnage converging toward Cristobal to enter the spacious approach to the Canal. Here, too, passed dugouts manned by San Blas Indians, sails set to the wind. Pelicans amused us by their antics (were they, too, afflicted by prickly heat?), man-of-war birds mounted to the clouds, cocopalms cast spidery shadows, imaginative, fantastic, along the embankment on the sea-wall. Happy voices of children rose from the hotel pool; seaplanes soared rapidly from sight; while, after dark, the light-house flashed and the pent-up heat of day found startling expression in thunderstorms portentously like cosmic cataclysms.

There was merriment as to the status of our hotel; not table and bed linen could agree as to whether the building were in Colón or Canal Zone. Geographically it stood, obviously, in the former, but, owned and administered by the United States, Canal Zone stamps were permissible. There seemed to be a special dispensation. Colón hospital, too, was strictly for the Americans—army, navy, and Canal Zone officials—other mortals depending upon one run by Panamanians or that smaller establishment on Melenez Street, the Samaritan, its name reflecting the outgiving personality of its guiding spirit, Dr. Harry Eno.

Drowsy by day, the sun-wilted, gregarious population of Colón rouses itself near sundown. Victorias clatter over the watered pavements. Bombay Stores tempt bargainers for Oriental wares, other purchasers seek extraordinary values in perfume. My Illustrator, ever endeavoring to avoid the clutches of merchants of silk pyjamas (not for a week did they recognize the futility of the pursuit), on the lookout for Cherikui prehistoric pots, myself intrigued by Chinese embroideries at Madura's, found it all but impossible to avoid the purchase of more and still more crocodile-skin items on meeting the sinister reptilian eye of the stuffed creature hung luringly street-ward in lieu of shop sign. Incense, idols, sandalwood, Manila shawls, Panama hats (sold here but made in Ecuador) were among the objects offered by the arcaded bazaars.

All that has been said of the depravity in evidence at Port Said and certain Oriental ports applies at Panamanian Colón. I beg to differ with an author who writes of night life on Front, the shopping street, of the roar of sound, of music, of drunks issuing from doorways: "All is gala, coarse, obvious—and great fun." However, this same distinguished gentleman admits, on walking through the squalid red-light quarter, where forlorn derelicts of women sit expectantly in theatrically illuminated doorways, that "if the onlooker has taste, kindness or humanity, the scene is not merry."

Driving away from the swarming, wooden-balconied native quarter of Colón—a third of the tenement district was destroyed by the 1940 fire—

In Colon

we visited of a late afternoon New Cristobal, with
its airy seaside cottages built for canal employees;
on another day Fort Randolph, via Coco Solo, the
government airport, where, too, the Pan-American
hangar stands. The road to the latter leads
through the horrid nightmare of the mangrove
swamps, traversed by inky-black ditches, sprayed
weekly with heavy oil in the never-ending campaign of man versus mosquito. Nothing lives in the
wetness of the swamps, it appears, but land crabs
and the mosquitoes that breed within the crusta-
ceans' holes. No blue heaven is Colón, or Cristobal
either, despite its modern housing for the American army and canal officials … the first a former

black hell, rather, of pestilence and profligacy; the second a miasmic swamp, but both redeemed, somewhat, by superhuman enterprise.

The *Kungsholm*, and a local trading schooner known as the "coconut boat," make a port of call of the Golfo de San Blas. The islands (about fifty of which are inhabited) of the San Blas Indians— Cunas—some seventy miles from Colón, stretch along the Panamanian shore toward the Colombian border. Erroneously called "white Indians," because of a number of albinos among them, the San Blas have kept their race pure by prohibiting their women from visiting the mainland and by not permitting strangers to remain on their islands after sundown. Death has, until recent times, been the penalty for disobedience to this rigid moral code. Easily mistaken for Japanese, short in stature are the San Blas fishermen who come habitually to Colón, mooring their *cayucas* overnight in a little cove. More rarely is seen a San Blas woman, gorgeous in cutwork jacket of rainbow hues, arms and legs bound ruthlessly with chains of beads, and, inevitably, wearing a golden nose-ring.

Any one who has traversed the Canal by cruiseship, or visited Gaillard Cut by government tug, or, indeed, followed the waterway closely by train on the Panama Railroad (its cars marked P. R. R. looking strangely familiar to Pennsylvanians!), or had a panoramic view by air, can hardly fail to

San Blas women are gaily costumed

acknowledge that he has seen an outstanding wonder of the twentieth century.

There is apt to be an old-timer at Gatun Locks who will be glad to reminisce of boats that he has seen pass through in the last quarter century: battleships, cruisers, aircraft carriers, pleasure boats, from the *Bremen* and *Kungsholm* down to the minute *Igdrasil,* the thirty-seven-foot sloop manned by that valiant pair who in it circled the globe, the *North Star* of the Admiral Byrd Expedition, from Boston bound to the Antarctic. All-absorbing is the business of passing through the locks, directed with despatch from conning-towers. Mechanized "mules"—ruthless in their disregard of cruise-ship passengers—replace their namesakes on rural towpaths. How unlike this Canal was to the Suez, this country to the Arabian vistas and truth-defying mirage, we exclaimed, at sight of the chief wonders: Gatun Lake and Gaillard (formerly Culebra) Cut, named, properly, to immortalize its engineer. The highest waters of the canal, eighty-five feet above the sea, are formed by the damming of the tempestuous Chagres River. The water-line has been raised sufficiently to drown a portion of the jungle. Stark trunks of dead monarchs enthrall the beholder by their imaginative appeal ... by moonlight how macabre; how eerie at all hours of day! Orchids cling to the withered arms of these ancient wraiths who in life may once have looked down on the passing of gold-trains, of the lash of Spanish goads, of more that had best remain unknown. At times a giant is seen to quiver and topple, carrying its freight of epiphytes—perhaps some of that precious variety with central "dove" known as the "Holy Ghost orchid"—down to a watery grave.

Balboa the Americans have named their modern town at the Canal's outlet to the Pacific—an outlet guarded by immense breakwater. Here, too, is one of the greatest of modern drydocks. Adjoining Balboa, as Cristobal adjoins Colón, upon a rocky peninsula is the capital of the Spanish-speaking Republic of Panama, called, by Americans, Panama City. An avenue of royal palms leads to the Administration Building and other offices at Balboa Heights—Capital of the Canal zone—a garden city on which the United States has expended $17,000,000. At adjacent Ancon, chief residential section of the zone, the hill of the name overlooks Panama City, the United States Government-owned Tivoli Hotel attracts Americans in greater numbers than the Washington at Colón, although, in summer, breezes blow there less frequently. Government officials and those of the Canal, officers of army and navy, and more especially their wives prefer the gaiety to be had at Balboa Heights and at Ancon to the more prosaic routine at Cristobal.

To the traveler, who may make headquarters at El Panama or else the Tivoli, the Canal Zone at

Panama ‡ The drowned

Balboa will offer no attractions to compete with
the lure of Panama City and, more especially, its
Plaza Central, the historic site where, in 1821,
Panama City declared its independence from
Spain. The façade of the mother-of-pearl domed,
eighteenth-century Cathedral gives stateliness to
the square, and local color is added by the thought
that its building was made possible by the savings
of a Negro archbishop who, by his own intelli-
gence, had risen from obscurity. The See of Panama is said to be the oldest in the New World.

On the Plaza Bolívar stands the ancient church

forest of Gatun Lake

of San Francisco (now used as a college). San
José, with its golden altar, is another of the time-
worn churches; as is San Felipe Neri, dating from
the seventeenth century, built to withstand sieges,
having weathered earthquakes; there is, too, the
ruined San Domingo, with its celebrated flat arch
—the secret of which is said to have been revealed
to the monk, its builder, in a dream. In the Plaza
Francia has been erected a monument to de Lesseps while, as at Saint-Malo, the people's favorite
promenade, atop a substantial sea-wall, this built
in 1673, affords refuge from the cluttered streets.

A statue of Balboa balances that of Columbus, the gift of the Empress Eugénie, at Colón.

Palaces—government, municipal, and episcopal —especially the residence of the President, with its luxuriantly-planted patio give the city a Spanish flavor. Once when President of the Republic of Panama, Arnulfo Arias, one-time minister to Italy, addressed a dinner of an American group in Colón, he stated that "there has never been a closer relationship between my people and yours than exists to-day." In commemoration of July Fourth, the National Assembly voted not to hold a session, and Señor de Roux, the Foreign Minister, gave an unprecedented reception to representatives of the United States, attended by President Arias and other officials of the Panamanian Government. The item is of interest, considering the importance of the goodwill of Panama to our National Defense. Work on a third set of locks progresses; but on the eight-hour transit of the Canal the tourist would not be aware of the armaments that surround him. Yet warplanes, concealed machine-guns, mobile forces of artillery, are not lacking. Forts Randolph and Sherman guard the Atlantic and Fort Amador the Pacific approach.

The King's Bridge over which the gold-trains passed still stands on the King's Route to Old Panama. The tower of a ruined cathedral, San Geronimo, built in 1626, destroyed on Morgan's

day, January 28, 1671; a few buttressed trees, by
their roots hastening the downfall of the ruins
where excavators were at work; and on one of
these, a cuipo, the emerald gleam of a young
iguana—surviving remnant of antediluvian lizards, the spiny "monster of the jungle"—such are
my meager memories of Old Panama; augmented
only by those of strolling on a lonely beach where
sea-birds dwell; and where, owing to an Isthmian
geographic quirk, the sun or moon rises, unantici-
patedly, from the Pacific.

Columbus, Balboa, what venturous spirits
theirs, braving hostile oceans, charting ways new
to men, joining the Old World to the New... had
we such men to-day! I remember the motto upon
medals given to the builders of the Canal: "The
land divided, the world united."

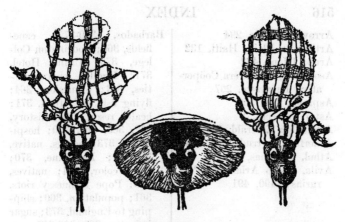

Index

515

INDEX

Fort Randolph, Panama, 505

Fort Richepance, Guadaloupe, 311

Fort Townshend, 219

Fortaleza, La, San Juan, Puerto Rico, 195

Francis, Henry, chauffeur, 278, 280

Frederiksted, St. Croix, 238

French Canal Company, 493

French West Indian Company, 253

Frenchtown, St. Thomas, 220, 223

Froude, James Anthony, 53, 288, 373

Gaillard Cut, Panama Canal, 501

Gandía, Mrs. Hector, 211

Gatun Locks, Panama, 501, 508

George I, 4

George V, 267

George, chauffeur, 271

Georgic, 346

Gloucester, Duke and Duchess of, 101

Goat Island, 418

Goethals, Colonel George Washington, 496

Gold Label Government Rum, 241

Gold Rush of '94, 493, 494

Golden Hind, 491

Goldberg, *An Anthology of Spanish-American Poetry*, quoted, 199

Golfo de San Blas, Panama, 506

Gómez, Juan Vicente, despot, 450, 451, 452, 455-457; anecdote, 466; family of, 440; road builder, 452; town house, 454

Gómez, José Miguel, 76

Gómez, Mariano, 76

Gonaïves, Haiti, 133

Gonâve, Gulf of, Haiti, 133

Gorgas, Colonel William Crawford, 496

Gosier, Le, Guadaloupe, 326

Gourbeyre, Governor, 311

Gourde, 127

Government Stock Farm, Trinidad, 398

Grace Line boats, 473, 501-502

Graf Spee, 113

Grand Étang, Grenada, 297, 299

Grand Fond Dolé, Guadaloupe, 319

Grand St. Bernard Monastery, Barbados, 370

Grande Chartreuse Monastery, Barbados, 370

Grande Coulée, Martinique, Musée Volcanologique, 350

Grande-Terre, Guadaloupe, 303; sugar factory, 326

Grands-Bois, Haiti, 153

Grant, President, 173

Grantham, the Hon. A. W. G. H., 90

Grantham, Sir William, 91

Green, Andrew, 278